PRAYER'S GONE GLOBAL

EXPLORING BIBLICAL PRAYER

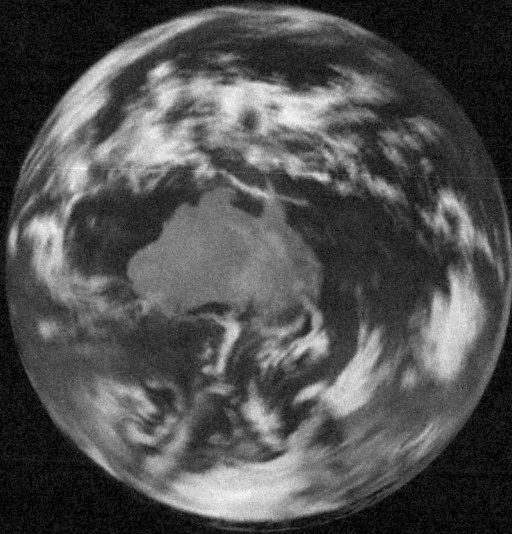

Steve H Hakes

Prayer's Gone Global

Exploring Biblical Prayer

~

Steve H Hakes

Paperback ISBN   978-1-8380946-9-0

Hardback ISBN   979-8-4477760-9-1

Kindle ISBN   978-1-8380946-8-3

V251128120238

Scripture quotations marked...

Thanks to...

- The Salvation Army: for the son
- C S Lewis (1898–1963): for the faith
- Leo Cecil Harris (1920-77): for the father
- Yonggi Cho (1936–2021): for the spirit
- Anne: for marriage

Life is a life of gratitude.

CONTENTS

Chapter 01	**Prayer and the Ancient World**	**10**
	No god please, we're British	10
	Ancient Mesopotamia and prayer	15
	Ancient Egypt and prayer	23
Chapter 02	**Prayer and Psalms**	**29**
	Covenant prayer	29
	Reflections of Lewis	35
	Give us this day our daily psalm	46
Chapter 03	**Prayer and Christianity**	**51**
	Entrance prayer	51
	Subpar prayer-songs	62
Chapter 04	**Prayer and the Trinity**	**72**
	Sabellius and prayer	72
	Petitionary prayer	75
	Ultimacy of the father	78
	Adding back the spirit	81
	The father first	84
Chapter 05	**Prayer and the Spirit**	**88**
	Improper prayer	88
	Proper prayer	92
Chapter 06	**Prayer and Authority**	**104**
	Authority commands	104
	Declare and decree	111
	Is God bound?	124
	Binding and loosing	127
	Prayer and power	134
Chapter 07	**Prayer and Blemishes**	**157**
	Theological blemishes	157
	Proseuchological blemishes	163
Chapter 08	**Prayer and Anselm**	**170**
	Set prayers	170
	Prayer meditation	179
Chapter 09	**Prayer and Malcolm**	**193**
	C S Lewis and prayer	193

Biblical Abbreviations

Ac. *Acts*

Am. *Amos*

Chr. *Chronicles*

Col. *Colossians*

Cor. *Corinthians*

Dan. *Daniel*

Dt. *Deuteronomy*

Ec. *Ecclesiastes*

Eph. *Ephesians*

Est. *Esther*

Ex. *Exodus*

Ezk. *Ezekiel*

Ezr. *Ezra*

Gal. *Galatians*

Gen. *Genesis*

Hab. *Habakkuk*

Heb. *Hebrews*

Hg. *Haggai*

Hos. *Hosea*

Is. *Isaiah*

Jas. *James*

Jg. *Judges*

Jhn. *John*

Jl. *Joel*

Jnh. *Jonah*

Job *Job*

Jos. *Joshua*

Jr. *Jeremiah*

Jude *Jude*

Kg. *Kings*

Lk. *Luke*

Lm. *Lamentations*

Lv. *Leviticus*

Mic. *Micah*

Mk. *Mark*

Ml. *Malachi*

Mt. *Matthew*

Nah. *Nahum*

Nb. *Numbers*

Neh. *Nehemiah*

Ob. *Obadiah*

Phm. *Philemon*

Php. *Philippians*

Pr. *Proverbs*

Ps(s). *Psalm(s)*

Pt. *Peter*

Rm. *Romans*

Ruth *Ruth*

Rv. *Revelation*

Sam. *Samuel*

Sg. *Song of Songs*

Ths. *Thessalonians*

Tm. *Timothy*

Tts. *Titus*

Zc. *Zechariah*

Zp. *Zephaniah*

Grades[1]

Percent	100-95	94-90	89-85	84-80	79-75	74-70	69-65	
Letter	A+	A	A-	B+	B	B-	C+	
Point	4.3	4	3.7	3.3	3	2.7	2.3	
Percent	64-60	59-55	54-50	49-45	44-40	39-27	26-14	13-00
Letter	C	C-	D+	D	D-	U+	U	U-
Point	2	1.7	1.3	1	0.7	0	0	0

---

[1]   For handier sorting in tables, I advise using A1/A2/A3 and B1/B2/B3, etc, for grade letters. I have put these here in the more familiar forms of, eg, A+/A/A- and B+/B/B-. For grade points, I round final totals to the nearest 0.5 points.

Preface

I like *Northanger Abbey*. It's a very simple story by Jane Austen, which hopefully will one day be truly filmed without lewdness added to sex it up (post 2007)—avoiding Andrew Davies' touch! It's basically about Miss Morland, a young 'average' woman of late teens, moving beyond family life into social life. If the true study of man is man—though it is not—we might say that Catherine's educational life curved upwards, toughening her up. In short, she rapidly learnt that good people—including herself—could be silly and short-sighted; that less good people could be downright scoundrels; that some good people were snobby; and that some good people were well worth getting close to (enter the godly Henry Tilney). Just who should we trust?

In her learning curve, she made some mistakes in choosing her friends, such as the syrupy sweet yet superficial Miss Isabella Thorpe. Having recently come under the fascination of Isabella, both women part with "a most affectionate and lengthened shake of hands, after learning, to their mutual relief, that they should see each other across the theatre at night, and say their prayers in the same chapel the next morning." I like this connection of social gaiety with church godliness, theatre with temple, panto and prayer, secular and spiritual. Prayer should be a natural part of our everyday life. Jane was herself a deeply religious Christian, slowly edging from Anglicanism towards Evangelicalism, and we have three extant prayers by her. Admittedly her prayers have, like Anne Elliot (*Persuasion*), generally not been attended to. The Spirit of the West seeks neither to heed nor herald the source of goodness.

I do go a bundle on Miss Austen. But I don't go a bundle on set prayers. Still, they can be helpful, though my personal focus is more on spontaneous prayer. In this book I have not fought shy of some personal formulations, offering readers much to agree and disagree on. And I confess that because some sections are substantially lifted from my previous books and here collected under one roof, there is some duplication—triplication, whatever—to be enjoyed or endured. I comfort myself with the thought that sometimes repetition in different words, helps to drive home the message. Yet my message itself is admittedly patchy, having parts perhaps better unsaid, and lacking parts perhaps better said. In short it's a mixed and incomplete bag, with much waffle—well, that is me.

For Bible texts, my main English versions (MEVV) are the CEB/CEV/ERV/LEB/NABRE/NCV/NIV/NKJV/NLT/NRSV. For grading, the best will be A+, and the worst D-: none shall fail. In quotes, I often amend [the LORD] to [Yahweh], and remove false capitals from nouns and pronouns. I sometimes take liberties when quoting generally: for example, updating gender style, adjusting tenses, standardising abbreviations, and simplifying bibliographies intext.

Steve H Hakes   mallon.detc@gmail.com

Chapter 01   <u>Prayer and the Ancient World</u>

<u>No god please, we're British</u>

"We do not believe in a god—for this would imply a possible or conceivable multiplication of gods—but only in God" (Tyrrell 76 slightly altered). Thus spoke Tyrrell. He was obviously unhappy with the way in which some Christians commonly spoke about God as being a type of god. I feel his pain. Polytheism—the idea that gods/goddesses are real—can be both the inside letter and the outside envelope, both what we believe, and how we speak: Hinduism (though a political umbrella religion) is a prime example.

The Bible reflects a form or so of polytheism within its ancient people. I like to think that those times were a little like an early-learning centre, using the children's familiar terms, while slowly weaning them into the unfamiliar. God had a special destiny for Israel; others could wait. Thus, it used the same familiar envelope, but you can see it mix in seeds of a very different inner message—that Yahweh alone is God. We still speak in envelope terms, as we have been taught, that Yahweh is this or that type of god, my god. It could help us if Bible translations changed the envelope—though not the letter within—at the point when Israel went global, when poetry married philosophy.

But the ancient world, for the greater part, never shared Tyrrell's pain, and happily worshipped the created, calling upon what we often term *gods* and *goddesses*, or just plain *idols*. Was that worship always evil, or simply barbaric at best, primitive? Abraham's father was that kind of worshipper, a moon worshipper. Abraham was better educated; Jacob's wife stole her father's idols.

Some strict Calvinists might say that before Abram/Abraham's call, every single human being, including Abraham, was as totally corrupt as could possibly be, worshippers of demons, and that all totally deserved ultimate hell. Had Abraham himself been so bad? Were all his contemporaries across the globe, really so bad, so blind? Might Yahweh have chosen another, had Abraham rejected the call?

Some would say that Abraham was incapable of resisting Yahweh, since, they say, grace was and always will be, irresistible. For my part, I suspect that with a plan to unfold, Yahweh looked for a man,[2] and chose one from among suitable candidates. The rest is history.

Dt.4:19 might read that Yahweh established a common level of worship, out of which, starting with Abraham, he selected an uncommon class of students to learn, or rather to relearn, monotheism. But only with Moses the teacher, did that class really settle down to study—Moses plus their new experience of God as Yahweh, provided the educational material. Sinai-School (or Sabbath-School) came well before Sunday-School. Looking back, we might say that Sinai was substandard to Christianity, even as the ancient world was substandard to Sinai. [3] Likewise, secondary education is substandard to tertiary education, and primary education is substandard to secondary education.

Indeed, irrespective of class level, God could and can respond with miracles in his "'goodwill' toward people of different faiths 'without necessarily endorsing them'" (Keener 2011:196). Yes, and even through false evangelists, through whom can come psychosomatic healings, and even deific healings when though inspired by false messengers, true faith reaches out to God, and God truly responds.

Anyway, before looking to the biblical world, let's look to the pre-biblical world—or why not just jump this chapter if uninterested? But even as looking at the Old Testament—the Tanak, or OT for short—can help our perspective, so can looking at what preceded it, yet please feel free to skip this chapter rather than getting bogged down.

For simplicity, imagine that the common world had Level 1 (primary) knowledge of God; that Sinai had Level 2 knowledge (secondary); that

---

[2]   In Is.63:5, the look found nobody suitable for the job, nobody doing the job.

[3]   Grades: Atheism allows a U for Unsatisfactory; the common level allows a D; Sinai allowed a C; Christianity allows a B; the age to come will allow an A. Jumping grades/levels by revelation, seems possible by the likes of Ac.17:30, where pagans were invited to skip Sinai and become Christians.

Christianity has Level 3 (tertiary); that the Age to come has Level 4 (quaternary): we have yet to know as we are known. For friendly names within this book, I'll call these levels of spirituality, the Common Level/Life; the Sinai Level/Life; the Christian Level/Life; and the Ultimate/Everlasting Level/Life, respectively.[4]

For their part, the Israelites were warned that whenever they looked heavenwards (a poetic way to say *upwards*) and saw the sun, moon, and stars—awesome sights above—they must neither worship nor serve them. Arguably, such things were simply not good enough for them, substandard, so to speak. Though—Moses added—"Yahweh your god lets the other people in the world do this" (ERV: Dt.4:19).[5] This idea is hinted at in the New English Translation's footnote on Dt.32:8. Similarly some of the early Christian philosophers—such as Justin Martyr, and Titus Flavius Clemens (a.k.a. Clement of Alexandria)—held this idea, that what had been fitting for Common life might not be fitting for Sinai life, let alone for Christian life.

---

[4] For argumentation, see my *Israel's Gone Global* (2018) or simplified, *Salvation Now and Life Beyond* (2024). Whether you got eternal life or everlasting life— in the KJV following Tyndale—was pot luck (eg Mt.19:16 vs Mt.19:29; Mk.10:30 vs Lk.18:30): the Greek word αιωνιος/*aiōnios* was translated both ways as synonyms, perhaps because of the overlapping meaning. For convenience, I often use them to express their contrast. For us, *eternal* is a quality of life we now have, and *everlasting* is the unlimited duration we shall have. God lacks unlimited duration, since he is beyond time, its surround, and the quality of life he has—he is—is eternal.

[5] Hebrew translator, W C Williams, strongly agreed with me in principle with translating out the false capitals we have translated in. He sadly reflected though, that translating as *god* in polytheistic settings would by bucking convention lose readership: why sink a helpful ship by adding too much helpful baggage? Those dedicated to providing first class Bible versions must sometimes only gently introduce improvements, lest their good work fall foul before the fickle court of human readership. Even Tyndale and the HCSB gently floated God's name, and the HCSB sank. With less risk involved, I shall adjust my citations to remove false capitalisation where I deem it helpful. I shall also take the liberty to adjust the term [the LORD] to God's name, Yahweh: God gave us his name; why should we sidestep it?

It was perhaps held by the apostle Paul. For instance, Ac.17:30 records him preaching to Athenians about such worship. He commended them for their dedication to worship, even to the extent of having at least one catch-all altar to an 'unknown god', perhaps lest they slighted any divinity.[6] They could understand that kind of talk. Then he added that primary education was outdated, for tertiary education had become global through Jesus. They could not understand that, and called him a babbler, a sponger. But he urged the class to move upwards to higher things. Long story short, the unknown, the unknown *god*, was in fact God, who was telling them to offer allegiance directly to himself. An abacus is fine for kiddie fingers, but not for college freshmen.

In looking back at common humanity, I tend to use the term *divinity*, a diminutive form of *god/deity*, to highlight the worship stage immediately below deity, though the Bible is less systematic.[7] Thus I tend to speak of *deity*, only as meaning God himself, and *divinities*, as meaning the next level down, such as angels.[8] Arguably some of the divinities were and are evil, dark, even as the term *angels* can refer to

---

6   Greek stories, eg *The Odyssey*, told how dangerous it was to overlook a *god*. Historically, there might have been several such altars in Athens (Marshall 1992:286). But had Paul deemed it demonic, would he have commended their worship? Arguably, demons, as defined in Christian circles, did infect substandard worship—a value system—and other texts should be considered for a fuller picture (eg 1 Cor.10:20-1; 1 Tm.4:1; Jas.2:19; Rv.9:20; 18:2).

7   Similarly, Roman emperors generally hoped for death to elevate them to the divine, divinity level (*divus*), not to the deity level (*deus*). Compare Greek *theotēs* to *theiotēs*.

8   In line with the Godbey New Testament (1902), the RSV (and NRSV/ESV offspring) used this term in Ac.17:18, to set off Athenian polytheism from Paul's monotheism. That's better than Wycliffe's *fiends* (*fendis*) or Tyndale's *devils* (*devyls*). The Greek is δαιμονιον/*daimonion*, which had a morally neutral meaning outside of Jewish-Christian circles.

    Rm.1:20 also has a history of the term, from the Latin *divinitas*. Some might prefer the neutral Sumerian *údug/údugs*, for some were benevolent (as angels), and some were malevolent (as demons). Sadly, the pejorative term *demon/s* is nowadays often applied to all údugs. Or maybe use *spirit/s* as a neutral term for demons and angels?

unfallen or fallen creatures. For instance, *Jude* 6 speaks of fallen angels (αγγελοι/*angeloi*)—more often called demons—while Lk.1:19 speaks of Gabriel as God's messenger (αγγελος/*angelos*) to Zechariah.

Sometimes words have a wider range of meaning than we are used to—*Jude* 4 calls Jesus (or God) our *despot*, but not in the common sense of the word today! Similarly, the Athenians assumed that Jesus was a good demon (Ac.17:18: δαιμονιον/*daimonion*),[9] a good term in some circles, but not one that Luke would have happily chosen for Jesus.

Words are like envelopes that can handle a range of inner messages, and need context in order for us to see how speakers/writers have intended them to function—meaning-content can greatly change over time and culture. Thus, in Eph.4:22, the 'conversation' of the KJV is the 'manner of living' of the KJ21, and 'the old man' (KJV) is not one's husband or father, but 'the old humanity' of the *New Testament for Everyone* (NTE).

C S Lewis suggested that God gave good dreams, myths, to the pagan peoples, the ethnic *goyim*, myths which became contaminated by Satan. If we follow this line, we could postulate that idolatry was in principle fine, and was perhaps fine to begin with, but not so fine in its later degenerative stages. Nevertheless, if we are to be guided by 1 Jhn.5:21—and John's wording might suggest that it was a starting lesson for all new Christians (1 Jhn.2:12)—we are to keep well away from idols. Did John warn here against backtracking to common humanity, even if for some it might be relatively harmless, perhaps somewhat virtuous?[10]

One might even suggest that Christianity, though God-given, has suffered corruption by Satan, while still retaining a core which may be called Common Christianity. Lewis pictured such mere Christianity as being the shared corridor which led to many varying rooms, denominational branches of the Christian Tree (*the church*), so to speak, with not all branches being equal. He himself tried to keep a convenient mediating profile, which he put as Anglicanism, neither

---

[9]   Translated as god/deity/divinity/demon—see the CEB/LEB/NRSV/MKJV in that order. The last is the *Modern King James Version* (1998).

[10]   Within this level, Atheists, Hindus, and Spiritualists, can all be virtuous.

high nor low. This positioning he found less easy to maintain in later years, as Anglicanism's counter-biblical post-Christian tendencies became more pronounced, tendencies he had warned his branch about in his talk named *Fern-seed and Elephants*.

Ancient Mesopotamia and prayer

If we jump back almost 4,000 years, we might have met Jacob arriving in Egypt (perhaps about 1700 BC: Kitchen 359). Within a few centuries, Yahweh put on record that he welcomed the use of stars in pagan worship, but not in ethnic Israel's worship (Dt.4:19).[11] In short, pagans were to be good pagans (not Israelites), and Israelites were to be good Israelites (not pagans), both people-types preparing the way of the lord/ Yahweh. Separation between a special people and a pagan people, was an interim plan.

But when messiah came, he would unite from both streams of humanity, a new package (Eph.2:15), redefining *kosher* and *goyim*. Paul, speaking into the heart of a deeply polytheistic and philosophical city (at the Areopagus in Athens), explained the plan. Amazingly some Athenians found instant release and fulfilment (Ac.17:34): their polytheistic road had led to the true gateway. And from the polytheistic world Abraham, ancestor of Israel, had begun the long road to philosophic monotheism. Let us look at prayer in the world into which he was born, by digging deeper back in time.

If we jump back 7,000 years, we could meet the Sumer, the people who perhaps invented cities,[12] in which at first priests ruled, each city having its own patron divinity. Within a thousand years, they were building ziggurat temples for worship within the heart of their cities, temples both important and convenient. Within another millennium, they went on to probably invent the first writing (about

---

[11]   Likewise Mt. Gerizim and Mt. Zion represented lower/higher levels of worship, but true (αληθινος/*alēthinos*) worship of God as father would supersede both (Jhn.4:21,23). Dt.4:19 can be taken in other ways.

[12]   Sumer's Uruk, dating around 4500 BC, is probably the world's oldest known city. Had science-based civilisation flourished much further back, the sands of time would have removed all trace. Archaeology has a very limited range, but I will generally give it the benefit of the doubt.

2,000 years before China began writing), and were soon using wheels and mathematics, the latter using a sexagesimal base, 60 instead of our decimal base, 10. Their records of their kings reflects this sexagesimalisation, presumably using mathematics to factor in the idea of importance, of impact on their world—figures after the great flood being more modest.

Thus, antediluvian King Enmenluanna reigned for 43,200 years; King Alalgar reigned for 36,000 years. To divide by 3,600 (*saroi*) might give the real lengths as 12 years and 10 years respectively. To divide by 600 (*neroi*) might give the real lengths as 72 years and 60 years respectively (Kitchen 446). Symbolic royal multiplication! Reigns after the great flood were more like 1,560 years, which would be 24 real years if later scribes had merely inflated by 60.[13]

If we jump back a mere 4,500 years (2350 BC), we could see the Akkadians,[14] led by Sargon the Great, beginning to take over the Sumerians, a people culturally like them though having a different language.[15] Little is known about the earlier Akkadians, who perhaps had been a minor northern neighbour in the days of Sumer's dominance. But when Sumer's king of Uruk attacked Sargon of Akkadia, Sargon turned the tables, forming the world's first kingdom. Knocked down but not out, about 200 years later the Sumerian city of Ur would put Sumer in control of this new empire.

Yet under Sargon, Sumer's religious life seems to have merged happily with Akkad's within the Akkadian kingdom, and for convenience we can sketch the kingdom's prayer life from the Akkadian perspective.

---

[13] We still measure degrees in 360, and minutes in 60s. Pharaoh Pepi 2 Neferkare reigned from 2278 to perhaps 2184 BC, 94 years. Long, but realistic. A superficial reading of ancient longevity and regnal lists, can move beyond realism.

[14] The name created before the takeover, when Sargon built Akkad in South Mesopotamia.

[15] Whereas Sumerian didn't leave survivors, Akaddian is directly related to Arabic, Aramaic, and Hebrew.

As it now seems, the Akkadians had three main types of professionals to deal with contact between earth and heaven. These were those seeking the divine will—diviners (*bārû*)—those seeking to expel evil—exorcists (*āšipū*)—and those offering up praise and gratitude—cult-singers (*kalû*). It seems that they were only men, were highly trained, and served both the temples and the courts.

There were a number of prayer-types that this ancient kingdom used, and those prayed to could include 'ghosts' (human spirits postmortem), divinities (good or evil), protective spirits, witches, and sages (Lenzi 9). Symbolism could combine with speech. Symbolic postures included ceremonially raising hands heavenward (*šu-il-lá*/*shuilla*)—symbolic perhaps of being weaponless, hence of surrender/submission? Symbolism could play essential parts in the prayer setting. Prayer often began with praise, closed with a promise of thanks, and had the prayer concern sandwiched between.

<u>Types of prayer</u>

Ritual Wording (a.k.a. Incantational): Ritual specialists would add formal structure (in the pattern, praise/request/thanks) to accompany the use of texts aimed to combat the likes of poison and ill health. They were perhaps built on the idea that rather than attempting magic, praying with all the trimmings would more likely incline the divinities to intervene. Similarly, the church has had a long tradition of praying the Paternoster, though not all Christians keep this tradition. When addressed to *ghosts*, the introduction was merely to identify, not to praise, the recipient.

Modern day Spiritualism also holds the idea that, while maybe asking *ghosts* for information rather than for help, that at least *ghosts* might need mortal help (intel rather than supplies) in getting over their deaths and getting on with life.[16] The OT records King Saul's belief (against Yahweh) that ghosts could intervene in human history, and arguably Yahweh took the exceptional measure of sending the real Samuel to

---

[16] Ex-Spiritualist medium Raphael Gasson explained such rescue mediumship, as well-intentioned mediums blindly being led up the garden path by deceptive spirits, ageless demons who pretend to be human *ghosts*, but which seek to spitefully mislead human beings into dead ends (Hakes 2020:58-62).

pronounce Saul's sin and soon death. *Job* 14:21 (incorporated into Israel?) highlighted the ignorance of the deceased from human events.

One such prayer incorporated offerings to the *ghosts* of parents, grandparents, sister, kin, and clan, of what they needed in the netherworld, along with praise. It went something like, *please ask the judges Shamash and Gilgamesh to deliver me from evil and from sorcery.* In return the petitioner would help the *ghosts* (Lenzi 143).

Ershaḫungas: These were prayers to pacify angry divinities (whether household or public) so that personal misfortune from them would end. They were composed by professional cultus singers. They were not sung, but kettledrums might accompany them. They began either by expressing the terror of the divinity, their charm, the general need, or grief and penitence resulting from unspecified sin. They expressed the desire to get back to a normal relationship, for which the restored would express their praise, and what word they wished to hear (eg 'ransomed', 'healed', 'restored', 'forgiven') was often told to the divinity: we too sometimes pray, *What is it you wish me to say?*

Related divinities, such as the principal divinity's spouse and advisers, could be asked to intervene. They might have been prayed to directly by the affected individuals, or indirectly by clergy. Such prayer could be based on not knowing which divinity one had offended, nor why, and so covered all bases.[17] In short, *whoever and however I've offended, please, I know that me and my people will keep making mistakes, but let me off and let us go back to as we were.*

One such prayer began by asking the offended divinity to relent, frankly admitting that the sinner didn't know whether they personally knew the particular divinity or not. The sinner assumed that they had offended badly and often, because they were suffering badly—they presumed suffering to be proportional to sin. Whichever divinity was so upset, it seemed good to let them know that the sufferer had tried other remedies but had failed before disturbing them—perhaps a legitimate process to try first to divine the source of their suffering?

---

[17]   Likewise the Athenians who had altars to unknown divinities (Ac.17:23)?

The sufferer might have waited long for the offended divinity to bless them in mercy, wondering how long it would take to be forgiven. They knew that humanity was rather dopey when it came to good relationship with the divinities, but prayerfully highlighted that though obviously they had offended, they hadn't meant to. They begged for understanding, the stripping away of sins—which even if seven times seven, could be forgiven by the divinity—and for a season of praise to follow as the divinity was reconciled to them as a mother or father to a repentant child (Lenzi 261-2).

Hymns: These were songs glorifying the divinities. One anthrodirectional song was sung about Ishtar—it smuggled in goodwill towards the king (Lenzi 126-7). In this song, she was the most awesome she-divinity, with oodles of sex appeal, temptingly kissable, with a winning smile and gorgeous eyes—and presumably enjoyed flattery! She was highly intelligent and influential, jam packed with motherly care. Her word was the word of heaven's queen, equal with Anu her husband, heaven's king. She had gained Anu's blessing on the mortal king Ammiditana[18] a devoted worshipper, to whom should be long life and lifelong dominion.

Royal Prayers: This is not so much a special type of prayer, as a comment on the prayerfulness of royalty. Monarchs would pray the standard prayer types, though some of their prayers neither fit the common standards, nor form a royal standard. The content could be kingdom concern rather than common concern. Some such prayers were engraved into buildings or onto clay cylinders. An instance of this is a prayer that Sargon 2—from the northern Assyrian part of the former Akkadian Empire—had engraved at the temple of Nabu (Mercury) in Dur-Šarruken. It asked the divinity to give the king his righteous attention, to keep him healthy for many many years, thus allowing him to long oversee the Assyrian Kingdom which he hoped to last as long as Nabu's temple, which he the king had built. It may be taken as an altruistic prayer—*please let me be a kingly blessing.*

Gottesbriefe: Sometimes requests were written out and individually composed. They were to so and so, from so and so, and could be from

---

[18]   1683-47 BC, a great-grandson of Hammurabi.

a commoner or from the court. The body of the text took the standard form of recognising the greatness of the divinity addressed, then explaining the situation and what was sought, closing with a promise that divine help would not go unrecognised. However, royal letters could function as military reports to one's personal divinity, hopefully of a satisfactory nature.

The individuality of these compositions tells of direct (bespoke) meditation of the human/divine relationship, rather than using an off-the-peg standard prayer form. Some Christians use the idea of writing letters directly to deity, or writing prayer requests for others to pray for. More formally, the Akkadians sometimes handed over their written prayer letters to be properly read out by professionals to the idol of the divinity, before archiving the letter.

Tamitu Prayers: These were *please-let-me-know* requests that tended towards standardisation. A reply was often sought through examination of a creature's innards (*extispicy*). The divinity was asked a very specific and clear-cut question, so that a simple *yes* or *no* would suffice. The diviners even added riders, *ezib*-clauses, short notes to the divinities not to get too caught up in minor details such as bad attitude, so long as they could either say *yes* or *no*, or not to bother answering unless they answered by the set time. The divinity could be flattered—and perhaps even warned that to ignore or to misdirect, could lead to bad publicity.

The simplicity of the idea of a yes/no reply, might find some parallel within the OT. Could the Urim/Thummim Stone(s) be cast to get a *yes/no/neutral* reply? And if cast within Yahweh's will—not as magic—would it/they not have been accurate? Perhaps there were two stones each with a urim/no side, and each with a thummim/yes side, which if tossed by the high priest would give Yahweh's yes (both *yes*), his no (both *no*), or his abstention (one *yes*, one *no*).[19] Unique ways

---

[19] 1 Sam.14: The priest Ahijah carried the ephod which carried the Urim/Thummim stones (3). Impulsive and well-meaning but a spiritual blunderer, Saul imposed a needless fast on his army. His son Jonathan unintentionally

were sometimes used by commoners to ask Yahweh directly and specifically, such as Gideon's repeated request for an affirmation or disaffirmation (Jg.6:36-40).

Namburbi: This was a prayer-ritual that sometimes lasted for days. It was usually to counter—to neutralise—any dire threat that hung over one's head, but sometimes it was for positive gains such as reconciliation of long separated couples. A professional exorcist would be in charge, and the ritual could involve great expense, besides the food and drink offerings. Prayer—perhaps of different types—was usually a component. A few divinities, such as Shamash [the just], Ea [the wise], and Asalluḫi [the magical], tended to be the ones asked for releasing the jinxed from their curse—indeed Shamash had to be convinced that the evil fate was unjust: the divinities couldn't simply be bought off.

Ritual purification through *holy water* was a part of the ritual, and a figurine was used to vicariously carry the curse away from the one accursed.[20] Akkadians were happy that petitioning could result in the predicted fate being avoided. For the Israelites, we can also find

---

ignored the command, then intentionally overruled Saul's order. Freed by Jonathan, the famished army both sinlessly ignored Saul and sinfully ignored kosher law. At least one stone was used to place the main blame. It worked, but—and Jonathan minimised his sin—Yahweh did not require his execution, *pace* Saul.

But note that some argue that the high priest at times spoke as a prophet—as Moses was a prophet who had acted as a priest—allowing one to hear the answer, and the two stones (or one stone) from his breastplate pocket would light up to verify his authenticity. Or that tribal lettering on the twelve gems would light up selectively, allowing one to read the answer.

[20] On this theme of negative oracles, Lenzi 415 suggests that 2 Kg.3:27 best reads as one god (Yahweh, behind the scenes) defeated by another god (Kemosh, behind the scenes) following a sacrifice. Moab might have believed so, but not Yahwists. Kitchen 34 suggests that the Moabites were frenzied to counterattack by Mesha's act of desperation, their do-or-die anger smashing into the Israelite Alliance, which retired. Moab would rebuild its shattered land, punished but not repossessed. Elisha didn't promise Israel Moab (Moab remained aloof), but promised defeat over Moab (Moab remained devastated).

examples where Yahweh allowed his mind to be changed (2 Kg.20:1-9/ Is.38:1-8;[21] Jr.18;[22] Ezk.33:12-5; Am.7:3). Prophecy could be interactive, fluid.

One example of a standard Namburbi-prayer is about snakes.[23] Shamash was addressed by his titles. The addressee's name was left blank, but the personal divinities were listed as Marduk (masculine) and Zarpanitum (feminine). A snake was hiding somewhere in the house, a foreboding of evil and a constant worry. Shamash was asked to save, and in turn would be honoured.

Ikribus: these were basically prayers that went hand in hand with divination, in effect praying that each step within the ritual would be acceptable, so that secrets would be revealed from the spiritual realm. They tended to be *I-wish-to-know*, rather than *please-bless-me*, and to end with *please-answer-me*, not *I'll-praise-you*.

<u>Short summary</u>

Without mapping the stages of ancient Mesopotamia's prayer life, from even the little which has been said we may pick up various prayer ideas which had floated around this area which has been dubbed, *the cradle of civilisation*. It looked beyond the mortal eye—perhaps with memories of Adamic times—with perhaps an inner eye of being in God's image/likeness. It valued experts in the field of prayer, such as sought to know, to do, or to honour, that which is

---

[21]   It is not said, and indeed probably implied otherwise, that Yahweh aimed to punish Hezekiah, who had fallen ill: normal ills come to normal people. Yahweh sent good advice to the king, but after godly Hezekiah begged for healing, rewarded him by healing him. The apostle Paul begged for deliverance, but happily bowed to God's will (2 Cor.12:8-9).

[22]   Yahweh mentioned interactive prophecy (v7-10—where his *repentance* would follow theirs), but added that they were so stubborn that he knew that they wouldn't repent in spite of his goodwill (11-2).

[23]   An Akkadian prayer is given in Lenzi 429. Probably sinful Judah's anti-Yahwism included magic charms, which could be the irony in Jr.8:16-7. Judah knew that the tribe of Dan had been protection like a snake (*nakash*) to invaders (Gen.49:19), but Yahweh's Babylonian army would slide through Judah's defences as snakes that could not be charmed (*lakash*) and would do the biting—they, and not some Danite army defending Yahweh's people from invaders.

higher than us. The divine was welcome within what we might artificially separate into sacred and secular. Prayer was deemed very important, so much so that getting the envelope—the approach—just right, was deemed to be of great importance, which was where expert advice and help was needed.

Regarding request, there was no one person or being to ask, and even the spirits of humans who had died, featured in suprahuman appeal. But certain chief divinities stood out as fairly basic to prayer. It didn't help anybody to offend transcendent powers, so apologies might be needed even if one couldn't pinpoint which power had been unintentionally offended. Normal life was best lived on the friendly side of such powers, and positive fellowship with the divinities was divinely delightful.

Those in high office could seek blessings for public wellbeing, and regularly remind the divinities of this set-in-stone desire. Sometimes urgent requests would be made, often needing no more than a general yes or no. Crises could lead to intense focus on extended prayer over several days, involving professional help and high payments, but prayer was well worth it. Individual purity was important to open the prayerway—ritual washing underlined this.

Ancient Egypt and prayer

Speak aloud of prayer life in Ancient Egypt, and you can still hear echoes of the idea that religion evolved from predynastic Egyptian animism (spirits in inanimate/animate creatures), to polytheism (spirits over creatures), and that prayer was purely subjective. What Edward B Tylor in the 1860's dubbed *Animism*[24] (or Primal Religion) is said by some to reflect an early stage of an evolution of religion. You might hear also the suggestion that perhaps the idea of post-mortem life began when

---

[24]   Predating this 'level' is said to be animatism, assuming that humanity simply evolved from pre-simian life, life that presumably lacked the concept, *deity*, which is assumed to have been created by man's imagination. Animatism is the idea that a fearful indefinable force—like in *Star Wars*—lurks around about us, which animism identifies as individual entities (spirits) living in natural objects.

some noticed the phenomenon of natural mummification, bodies having been remarkably preserved in hot sands or in ice.

C S Lewis chuckled at this idea in Mr. Enlightenment's pontification about guesswork dressed up as science. "Hypothesis, my dear young friend, establishes itself by a cumulative process: or, to use popular language, if you make the same guess often enough it ceases to be a guess and becomes a Scientific Fact" (Lewis 1944:36). Enlightenment was foolishly arguing that *God* is but a primitive idea of primitive follies, prescientific follies. Enlightenment guessed about how some images of deity arose (etiology). For instance, that God had a trunk (Hinduism's Ganesh) because some drunk seemingly spied an escaped elephant in the hills. And maybe someone bitten by a snake imagined a satan. Enlightenment then guessed that deity itself was a foolish image.

Such ideas as everlasting life being based on mummification, are impossible to verify, since no literary evidence exists for preliterary times. The preliterary years are to us, very speculative times. It has in fact been argued the other way, that an original monotheism fractured into polytheism, with the stormy wrath and the sunny blessing of one god, being split into the idea of a storm god and a sun god. Anthropologists speak of primitive tribes having "a memory of a 'high god', a benign creator-father-god" (Alexander 31).

From the ancient kingdom of Egypt, only two humans seem to have risen to the cultic level of divinity, namely C27 Imhotep the builder and healer, and C14 Amenhotep, son of Hapu. But all the pharaohs were held to be at least worthy of worship as semi-divinities. Although divinisation was deemed to apply to some, most divinities were deemed to have begun in heaven (top down) not earth (bottom up). Once, it was said, heaven was pure water from which a hill of land came forth, and the divinities came forth from the water—or the land—and multiplied.

Ancient Egypt had a rich polytheism. Indeed it was too rich for one pharaoh (Amenhotep 4, a.k.a. Akhenaten), who tried to pare polytheism back into one god, God as represented by the sun, Aten. Pursuing perhaps the policy of rapid gradualism, eventually the pharaoh disallowed even the worship of Amun-Ra as father of the pantheiion, although it was fine to call Aten simply Ra, as he had been before the alleged merger with an Amun.

Whatever the politics involved, the priests of polytheistic temples had their beliefs and livelihoods undermined, and so monotheism died soon after its pharaoh. Then temples got back to the usual busy routine of serving their divinities. That included getting them dressed for bedtime and dressed for daytime, making sure they were well fed and watered, ready to receive visitors and petitioners, and ready to enjoy their calendrical outings, such as trips along the Nile, and husband-divinities embracing quality time with their divine wives. This mentality underlines the biblical jest about Baal (a Phoenician divinity) being busy on the toilet (CEV: 1 Kg.18:27).[25]

The divinities seemingly needed protection. Temples were built on sacred land into which charms (magic amulets) had been sunk, and the corners had protective elements such as animal sacrifices. Temple roofs were well drained, and shrines were solid buildings within temples. In short, there were layers for mutual protection of contact. There was ongoing war between the dark and light side, with the good Osiris opposing the evil Set. Each temple could house an entire family of divinities, perhaps for companionship.

How close the common people got to divinities is unclear. There were of course annual festivals, such as when Amun had an annual boat trip from his main temple (Karnak) to his country estate (Luxor), in order to visit his wife who lived next door up along the Nile. Then common folk might catch a glimpse of Amun. So with luck you might have seen a divinity along the public highway. If so, you could have shouted out your personal requests. But these were perhaps rare sightings, too sacred for everyday life, although most commoners kept a small idol or two at home for webchats. Even in public access temples, the inner regions required payment for purification rituals, precluding the lower classes. Perhaps their main comfort was in knowing that the ruling classes were keeping well in with the divinities, assuring goodwill over Egypt.

---

[25]   Somewhat related is the ploy of turning temples into toilets (CEV: 2 Kg.10:27), thus contaminating their sites. In 2016, physical evidence of one such toilet was found to have been built above a demolished pagan temple at Tel Lachish.

Egyptians at large had a special affection for Hapi, who looked after the Nile. The state of the Nile was the state of the nation. As Rudyard Kipling put it, "Until one has seen it, one does not realise the amazing thinness of that little damp trickle that steals along undefeated through the jaws of established death.... The weight of the desert is on one, every day and every hour." Death was ever present, inclining perhaps the people to develop an obsession with it alongside normal life.

Thus we still have their prayers for life after death, and prayers after death for life. Of the latter prayers, it became imperative that one must know the name of Death's doorkeeper, and what and who one was to see—Thoth. Other knowledge keys (prayers) would then be needed to unlock Thoth, so to speak, and in turn Osiris' grace. While some speak of these as spells, they were (at least in later times) not magical, but were more like sign and countersign, a catechism used to distinguish between friend and foe.

Although essential, individuals were still judged (by Anubis) according to their hearts.[26] The pure in heart—those as pure as the Bennu bird, who pleased the divinities, who had given bread to the hungry,[27] water to the thirsty, clothing to the naked—would be welcomed by Osiris into the fields of peace, until Osiris returned to Earth. Damnation would be into Apophis the Terrible's pits of fire.

Prayers were never meant to be magic, although some tended to the hope that writing the word 'innocent', should be enough even for the chief of sinners. Besides positive virtue, there was a list spoken to 42 divinities of 42 sins avoided (negative confession; Job 31), listed in the Papyrus of Ani (in the Book of the Dead): "I have not"...*stolen, or lied, or*

---

[26]   Perhaps the story of the son Se-Osiris teaching Setna his father, indicates a shift in belief, since the older generation envied the pomp and ceremony of the rich. Setna hoped to enter Duat as a rich man whom they had seen escorted by heaps of priests, hymns, prayers, and offerings. But his son hoped that Setna would enter as a poor labourer whom they had seen escorted by only a few family members. That was because the particular poor man had been a good man, while the particular rich man had been an evil man. See Roger L Green's *Tales of Ancient Egypt*, 1995:122-31.

[27]   It was believed that Ma'at taught that the rich should give bread and clothing to the deprived, to care as husbands to widows, and as parents to orphans.

sinned by homosexuality, or slandered, or blasphemed, or been arrogant, or deprived children or divinities.... In short, Egyptians assumed that sins were to be avoided and virtues were to be embraced. Family members felt a responsibility to continue feeding the deceased, and to pray for their wellbeing.

But the divinities could be loved as part of everyday life. One song of reflective praise went a bit like this: "Praise Hathor of Thebes, bow to her. I pray to her because she is awesome and her power is strong. The people love her, a beauty among the divinities. The Council of Divinities go to her, bowing down to her greatness. While thinking about her I saw her beauty, I saw the Lady of all Egypt in a dream, and she filled my heart with joy. Then I was refreshed by her food, without such we would truly lack real food. The wise honour her at the yearly festival; her wisdom truly feeds the people. Let us tell the next generation how beautiful she truly is, we who are bathed and intoxicated by the very sight of her."

Did the Egyptians live in a sense of the divine, sentiments triggered by association? Their very icons portrayed the divine as uniting man and the natural world. To see a jackal could remind them of Anubis, an important divinity after death; seeing a lioness could remind them of conversion[28] from military (Sekhmet) to family life (Hathor), and the evil of man.

There were evil divinities, such as Set, all too easy to sinfully join. Stela BM EA 589 (an inscription stone about the size of an A5) tells on one side that a certain Neferabu was a good man, but the reverse side tells how he had been rightly punished (probably by spiritual or physical blindness) for oath-breaking by Ptah, in whose name he had made an oath. The story ends in a one-line prayer asking Ptah for mercy, and signed off either in relief of being *justified* before Ptah, or (translation varies) by the still hopeful priest-mortician simply saying that Neferabu was *deceased* rather than justified. Written confessions of personal sin probably began in the Ramesside Period.

Like the Akkadians, Egypt had royal requests put to the divinities: "Please look at me and hear, O lord, Ptah, father of fathers...hear my plea

---

28   A number of divinities—often keeping their names—went through different jobs, so to speak, varying associations with the physical world.

who am your beloved son. Please install my son Ramses 4 as king." Here, Ramses 3, facing challenges to the succession, desired his son to reign as a strong divinity over all Egypt, leading a healthy and happy life—life, power, health to him—with Egypt's neighbours subjugated to him as to the mighty Horus.

Prayer could be, or at least begin with, celebration of the divinity: "Greetings to you, exalted ancient one, O Tatenen, [29] father to the divinities, eldest divinity of the primeval time. You shaped humanity; you made the divinities. You began history as the first primordial divinity—every event that occurred came after you. You created the sky according to what your heart imagined, and raised it up like one lifts up a feather. You founded the world as your own creation, encircling it by the ocean and the great green seas. You made the underworld, provided for the dead, allowing Amun-Ra to sail across below, to comfort them as ruler of eternity, lord of forever, lord of life.

"You cause lungs to deeply breathe in the breath of life, letting all people live through your provisions. Time, fate, and fortune, are under your control. We live by your decrees. You created the offerings for all the divinities, when you embodied your form as Nun, the primal waters, lord of eternity. The everlasting is under your care. You breathe out life for everyone, and guide Egypt's king to his great throne, obedient to you, king of all Egypt."

And as with the Akkadians, we can find tamitu type prayers. That is, Egyptian divinities were asked for a simple yes or no, useful in difficult court cases. But if human judges could be bribed, what assurance was there that heavenly judges couldn't be bribed—or at least their priests? But whatever shenanigans might have went on, might it at least have been that though they asked with little true knowledge of God, God heard them, and was gracious to them, according to their faith and heart? Does he stop his ears from those who truly seek him?

---

[29]   Egyptian divinities sometimes swapped offices around, and sometimes joined up names. The names *Tatenen* and *Ptah* were sometimes used for one divinity.

Chapter 02   <u>Prayer and Psalms</u>

<u>Covenant prayer</u>

In the beginnings of the Bible story, we read of human society, as a priesthood in a garden temple, having two-way prayer with Yahweh—dialogue, chatter? This priesthood soon fell into sin— relational disconnect—and was significantly cut off, dying to that special relationship (Gen.2:17). It can be interesting to see how clusters of the terms, *Yahweh, God, Yahweh-God*, occur in *Genesis*. And also interesting to see how sacrificial practice was made, and for what reasons. I have covered such elsewhere, and many have done so far better than I. That is backdrop. Let's jump to Abra[ha]m.

Yahweh looked for a man to begin a chosen line, and befriended Abraham. I take it as a given that Abraham had grown up with prayer, in that his father—and presumably mother, kith and kin—prayed to divinities. That would have prepared him for Yahweh as a god, although I would guess that he was unprepared to have deity speak to him (Gen.12:1-3,7). If the common light was Level 1, I would rate Abraham's as Level 1+, predating Sinai's Level 2. At some stage Abraham moved to two-way prayer, dialogue (15:1-2).

Gen.24:63 is possibly a reference to prayer, for the Hebrew might be translated as *pray*: "Isahac was gone out to praye in the felde at the euen tyde" (Great Bible), which unlike the KJV the Geneva held too. Wycliffe had translated as 'think', and Tyndale as 'walk in meditation'. Ethno-Jewish messianic-type versions have 'walking' (CJB/ISV), 'meditate' (OJB/TLV). But the Hebrew *suach* remains an uncertain word, not one on which to build certainty on. Yet there seems ground to picture Abraham's early rise, Isaac's meditation in a field, and Jacob's vision at night, as depicting prayer to deity. Clearly we read that Isaac prayed pleadingly (25:21).

The one-on-one covenant began to expand with Isaac's son, Yakob/ Jacob, whose twelve sons became ancestors to twelve united tribes. For a while they were praised in Egypt. For a while they were enslaved in Egypt. One can see a broad pattern of Yeshua/Jesus, who even in his crucifixion week was praised by Galilee, and cursed by Judea, so to speak, and whose *exodus* and *Canaan* followed on the heels of the cross (Mt.21:11; 27:22; Lk.9:31).

All the while the covenant people [30] were being shaped in their community psyche. At last they were given new land to live in, in what could be said to have been rental tenancy: the former tenants (Canaanites being their corporate name) had proved unworthy; the new tenants—Israelites—were warned not to follow suit. Indeed after they suffered eviction into Babylonia, South Israel (Judah, the Jews), basically dropped God's covenant name, as those unworthy of it.

While within their gift of tenancy land—Canaan renamed as *Israel* after their united name—many reflective songs were written, some of which have been collected and arranged into what we call the Psalter, or [the Scroll of] Psalms. There are a few other psalms scattered about the OT—for example Ex.15; Am.2:2-9.

The Psalter is a mixed bag of song types, and has gone global. "Jesus and his disciples loved the psalms. So also did the covenanters at Qumran, to judge by the many manuscripts found in the caves there" (Blair 149). Martin Luther called *Psalms* a Bible in miniature. "The psalms...are of great benefit to any believer who wishes to have help from the Bible in expressing joys and sorrows, successes and failures, hopes and regrets" (Fee & Stuart 2003:205).

But while seeking to hear its old voice *under Sinai*, our focus is its new voice *under Golgotha*. The psalmist's burnt animal offerings (with their link to obtaining forgiveness), are now meaningless. We are *not* under Sinai: offer yourself, *not* burnt animals, to Yahweh (Ps.66:13); meet at your local church-Jerusalem, *not* at Sinai's Jerusalem (Ps.122:2).

---

[30]   Covenant morphed in various ways. From person (Terah's son, Abraham's son; Isaac's son) to people (Jacob's sons), then via Moses (Ex.34:10), yet based on the less formal covenant. The earlier was an *El Shaddai* covenant; the latter a *Yahweh* covenant (Ex.6:3-5).

Let's first look a little bit about its general setup, before seeing something of how it relates to prayer. *Psalms* is somewhat artificially divided into 5 sections, perhaps to remind readers of the fivefold Pentateuch. Emphases vary somewhat between sections, yet the borderlines can be a bit fuzzy. For instance, you might see how borderline Pss. 106 and 107 are similar. Content elements can be basically seen as shared between sections.[31]

- Section 1   1–41   Mainly Yahwistic
- Section 2   42–72   Mainly Elohistic
- Section 3   73–89   Mainly Elohistic
- Section 4   90–106   Mainly Yahwistic
- Section 5   107–150   Mainly Yahwistic

The psalms had message and meaning written in, and that was written in what we might call poetry. C S Lewis called Ps.19 one of the best poems in the world. However, their poetry was not such as we might write nowadays. Their poetry had a rhythm of sound (syllables are stressed) and of sense (often using types of *parallelism*). Psalms are a kind of spiritual art. To understand them, it helps to be aware and to understand how they worked. For example Ps.27:3:

	A	B	C	Beat
1	Though an army	besiege	me	3
2	my heart	will not fear		2
1	though war	break out	against me	3
2	even then will I	be confident		2

---

[31]   Some reworkings were permitted. For example, Ps.53 is basically Ps.14 detetragrammatised, once Jews moved away from God's name. Also Ps.40:13-7 parallels Ps.70, and Ps.57:7-11+60:5-12, parallels Ps.108. Corrie ten Boom said that a WW2 rabbi they hid, liked to ask folk to read verse 1 from "psalm one hundred and sixty six". The 'trick' is that the first verse is the same in Ps.100 as in Ps.66. But no not quite, since one shows the older Yahweh style, while the other shows the less covenantal Elohim style. We should keep that theological distinction in mind.

Note how the thoughts in 1A (though an army/though war), 1B (besiege/break out) and 1C (me/against me) are parallel, and likewise in 2A (my heart/even then will I) and 2B (will not fear/be confident). Perhaps semi-poetry is a better term, since their poetry could overlap into prose; and, in writing prose, many prophets overlapped into poetry.

I suspect that none of the psalms were written on the fly, and that some were worked and reworked over one or more lifetimes. Consider for instance Ps.119, where "each stanza has eight two-part lines beginning with the same letter", and which step by step worked through all the 22 letters of the Hebrew alphabet (Bruce 638). They could incorporate existing material: compare 1 Sam.2:8//Ps.113:7.

"The Psalms must have been used in a number of different ways. Gunkel, for example, assumed that they were mostly personal expressions of piety—the sort of poetry that any worshipper would use to express their deepest feelings about life and about God. Others have argued that the psalms do not reflect individual experiences, but the experiences of the whole nation of Israel over a long period of time. It has even been suggested that they are a kind of spiritual temperature chart of Israel's history from the earliest days up to the time after the exile. Both these elements are no doubt present. But what is fundamental to the various thoughts of the psalms is a deep religious experience that their authors knew to be relevant to the whole of life. For the sense of God's reality can come as readily from Israel's history or from the writer's own private experiences" (Drane 97). And add to this last line, 'nature'.

Gunkel—followed by Westermann, Brueggemann, and many more— has helped us to group the psalms into distinct types. But in looking for patterns, a danger lies in squeezing them into cultic modes of ancient civilisations, overlooking their unique content as well as their democratising nature. The latter made many psalms workable in homely settings, unmediated by priests.[32] It may be that psalms were most if not all, composed substantially or exactly as we have them now in Hebrew form, even if composed within the world of the

---

[32]   Something which C11 Anselm sought to do with set-prayers.

priestly and royal, and shaped *de nova* by such influences.[33] Some were reworked even as we can rework song lyrics: I'm a song rewriter. They sought to promote reflection and the eschatological hope of Yahweh's reign through an ultimate messiah. Although they are more diverse than this, we can say that the main types of psalm are Glory, Groans, and Gratitude. They had a rich meditative prayer life.

Glory hymns, extolling Yahweh and his works (eg creation, cultus, city) typically began and ended in praise. For example, Ps.117:

- Introductory summons   Praise Yahweh
- Main section   For great is his love towards us
- Summary summons   Praise Yahweh (Hallel u Yah)[34]

And note Ps.8: "An important hymn because it regards people as the occasion for praise and, incidentally, explains the basis for the possibility of our experience with God" (Martens 170).

Other such hymns include Pss. 105, 111, 113, and 114. An Egyptian hymn to the god Aton is an example of non-Israelite hymns, but the covenant relationship of Israel was unique.

Groaning psalms are of laments, and begged for Yahweh's help. They all—except one—end with assurance. For example, Ps.13:

- Direct question   How long, Yahweh?
- Situational complaint   Will my enemy triumph over me?
- Petition   Please look to me and answer
- Covenant confidence   I trust in your unfailing love
- The praise   I will sing

Other such psalms include Ps.22 (Complaint (1-8); Confidence (9-10); Prayer (11-21); Praise (22-31)).

Gratitude psalms express thanks in three parts. For example, Ps.30:

- Thanks intended   I will exalt you

---

33   I think of how Luke, guided by the spirit over some period of time, assembled his research material into a cohesive whole (Lk.1:1-3).

34   I fondly recall my 1960's days in the Salvation Army, where with waves of tambourines we sang *"Hallelu! Hallelu! Hallelu! Halleluyah! Praise ye Yahweh!"*

- (Usually) help given   Salvation from death
- Thanks promised   I will give you thanks

As a whole, the psalms show that "God was not marginal but a vital reality of Israel's life. The [OT] does not contain lengthy philosophical or theoretical essays about God. We hear about...God not from the essayist but from the worshipper. An annunciation of his attributes, even, is always in the context of prayer or praise" (Martens 171).

A prophetic element was also picked up by various of the psalmists (see Ac.2:31). On the NT citing the OT, it may be said that there are genuine doubts about how accurate the names are that now introduce the psalms. I no longer assume that headings naming names, vouchsafe such authorship. Nor if I quote Mr Pickwick, do I deny Mr Dickens as the true author. Traditionally, appended names may bespeak a name-related psalm, as perhaps a psalm written *about*, rather than *by*, King David. A Davidian psalm might speak one way to ancient ears, and another way to our untrained ears.

For the writers did not add their names, and the "headings have been added editorially" by a later generation (Carson 1997:485).[35] It could well be that memories were reliable, and that the earlier generation had passed down the line who had written what. But by and large we accept the psalms, not because of who composed them, but because God has inspired their inclusion into his book, and we see verification through the church. And if we discover that the sons of Korah—not Asaph—wrote Ps.73, so what?

The paradigms within the psalms were, by the spirit, sometimes such as could speak powerfully about messiah himself: truth and prophecy were woven in. "From the apostolic use of the psalms, it is abundantly evident that they figure prominently in the preaching and teaching of the early church. The apostles established Jesus' suffering (Pss. 22; 35; 41;

---

[35] The Masoretic Text—ie the Hebrew textual tradition begun in the C1 AD—put these titles as a verse 1 of each psalm. This is why when quoting psalms, books sometimes give a reference to the Hebrew text and to the non-Hebrew texts. While this broke the poetical balance, especially with acrostic psalms, it shows the high regard that at least C1 ethnic Jews felt for the titles, which Jesus also reflected.

55; 69; 109), messianic claims (Pss. 2; 72; 89; 110; 132), priestly ministry (Ps.95), his being the Son of Man (Pss. 8; 16; 40), and the coming judgment and redemption (Pss. 18; 50; 68; 96–8; 102), by appealing to the psalms" (VanGemeren 2417-31/30250).

Reflections of Lewis

Let's zoom through *Reflections on the Psalms*, by C S Lewis. Though I much admire this book, and have been blessed by it, I do find four features in it quite repellent—four fat flies in rich perfume. These are the use of *Jew(s)*, when an anachronism for *Israelite(s)*; the degrading of God's name even from Tyndale's lower option, to [Lord]; the term *Judaism*, when an anachronism for what in AD 70 replaced Pharisaism; the concealed polytheism of *God*, when contextually it should be put as *god*, as open polytheism. Common enough errors, sadly, among current top-notch scholars—one must live with them.

In reading *Psalms*, we might pick up that the psalmists were more likely to beg for Yahweh's judgement, whereas we might be more likely to beg to escape Yahweh's judgement: do we not deserve his condemnation more than his commendation? But this different perspective is based on different aspects of his justice. One is the social level. The other is the heavenly level. Both can be spiritual. Indeed, atheists calling for justice are naive to the fact that if there is *no* god, there is *no* justice, so there would be no *sense* of justice. You can't logically hang an absolute on randomness. Ethics exists because the universe is built within moral supernature.

We can only perceive a justice or an injustice because we perceive God's just nature—an absolute. We can be mistaken about what is unjust, only because we are not mistaken that there is an absolute standard, justice, inexplicable if the universe is merely a random construct from nothingness. If we accuse the Just of being unjust, we commit a logical fallacy of accusing God of not being God. In such accusations we are usually either wishing God not to be, are unhappy with his interventionalism being limited, or both.

Job only came to the end of his dark tunnel once he compared his wisdom to Yahweh's, and realised that without sufficient wisdom he himself was calling unjust the Just (*Job* 40:8). He might not have realised that the satan had needed a lesson in human virtue, but he realised that he himself—and his immediate world—had been given some important upgrade.

The psalmists pleaded for God's justice, and from such as Pss. 67:4 and 96:12-3, we can see that "judgement was apparently an occasion of universal rejoicing" (Lewis 1958:15). This in turn warned the unjust to repent and to make restitution, and warned those tempted to injustice to think again. In a Christian perspective, we may more often see that though those unjust towards us might be adjudged to have been in the wrong, we might well be adjudged to have been in the wrong towards God. Yet the psalmists were not without that perspective (Ps.143:2).[36] That raises questions about pardon from the righteous judge of the universe.

But the coming judgement does not mean that our civil disputes will be sorted out, although they will be entirely ended as issues. But for the psalmists, issues were important, and should be important for us both sides of any dispute. And the psalmists saw that beneath human conflicts, God was concerned with just treatments and outcomes, whether on individual or international matters. Even Yahweh's people could internationally be in the wrong, and at times Yahweh would step in with justice for the wronged.

Sometimes individuals and nations are treated deplorably, and get no justice. The fact that God is as a father of the fatherless, and a protector of widows (Ps.68:5; Jas.1:27), does not mean that each orphan and widow will as such get due justice in this world, or even recompense in the age to come.

But this tells us about whose side we ought to be on, in principle if not in practice, even as God is on the side of the needy in principle if not in practice. Sometimes it can be difficult or impossible to claim to be the former, without being the latter. Sometimes there can be good and sufficient reasons to forgo a good action in line with good

---

[36]   Here I think it was a case of the psalmist saying that they were suffering enough unjustly, and hoped that Yahweh would not add just punishment. There are seven penitential psalms (Pss. 6; 32; 38; 51; 102; 130; 143). But generally, the psalmists focused on unjust attack (Ps.7:3-5). Our prayers should confess both our guilt and our innocence.

attitude. Sometimes in God's calling, we ourselves might be bereaved or orphaned, whether by death or divorce.

The theme of getting justice can and should be factored into our prayers, even as it was factored into the prayers of the psalmists. For us it might include lament, petition, repentance, even joy.

From psalmists suffering injustice, Lewis moved to the psalmists being vindictive. Ps.109 is a prime example of individual lamenting and seeking of vengeance. In it we see within the context of prayer, a powerful unleashing of revengeful rage. Is such prayer justified? Those against the psalmist had been extreme in their evil injustice against he who had been friendly towards them. To them who were satans towards him (4), the psalmist prayed that a satan—perhaps one of their number—would betray them unto death as their just deserts (6).[37]

Bitter emotion went into these prayers, piling on imprecation upon imprecation, curse upon curse. It even extended towards any families involved, in fact begged Yahweh to multiply widows and orphans— the more the merry less. Was it so that dependents should not benefit from ill-begotten gains, perhaps even that by beggaring them they would come to publicly condemn the sins which had given them previous wealth, so making them sadder yet wiser people: "sorrow worketh repentance unto salvation" (ASV: 2 Cor.7:10)? Alas, the psalmist wished simply to deprive the bereaved of any such charity (12-3).

Lewis called that attitude, demonic (Lewis 1958:23). But he also admired their openness about anger, when contrasted to a lame attitude in the West where anger must be denied even against moral evils. Moral insensibility fails to take right and wrong seriously. It can be healthy to be angry with spiritual indignation, but Paul said that in our anger we ought not to sin (Eph.4:26). It can be sin *not* to be angry over injustice, whether to yourself or to others.

In a communal lament, a psalmist went so far as to desire a blessing on any who bashed in the brains of Babylonian babies (Ps.137:9). Sure, Babylonia had done as much to countless hordes of babies, but its

---

37   From the Hebrew behind 'accuse' in v4, we get the word satan (accuser).

babies had not done the dirty. But in the mindset of the day, solidarity was key. Blessings were wished on the kith and kin of those who did good; curses were wished on the kith and kin of those who did evil.

The psalmist wished a quick retaliatory strike against Babylonia— only by conquest would her babies be brained. After death those slain as babies (or as adults) would be judged rightly by Yahweh, based on what they were, not on what their people had done. Even so we are to commend neither savage psalmists nor their singers, for their brutal prayers for brutal outcomes of war upon the innocent.

We have been taught to bless those who sin against us, and to love our enemies. But in prayer, we can with the psalmists let our hair down, and get the bitterness out of our system (emetic). Before God, we can acknowledge our demonic temptation both to curse those who sin against us, and to hate our enemies. Expressing that anger, Lewis argued, is a lot safer psychologically—for us and for our enemies—than hiding our anger from God and from ourselves. And also better to ask God to avenge—if he sees fit—than to pay back tit for tat, curse for curse, eye for eye.[38] And fortunately God doesn't always answer either our divine or our demonic prayers.

And woe to others, if we eke out our resentments in our actions or attitudes against them, in petty or powerful ways. "I am exceptionally blessed in having been allowed a way of life in which, having little power, I have had little opportunity of oppressing and embittering others. Let all of us who have never been school prefects, N.C.O.s, schoolmasters, matrons of hospitals, prison warders, or even magistrates, give hearty thanks for it" (Lewis 1958:27).

Our righteous or unrighteous anger, given free rein, can also show us our inner darkness. That can lead to prayer for the light of Christ to cast out our darkness. In *The Holy War*, John Bunyan showed how Christification comes post-conversion, bit by bit, as our soul is slowly captured and guarded by the forces of Light. So in some ways, our

---

[38]   Incidentally the *lex talionis* was an improvement of the surrounding nations' idea of two eyes for one eye. It limited revenge to what had been done unto you, instead of going the extra mile in anger. It set the *just deserts*, with literalism usually downgraded biblically to mere financial penalties.

angry prayers are healthy, enlightening, and can lead to a blessed improvement. There were, incidentally, correctives within Sinaism: Ex.23:4; Lv.19:17-8; Pr.24:17.

Lewis' next chapter—on death—makes some good points, not least on how unreligious the ideas of hell and heaven can be, if preached as sticks and carrots to accept God. And he noted how "Buddhists are much concerned with what will happen to them after death, but are not, in any true sense, theists" (Lewis 1958:39). Indeed, inner preparation for postmortem life can be as mundane as insurance policies, and buying into God can be like marrying for finance rather than for affection. Irreligious conversion is more likely to be into mere Churchianity than into Christianity. For his part, Lewis was allowed for a whole year to believe in God and to try—in some stumbling fashion—to obey him, before any belief in the future life was given him.[39] And that year always seemed to him to have been of very great value (Lewis 1958:40). This chapter raises issues such as how much should we pray for our own benefit, but I shall skip it.

From *The Canterbury Tales*—and reflected in *That Hideous Strength*—we read: "Now let us stint all this and speak of mirth".[40] Thus Lewis moved us on to the fair beauty of Yahweh. The psalmists spoke of his beauty, his wonder, his goodness, their delight and their gusto. They revelled in him. A good question for us is whether we do too. Some who come to him for the offer of heaven, might need to learn that love which says, *Better to die for you now and perish in blackest hell, than to live forever in paradise without you.*

Partying is part of the psalms. "Every temple in the world, the elegant Parthenon at Athens and the holy Temple at Jerusalem, was a sacred slaughter-house.... But even that had two sides. If temples smelled of blood, they also smelled of roast meat; they struck a festive and homely note, as well as a sacred" (Lewis 1958:42). We may make merry in Yahweh, even more so than did the ancient Israelites, for we are closer to joy and have more reason for thankfulness. If we do not

---

39   Anthony Flew, also a convert from atheism, made clear his nonbelief in postmortal life, and indeed his wish to deny it.

40   In *The Nun's Priest's Tale*, and where the Pendragon speaks with Jane.

dance at the butcher's, we can still, metaphorically, dance in our prayers, though some, like Michal, might ridicule our gladness.[41]

And such delight in him is miles better than "the merely dutiful 'church-going' and laborious 'saying our prayers' to which most of us are, thank God not always, but often, reduced" (Lewis 1958:43). Our prayers can be at times a burden, but at times they can be a sparkle. Prayers and practice can combine. The psalmists made merry together (Ps.27:4), and—to borrow a few words from William Wordsworth—a poet could not but be gay, in such a jocund company. Indeed their integration of holy rolling with holy reflection, might be a more holistic life than a Sunday-only or Prayer-only time of *worship*.

"Their fingers itch for the harp (43:4), for the lute and the harp—wake up, lute and harp!—(57:9); let's have a song, bring the tambourine, bring the 'merry harp with the lute', we're going to sing merrily and make a cheerful noise (81:1-2). Noise, you may well say. Mere music is not enough. Let everyone, even the benighted Gentiles, clap their hands (47:1). Let us have clashing cymbals, not only well tuned, but loud, and dances too (150:5). Let even the remote islands (all islands were remote, for the Israelites were no sailors) share the exultation (97:1)" (Lewis 1958:47-8). Are our hearts ever merrily on fire when we pray?

If cut off from the temple, a psalmist could feel like a parched deer agonising for free flowing water: "My soul thirsts for God, for the living god. When shall I come and behold the face of God?" (NRSV: Ps.42:2).[42] Perhaps they had a sense that in seeing God's temple, they were seeing God (Jhn.14:9). Ps.63 spoke of a longing for God that felt like being parched in a desert. Whether his covenant love meant more than individual life (CEV: 3), or whether the psalmist meant he'd risk his life for God's covenant love—as one risks their life for love of country—I presume that *life* simply meant mortal life. To lose mortal life is not to lose Yahweh's love. Indeed we may speak of a hunger and thirst for Yahweh, an "appetite for God" (Lewis 1958:47).

---

[41]   Incidentally, the king was not naked.

[42]   There is disagreement about how to read the text: seeing God's face, or God's face seeing?

For communal thanksgiving, the psalmist spoke of being "filled full" by Yahweh's goodness and his holiness in his temple (CEB: 65:4). Envy the swallows which nest in Yahweh's temple: *Oh to be like even a lowly bird nesting in such glory* (84:3)! A mere temple doorkeeper for even one day, was more enviable than 10,000 years of mere fame.

Lewis' next chapter—on regulations for life—makes some good points, not least how law and order help society to flow well within their channels: harmony tastes sweeter than honey (Ps.119:103); sanity is sweet after a nightmare. Order gave firmness for feet which had long slithered in muddy fields. Yahwism was a healthy mix of global laws—such as honesty—and symbolic covenant laws—such as observing the sabbath. The latter were good in focusing minds upon facets of spiritual life, though as Charles Williams warned, "when the means are autonomous they are deadly" (Lewis 1958:52). They were also prophetic pointers of fulfilments to come with messiah. For instance we may look at the kosher laws of foods, and see how once they spoke of the Gentile peoples as unkosher, but Yahweh's people as kosher, and forbade certain types of contamination to her holy mission. That ended socially once a new spiritual order was birthed (Ac.10:28). This chapter raises issues such as self-righteousness when we pray—and when we don't—but I shall skip it.

Lewis' next chapter—on hypocrisy—makes some good points, not least how we can be tempted to fit in with the spirit of the age, as lambs dressed up as wolves. We should beware lest we stride along with the shameful, stand around with sinners, and sit silently with scoffers (Ps.1:1). Are we not not good enough to help them, and too weak not to become bad like them? This chapter raises issues such as how we must pray for strength and wisdom to keep our integrity, both for our sakes and for that of others—but I shall skip it.

When it comes to the fair beauty of the world about and the heavens above—natural nature—we have much to praise God for. In one way, to enjoy the country you must live outside of it—enjoy by contrast. Does a crab book a beach for a holiday? Of course, in another way, by living in the country one can enjoy different aspects of it, such as its fruitfulness in food—living off the land—like Homer and the psalmists did (Lewis 1958:66-7; Pss. 65:9-13; 104:16).

But one way or another we can become too enamoured with nature. To the ancients, too often they mentally divinised nature, and then worshipped it on impulse (*Job* 31:26-8), rather than in context of created to creator.[43] Did God overlook such folly and accredit it to them as indirect worship, the babbling as children of those who were children? Job had come to know better, and so to him it would be a throwback to pre-enlightenment (Rm.14:23).

The biblical doctrine of creation divests nature of any pretence of being self-existent, of having intrinsic deity. Yet it clothes nature as a handmaiden of her creator, as a work of his art, "an index, a symbol, a manifestation" of God (Lewis 1958:70). In Ps.19, the image of the searching and cleansing sun doubled as a symbol of the searching and cleansing Law. In Ps.36:5-6, it is Yahweh's inescapable permeation from the highest heavens to the deepest earth: "God's judgements are an abyss and a mystery like the sea" (Lewis 1958:70), and thunder and lightning can be an image of his voice (Ps.29:3-5).

I affectionately recall a jolly old song which thanks Yahweh that *he has given me the wine to make my heart rejoice / and the oil to make my face to shine*. More of a Jesus-song actually, though based on Ps.104:14-5. Yes, we can thank God that nature provides blessings to man, but also rejoice in the full reading of this psalm, that the biosphere is so wonderfully self-catering.[44] It is a wonderful world within the wonderful universe.[45]

---

[43]   Paganism rarely bothered with a First Cause. When it did it usually assumed that divinities came from something rather than someone. "The difference between believing in God and in many gods is not one of arithmetic", for they were created *gods/goddesses* (Lewis 1958:71).

[44]   Scientifically the first cell was created capable of reproducing and restructuring into a balanced ecosystem, but behind its coding Yahweh is its ultimate source. "If the universe booted up the first cell without the action of a designer, then the universe itself must possess directional qualities that nobody yet comprehends" (Marshall 2015:151). As the psalmists, let's rejoice in the harmony of God's creation.

[45]   Lewis noted the similarity of this nature psalm to a monotheistic hymn by

Lewis' next chapter is perhaps my favourite. Why ought we to praise Yahweh? We might simply praise him because we're told to, no questions asked. Fine, but if we ask why, can we find good answer? For some are genuinely puzzled. After all, if God begs to be told how good and how great he seems to us, is he some kind of cosmic narcissist, the supreme egotist? [46] Should we treat him so? Is it flattery, as a man might flatter a girl? Will God be swept off his feet?

Another line of thought is that our foolish praise could objectively be an insult, but graciously pardoned by God. I have in mind a song which basically says to deity: *You are worthy of my praise*—as if *my* praise is of great value—for happily deity manages to match my standard. I should rather ask, *Is my petty praise worthy of deity?*

The psalms certainly encourage us to praise him, and might even make it sound as if it's bargaining: "You like praise? Do this for me, and you shall have some" (Lewis 1958:78). In Ps.54, was the psalmist's response of praise (6), their payment for being rescued (1)? Did they reckon that for Yahweh's sake—do kindly remind him—he really should rescue his flatterers from death, since otherwise he would lose his fans (Pss. 30:9; 88:10; 119:175)? In short, it could sound as if praise was a lollipop we had, and that God had a sweet tooth. I have heard some Christians say that God needs us, needs our fellowship, our company, lest he be lonely. That, they have patiently explained, is why he created us—as if he has a man-shaped void.

Let us question the understanding of the psalmists. Had they misunderstood Yahweh? Let us consider why, perhaps, we ought to praise Yahweh, by looking first at lower objects of praise. Take an unusually vivid sunset. We might invite others to join in our praise.

Pharaoh Akhenaten—though he had a touch of dualism. Unlike Henry 8 who plundered the abbeys, the temples of Egypt swept back into power once Akhenaten was gone. Some wonder whether his light from on high might, in God's design, have helped Moses grasp the oneness of God.

[46] Even if we account him to be the supreme egotist, he is the opposite pole to being the supreme egotist—he is the supreme altruist. Some songs mislead. At least Bob Kauflin excluded the trinity—*the praise will all belong to you*—but even picturing God the son as ungraciously egotistic, hurts—*Grace..called..me to bring you glory* (*Grace Unmeasured* (2005)).

Likewise for human artistry. In such instances, we have not praised the object *to please the object*, but to soak in, to even enrich, our own pleasure. The connoisseur of wine will see, swirl, sniff, sip, and savour. If they praise the wine, though it is not enriched by praise, others might join them in a glass. And if the wine could speak, and was altruistic, might it not say *praise me, that others may enjoy me though I'm best only in moderation*? The more thumbs up a YouTube podcast gets, the more the algorisms promote it to others.

Since Yahweh can speak, may he not as altruistically command us to praise him, as a duty we have to others? And such, incidentally, would extend to our lifestyle: let our light shine (Mt.5:16).[47] Public prayer is one forum in which to praise him to others as a recommendation; private prayer is a forum to praise him to ourselves, to feast on him.

"The miserable idea that God should in any sense need, or crave for, our worship like a vain woman wanting compliments...is implicitly answered" by Ps.50:12: "If I were hungry, I would not tell you..." (Lewis 1958:79). It is for our benefit to praise him, even as it is to praise a scintillating sunset. To harden our hearts against praise, can damage our souls. Not because the sunset or Yahweh seeks our damage or is offended, but because we fight against our own wellbeing. To enjoy, to appreciate, is part of human nature: "...praise almost seems to be inner health made audible" (Lewis 1958:80); breathing out having breathed in.

Thus the idea of *in heaven* praising deity eternally, is about enjoying him eternally, and him delighting in our praise is simply because he delights in our wellbeing and enjoyment. It might even be that the psalmists, fearing that death would terminate their enjoyment of Yahweh, pleaded with him to extend their mortal years. We now know that death opens the door to fuller joy (Php.1:21).

Lewis' next chapter—on extended meanings—makes some good points, not least how so far as able, we should both engage with the psalms *as if* among their original audience, and *also as* Christians

---

47   Incidentally this was first taught to non-Christians, encouraging them at Level 2 to be the light of Sinai in their dark world (Is.60:1). How much more at Level 3, are we the light of/to the world (Ac.13:47)?

with the hindsight of extended meaning.[48] And even pagan writings have elements which fit the Christian story: were thoughts beyond their thoughts to those high bards given? This chapter raises issues such as unbiased and insightful reading of whatever God has coded into *Psalms*, without reading into *Psalms* what he has not coded in—but I shall skip it.

Lewis' penultimate chapter—on Scripture—makes some good points, not least on how we have different genres in Scripture, such as the historical and the mythical. And he lamented that, having dropped atheism and its philosophy of dismissing all claims of miracles as nonhistorical, some had labelled him a Fundamentalist. This chapter raises issues such as how we should read extended meaning from the psalms when attested by the NT, since granted that miracles can happen, there is no good ground to dismiss predictive psalms (eg 16:10), and good messianic reason to accept them—but I shall skip it.

Lewis' ultimate chapter—on intentional extended meaning within the psalms—makes some good points, somewhat prepared for in the previous two chapters. We can see that messiah would exceed his own dynastic father, would suffer terribly,[49] rise from death, and would head an order of priesthood over and above Aaron's. This final chapter raises issues such as how the psalms connect to prophecy—

---

[48]   Similarly, with the eucharist I picture myself first as a slave on the doorstep to the exodus and the freedom of our own country. I chew the bread thinking, *it won't be long now*. Then my mind moves—if only the musicians' unheavenly anthem drowns not all music but its own—to the spiritual freedom of a life of exodus and of Canaan we now enjoy (Christian Life), with hints of the final exodus into the final Canaan (Everlasting Life).

Sadly the musicians sometimes itch to interrupt such reflection. If they play a prayer-song, I wish to pray. If they play a non-prayer-song, I still wish to analyse the words. Either choice, my reflections are interrupted. And if it's a prayer-song when the elements are taken to the congregation, I do not wish to interrupt prayer to take the elements. Then I simply partake "in my mind".

[49]   Sadly Lewis 1958:106 assumed as fact the theory that Jesus became sin. No, he became a sin offering (NLT: 2 Cor.5:21). And he became cursed, not a curse (NLT: Gal.3:13). Many myths, such as his body being broken, still plague us.

---

but I shall skip it. It does, however, add meat to the bone, some rich christology and huiology which can factor into our praying.

Give us this day our daily psalm

How then should we pray through the psalms? A lot of elements have already been mentioned, but do do do remember to make some adjustments between their covenant and culture, and our covenant and culture, for messiah has both enriched our appreciation, ended certain things, and recontextualised certain things. It's a different ballgame. Science, moreover, is a useful new handmaiden to Scripture, enriching our appreciation. And it is also basic to try to factor in their perspective, holding them in some kind of comparison. Let's take an example, Ps.8.

Now I would at times mix Bible versions—each have their strengths and weaknesses, and yes, educated guesswork. If we combine the strengths of different versions, we sometimes build a stronger reading, and comparing them helps us to mull over meanings. So let us begin this psalm of creation praise, where we leave "the world of enemies, wicked people, and distorted justice (Ps.3–7) for an image of the world as God originally created it" (VanGemeren 5947-8/30250).

If we begin with say, the NIV, we first must move from [LORD our Lord] (1). The HCSB/LEB improve by putting [Yahweh], but from the Bishops Bible onwards, none seem prepared to decapitalise [Lord] to [lord]. When they prayed *Yahweh our lord*, they prayed with their covenant with God in mind, their special spiritual relationship, their identity politics.

Thus when we pray through this aright, we can see something of salvation history, how God had established an ethnic race and nation to carry his glory and his plan: husk. We can move to how the plan unfolded with messiah, and see the new covenant mediated by Yeshua: wheat. We can see that Yahweh was lord to that ancient people, and that lordship—governance—has been focused in the person of Jesus—Jesus is lord, Yahweh's appointed lord over the church. We can then reflect on aspects of him, such as his connection to deity, and to humanity.

We see that though Yahweh was supreme above the earth, only ethnic Israel was privileged to *know*—in the sense of covenant knowledge—his name.[50] Are we not more privileged to further know the name of our messiah, who shares the Yahweh-term *lord* (Php.2:9-11)? Incidentally, with Paul we acknowledge that Jesus' name, lord, is held under God the father: it was a gift to Jesus.[51]

Moving through the psalm, we see that even the heavenly universe is glorious because created by God. But quickly the psalmist pictures weak little children, not even soldiers: "the praise of children and infants" (NIV: 2). And "the sound of opposition is silenced by the babbling and chatter of children" being witness to the fact that God has established a stronghold on Earth, has established his rule (VanGemeren 5989/30250). Did that mean the fact of humanity planted and preserved on Earth against a cosmic foe? Do we look thus at the solidity of God's creation plan? Or did that mean the children of Sinai, even as later Jesus would say that his church would never die off (Mt.16:18)? Do we look thus at the solidity of God's salvation plan? Think it through, then pray through it.

We too should stand amazed that he who created the universe, should be concerned about us (3-4). Some might be puzzled by the anthropomorphism of Yahweh having fingers (3). In poetic way, the psalmist likened Yahweh to human artisans, focusing on skill over brute force. Though they didn't know the mechanics, they could see that the universe (night sky) was a profound work of design.

We might stand amazed over the Big Bang,[52] and our anthropic universe, and reflect on the designer having sparked off an event which, unfolding over billennia according to his implanted laws, has naturally resulted in stars, planets, moons, and on which planets—ours at least—he has planted life. Macromanagement. If we plant a seed, under friendly conditions it grows according to its inner laws.

---

[50] Anyone can know Penny as a woman, but only her husband will know her as a wife. Ethnic Israel knew Yahweh as their exclusive husband, even though his name had wider circulation.

[51] Systematic theology would say that the title was given at conception/birth, but only activated after his death/resurrection.

[52] Whether driven by science or philosophy, alternative ideas have been mooted. For convenience I will assume that Big Bang theory is substantially correct.

Has the universe not been like that seed? And if the universe, has he not designed a cell which has unfolded and multiplied in many divergent ways—intelligent evolution? Has God thus through kickstart, brought forth the human race, giving it his *image*? In *Mere Christianity*, C S Lewis suggested that raising humanity into Christ (*imago christi*) has been the next step in evolution (2.5).

Or we might favour the micromanagement model, and presume that God has specifically designed our planet, or at least humanity, giving man his *image*. But whatever his *modus operandi*, how amazing is the biosphere—here particularly man, and perhaps elsewhere within the universe? With the help of science, we now understand more about biology than did the psalmists. And yet compared to the sheer size and significance of the universe, "what are human beings that [God is] mindful of them, mortals that [he cares] for them" (NRSV: 4)?

On this last text, D A Carson argued the point that the term *son of man* did not always carry a messianic link in the OT, that it was not used thus in Ps.8, and that when this text was used in the NT, it was not used thus. Hence, and in light of Hebrew parallelism and parallel expression in Heb.2:6 in a non-messianic way, I think it better to avoid the son-of-man expression here.[53]

You might, if comparing Bible versions, wish to ponder in prayer whether Yahweh deems humanity important (to whom or for what), as the ERV/NCV assert (4). Perhaps the wonder is that we have no importance to him, yet he cares? Though you might think an amoeba insignificant compared to a galaxy, Ps.8 goes on to show how glorious we are even now.

What have we been made only a bit below? Is it the unfallen angels (NCV/NIV/NKJV)? Is it the heavenly beings (ESV/LEB/NET)? But who or what are *they*, if not unfallen angels, perhaps even helping locally to govern the world? In fact, the Hebrew term *elohim*, can mean *God*. Are we a wee bit below God (ERV/HCSB/NASB/NLT/NRSV)? Heb.2:7 has

---

[53]   After reviewing humanity's status, the writer considered Jesus (Heb.2:9) in distinction to humanity at large. He has been exalted to founder of the new humanity, which will be above angels. Overall MEVV Grades: NRSV (A+); CEV/NCV (A-); CEB (B+); NIV/NLT (C+); ERV (D+); LEB/NABRE/NKJV (D-).

angels, but maybe was a working idea about *elohim*.[54] Of angels, it was understood that a touch from them could reduce us to dust, so even this lower reading would be awesome.

However it read, it read that mankind stood crowned with glory, standing as high rulers in our world which had been subjugated to man. We share the reign of God. In reality, this sovereignty we have is subject to abuse. Though in God's image (Gen.9:6), we have murdered one another and butchered the earth, in ways in which no mere animal is capable. C S Lewis suggested that ours might be a quarantine planet, for he postulated planetary sentient-conscious and unfallen life on other planets, safe from our contamination.

But our very ability reflects a higher possibility for good, too. To stories of animals fleeing from us, there are stories of animals fleeing to us. Seeing our possibilities to rise because we are in God's likeness by his design, is a useful corrective for demeaning our status as a species on Earth and within the universe. Let us not, in common humanity, undermine our hidden divinity under deity.

The animal kingdom is subjected to us and is fair game, but our rulership should not be badly oppressive—to oppress wheat (or cattle) by harvesting is permitted for our needs: a fair-use policy exists. When our rulership is badly oppressive, is it not because we are failing to carry out the duty of care that our king commands? Is even 'Firework' Night not a terror inducing abuse? And speaking to power, when we see our brutal treatment of the animal kingdom, the psalm reminds us that we have fallen short of God's glory. For the world has been placed at our feet, at our royal footstool. Should we not treat the creaturely world as petitioners seeking to receive our blessing? Did not Paul later say that the creaturely world looks forward to the day when we, who are in Christ's image, will come into our own when Christ our king returns (Rm.8:19)?[55]

---

54   *Elohim's* range of meaning includes human spirits (1 Sam.28:13).

55   Imagery elsewhere of cataclysmic destruction upon the earth, of the earth, I take to be metaphorical. Ps.8 speaks of creatures of the land, sea, and sky.

Ps.8 closed as it began, on the majesty of Yahweh's name in all the earth. We could easily tie in this psalm with the extra data of Heb.2, affirming that though now our glory lies largely hidden, in messiah we see how the story is to unfold. But even without this, we have much material to focus prayer through this psalm.

"Yahweh, you are supreme, the king of the universe. We might not like the term king, and yet is there a better? You have not been elected. You are the creator. And you care amazingly for your creation. We can see something of your glory just by looking above in wonder, stargazing. How blessed we are by telescopes and astronomy.

"And yet there is more glory within our world, the biosphere, even in the humble amoeba. And we should not overlook ourselves, for humanity is crowned with your glory. Even the most evil has your glory, though reign as evil kings within their petty kingdoms, abusers, defilers of the earth. Please help us to reign in our little kingdoms, as representing you. May we be blessings to our fellow man, to the land, the sea, and the sky. May we receive your blessings of care, and bow to your will. Thank you."

Interestingly in *Revelation*, there is talk of demon beasts of land, sea, and sky. On balance, is it that the demonic inclines human beings to exercise their royal authority to harm land, sea, and sky, until Christ returns to bring peace and prosperity?

Chapter 03   <u>Prayer and Christianity</u>

Mrs Potato had recently died in a car smash, leaving three Miss Potatoes, and Widower Potato. Looking back at how his life had been blessed by his marriage, he urged his three daughters to get themselves good spouses. Soon Nadine the eldest, told him her good news. She was betrothed to a King Edward. That was very good, said her father, himself a Royal Blue. Soon Nicola the middle daughter, told him her good news. She was betrothed to a Royal Jersey. That was good, said her father. Soon Desiree the youngest, told him her good news. She was betrothed to a Gary Lineker. That was bad, said her father. Why, he was merely a common tater.

Are you *merely* a Christian? Have you heard the good news? All people were once commoners, spiritually speaking, but "...God has been so kind to us, and he has accepted us because of Jesus. And so we will live and rule like kings" (CEV: Rm.5:17). So while we shouldn't be snobby about it, we should rejoice in the fact that in messiah, we have been raised into spiritual royalty. It's good to get to know they who have raised us up, brought us in. And who would that be, you ask? Well, that would be the trinity. "The trinity is the highest revelation God has made of himself to his people" (White 14).

In *My Fair Lady*, Eliza sings to Freddie: "Don't talk of stars, burning above; if you're in love, show me!" (*Show Me*). Likewise I say, don't *tell* me you're a trinitarian, *pray* like one. If trinitarianism's not rooted in your prayer life, then it's not that deeply imbedded in you, even if you can recite the ancient creeds off by heart, and teach them from the pulpit. I have heard pentecostal, Nazarene, and FIEC leaders, all publicly crucify the father in their prayers (*patrem crucifixit*). Yet they would swear blind that they were trinitarians. Fact is, it's in their head, but not in their blood.

Gordon Fee once said that "trinitarian Christians are not simply those in the theological sense of being able to affirm, and perhaps even explicate, this deepest mystery and most powerful truth of our faith, but also internalize this experience and live out their faith in trinitarian terms—as those whose whole lives are determined by, and thus lived in the light of, the experience of God himself: God, Father, Son, and Holy Spirit" (2000:24-5: slightly adjusted).

Looking back only a few centuries, we see the idea of early year teaching about the trinity. For instance, in the second volume of John Bunyan's, *The Pilgrim's Progress*, there is a place where Prudence 'catechises' the young lad James:[56]

Prudence: "James, can you tell me who made us?"
James: "God the father, God the son, and God the spirit."
Prudence: "Very good. And can you tell me who saves us?"
James: "God the father, God the son, and God the spirit."
Prudence: "Excellent. But how does God the father save us?"
James: "By his grace."
Prudence: "And how does God the son save us?"
James: "By his righteousness, death, and life."
Prudence: "And how does God the spirit save us?"
James: "By his illumination, his renovation, and his preservation."

All good biblical stuff, but it's stuff which should get prayed into us by us, and not merely taught to us. I hold with Donald Bloesch, that ideally "theology that is biblical and evangelical will always be nurtured by prayer" (Walter A Elwell's *Evangelical Dictionary of Theology*, 1985:866). It almost goes without saying, that the process is somewhat circular— or spiralling, whether decreasing or increasing. So true prayer—

---

[56]   I have largely updated the wording, and slightly amended it. As to the first question, it's based on ultimacy, not direct biology (Eph.3:14-5): "When I think of the greatness of this great plan, I fall on my knees before God the father [*patēr*] (from whom all fatherhood [*patera*], earthly or heavenly, derives its name)..." (J B Phillips: adjusted).

prayer that is biblical and evangelical[57]—should always be nurtured by theology. In short, we should seek to grasp what is biblical, and then to pray it into and through our lives. That, in turn, should nurture and grow the truth in us and through us.

So, what is God's tripersonal and monosocietal identity (triunity), and how should we pray it? Let's begin at the beginning of Christian life. Though possibly a little late in the day to talk about entrance prayer, something brief should perhaps be said. For at the end of the day, entrance into Christianity, is entrance into the trinity.[58]

<u>Water-baptism entrance?</u>

First I wish to consider a rival idea, one which does not hold prayer to be the way into Christ's kingdom. Some say that water-baptism[59] in infancy, not prayer, is the entrance into God's kingdom.[60] At least—to illustrate with vaccination—they say that it gives eternal security in the first few years, even if those baptised need a booster (for example, *confirmation*) or so, in later years.[61]

I suspect that this general pattern quickly formed from parental pressures. When you think about it, it's obvious that before infant water-baptism could begin, there had to be Christian parents who hadn't been baptised as infants: the chickens came first! If there was a way to be a Christian without being water-baptised in infancy, is that way still open? I think it's also obvious that biblically, there was a strong connection, even an assumption, between personal belief

---

[57] By the latter term I do not mean a political evangelicalism distinct from Christianity, but a Christian emphasis that, holding to the physical resurrection of Jesus and exclusivity of Christianity as the way to the father, promotes spiritual conversion individually elected, as the way in.

[58] A Christian doesn't have to be a trinitarian, but it's better to be both.

[59] For convenience I'll not tackle a distinction sometimes made, between water-sprinkling (*rhantism*) and water-immersion (*baptism*).

[60] More fully covered in Hakes 2018.

[61] *Pace* King Henry 8's *Defence of the Seven Sacraments* (1521), I see no biblical grounds for confirmation. That it can be a significant act of wilful dedication, I happily accept. Some thank God for their confirmation.

and water-baptism.[62] I think that the link was that having gone through the door by personal faith, water-baptism was the standard public commitment to Jesus as lord, a waving of the Christian flag. And I can see how one could be confused as to which connected factor was, if any, the actual door into Christ's kingdom.

Had I been a C1 Christian father, I might have asked myself, *has my personal faith simply led me to the door of water-baptism, or has my personal faith been the door.*[63] Still, so long as we went through that door, did it matter what prompted us through it? Should I not, as a responsible father, push my children through it to get them into church, even if not into heaven beyond earth? Did not the master say that we should "compel them to come in" (Lk.14:23)?[64] Having personally believed myself into Christ's kingdom, and especially if equating that with everlasting life, naturally I would wish my offspring to have everlasting life too.[65]

But if they had found the entrance as *personal belief*, why create another entrance—*parental belief*? I suspect that in early years, the

---

[62] Can you only have one side of a coin? However, I would discount the idea of water-baptism being one side of the Christian coin: welcome and commitment are the two sides, and I do not argue that water-baptism is essential to commitment, howbeit being on the side of commitment.

[63] A point-of-salvation, question.

[64] This parable was not addressing Christianity (which did not exist), nor was it saying "drag them in" (MSG) as if to a tyrant's banquet. It was, in the story, a message to encourage in (CSB/ERV/NCV/NLT) such as the lower classes, who might not believe it was for them.

[65] Those holding water-baptism to be the entrance to ultimate salvation, would generally allow that it works both for babies (through parental faith) and believers (through their own faith). But if one believes and is spirit-baptised (Ac.10:44,47), but dies before water-baptism, are they ultimately damned? Some speak of *intentionality* as key, of God accounting as water-baptised, all for whom water-baptism was sought, or who sought water-baptism, or would have sought water-baptism had they known about it (Ac.19:1,5). That raises its own set of questions, such as, what if the believer had never heard of water-baptism; what of Salvationists, if they believe General Booth's line that water-baptism was not key? And why, if we can be saved by intention, do we need the act? After all, if we can survive on the *intention* to eat, food isn't needed.

idea of personal faith subsequently shown by water-baptism, shifted to water-baptism subsequently shown by personal faith. Such a shift would lead to questions about whether personal faith was in any way, shape, or form, needed to precede water-baptism. Was not parental faith enough for everlasting life, with personal faith being grown into by the water-baptised children, implanted in the faith even if the faith was not implanted as a seed within them?

But, I ask, for those who die in infancy, is it fair of God to give heaven to the privileged few who have been water-baptised, and hell to those who have not been water-baptised? Does ultimate destination depend so much on one's choice of parents? Does God run a postcode lottery? [66] That is, if water-baptism really is indeed essential for ultimate life, for life with God beyond death. The church has long lived with this ethical puzzle.[67] Those who hold the puzzle, often offer a small cluster of proof-texts for a solution.

Well, what about household water-baptisms, of which there are five biblical reports? [68] These are sometimes used as supporting arguments. Surely, some say, babies were included in the biblical examples? Let's whizz through them.

---

[66] Some have reduced this postcode objection, by reckoning that God must have an in-between fate for them: then it's a postcode lottery *with a consolation prize.* A similar puzzle exists in evangelical circles, where for anyone dying without hearing the gospel, hell is deemed to be their lot. Again, various suggestions have been made to soften this, such as exempting people who die in the 'age of innocence'—even if they were conceived with a sin-bias—or suggesting ideas such as middle-knowledge, choice after death, or annihilation.

[67] Those who argue that infant water-baptism is to the Yeshuic Covenant, what infant son circumcision was to the Sinaitic Covenant, can have a compound puzzle. Why was the essential to ultimate heaven, precluded from non-circumcised Sinaitics (of female gender?), why is it precluded from non-water-baptised infants (of both genders), and are physical-circumcision and water-baptism equal alternatives to gain everlasting life? Indeed, were they ever gates to everlasting life?

[68] Wayne Grudem's, *Systematic Theology,* covers this well, except for missing out Cornelius' household, and his unwisely irenic attempt to pacify all denominations by a doctrine of equal validity (1994:982). His 2020 edition acknowledged and retracted that latter folly.

- Ac.10: the water-baptised had first been *listening* to Peter's message, when out of the blue that heedful household had been spirit-baptised and *spoke* in language(s) they had not learnt (44; 11:14-5). On that basis, they were then water-baptised. Had babies really *heeded* Peter, then been spirit-baptised and then *spoken* God's praises? And did not spirit-baptism confirm conversion, prior to water-baptism?

- Ac.16:32-4: all in the Jailer's household were old enough to *understand* Paul, and to individually *rejoice*.

- Ac.18:8: the entire household of a synagogue leader, Crispus, *believed*. Even had they had a baby who *believed*, would Paul's team have known that it had believed, and would it not then have been water-baptised, based on its own faith? The text adds that other Corinthians—including Gaius—*heard, believed,* and were water-baptised.

- 1 Cor.16:15 specifies that Stephen's household *helped* other Christians—pray tell, how did any babies help out?

In fact the only household description that doesn't implicitly rule out babies from water-baptism, is that of Lydia's household (Ac.16:15). But with four negative accounts, why assume that the fifth had any baby, then assume that Luke would have counted any babies into his report? I visit a family which has a baby. I tell you that while there, we *all* played Monopoly. Do you assume that baby joined in?[69] To support a big doctrine on a hypothetical little baby joining the party, is a very big ask indeed. Moreover, physical circumcision guaranteed only an earthly kingdom (Dan.12:2?).

The infant-water-baptism idea, sometimes called pedobaptism, has become a dominant culture. But when dropping out is permitted, the dropout rate can be high.[70] "Countless hordes of babies have been

---

[69]   It could perhaps move a token, but that's hardly playing the game.

[70]   Picture a spiritual circle within a cultural circle. Where allowed, I suspect that many would drop out from the larger circle, whether of Christianity or of

baptised without ever coming into living membership of the covenant community of Christ" (David Wright: *Themelios*, 2004:29.2.36). In itself, Wright's assertion no more disproves that they once had life assurance, than my not having life insurance (I don't) disproves that I once had it (I did). Who knows, maybe water-baptism, like some vaccinations, gives selected babies at least some shortterm cover— even if sometimes some serious collateral harm is hidden from the public. It's just that I don't get that from Scripture.

But if the rite covers even a first few formative years, it'd be nice to know why that *wasn't* promoted biblically, whereas believer-water-baptism *was* promoted biblically. Yet promote it or promote it not, a sad truth remains that many criminals in adult years were christened in infant years, and drug pushers can wear gold crosses.

When dropping out is not culturally permitted—as say in State Islam—the hidden volitional dropout rate is perhaps high—perhaps because cultural dropouts at heart, were never spiritually in in the first place.[71] Even as one can play at being an aeroplane, without being one, so the outer signs of Christianity, or Islam, do not a true devotee make. Being born of human parents makes one human; being born of Christian parents does not make one Christian, even if water is added.[72]

Islam, yet fewer from the inner circle.

John spoke of some dropping out of Churchianity, who had never been within Christianity (1 Jhn.2:19). That was the outer circle. Paul spoke of Demas having dropped out (2 Tm.4:10), although perhaps only from Paul's apostolic team. *Hebrews* warns against exiting from the spiritual core: I hold that re-entry is neither impossible nor guaranteed.

71   Cultural dropouts, vs spiritual dropouts. Some Christians don't always understand their true orbit. I recall one girl—in my Fig Tree Gospel Hall (Hull) days—saying how she had been riding her Churchian bike, and had finally twigged that she should be riding her Christian bike. That's an example of getting real, of waking up.

72   Jhn.3:5 speaks of being "born of water and spirit" (LEB). Some have believed that *born of water*, means baptised with/in water. However, it harks back to

There are other reasons given for supporting pedobaptism.[73] On the other hand, believer-water-baptism (credobaptism) confines water-baptism to postconversion. Yet some credobaptists share the idea with their pedobaptist friends, that for converts water-baptism is the doorway into Christ's kingdom (Christian Level), even assuming that that doorway is the only way to heavenly life beyond death (Everlasting Level). Still, debates run deep, and should be carefully examined by thoughtful Christians. It touches on how human beings, if they die in infancy or before birth, can or cannot enter God's kingdom. Is there no way for parental faith to help them?[74]

I have but briefly looked at infant-water-baptism, to at least raise some doubt about it. If you have held this platform, you might resolve such doubts and hold to it the firmer. All such matters are parts of the doctrines of sin and salvation—of hamartiology and soteriology—and are worthy of reflection. But even if you fully affirm water-

---

Ezk.36:26 and Jr.31:31, so Yeshua reasonably expected any top-notch OT scholar—like Nicodemus—to immediately see (10). Had Jesus meant Christian water-baptism, it would have been unreasonable to have expected Nicodemus to see what didn't exist.

Some believe that Paul backed third-party faith for ultimate life for unbelieving *children*, and cite 1 Cor.7:14-6. However, by claiming that the same level of holiness applied to unbelieving *spouses*, Paul simply meant a set-aside-ness, a holy—and thus helpful—environment (Mk.9:50).

[73] Such as a water-baptism for infants being the new covenant equivalence of physical-circumcision for infants born into the old covenant.

[74] For what it's worth, my own suggestion remains predispositionalism (predilectionism), which precludes any third-party help or hindrance. It assumes individual choice to be concomitant with individual nature, and discounts ideas of either all who die in infancy going to hell, or all who die in infancy going to heaven. Briefly, it postulates that we are conceived either spiritually towards, or against, God, who places us according to our own inner disposition from conception, whether we are able to enjoy heaven, or not. In a sense, I favour both Augustine's idea of *limbus infantium* (but for *all* the lost), and Calvin's electionism (but as *our* disposition electing us at conception): horses for courses. Calvin argued, and I agree, that many more must be ultimately saved, than lost, since the death of Christ must be more potent than Adam's sin.

baptism as key to entrance (baptismal regeneration), for this next section I hope at least that you will consider that it might not disallow another entrance point. For now I move to focus on prayer as the final human step to enter Christianity, our door knock on Christ's door.[75] Within this idea, let's kick off with what some call, the Sinners Prayer.

Prayer entrance?

A feature in some evangelical circles is called the Sinners Prayer. Popularised by Billy Graham, it goes back to D L Moody, and even links to John Bunyan (*Pilgrim's Progress*).[76] It is connected to the idea of individual conversion-confession, as being the required request to enter God's kingdom, and links to the idea that salvation is a gift—a free opening of the door—based on mutual welcome.

Some opponents of this idea say that salvation is better based on ongoing performance (such as a package deal of entrance-rite, ongoing godliness, and confessions).[77] After all, why should God make salvation so simple, so unretractable a gift that neither commits receivers to godliness, nor to the church? Hello, thank you, goodbye? Aren't there many Billy Graham dropouts, thinking they're heavenbound?

Put simply, this divide in thinking pits the corporate (we decide for you), against the individual (you decide for yourself). Both sides can fear that if any go through the wrong door, they will not go through the right door, and so will be everlastingly lost. My own position, inexclusivism, holds both proponents and opponents to be based on dubious suppositions. But anyway, what is the Sinners Prayer?

It is a fuzzy pattern, is extrabiblical, and its exact words vary, but in essence it is a formal request to God to enter Christianity—in biblical

---

[75]   Rv.3:20 uses the door-knock picture for Jesus knocking on *Christian* doors.

[76]   Somehow I cannot bring myself to picture Peter, on the Day of Pentecost, leading the crowd in a Sinners Prayer. But times have no doubt changed.

[77]   I would agree, incidentally, with those critics who say that although water-baptism has never been conversionary, under the new covenant it has always been biblically normative as initiatory into lifestyle, ideally, a public expression of having come into Christ's kingdom (Col.1:13).

parlance, for sinners to become saints.[78] The formulas are open to debate. Personally, I'm not happy with formulas that begin what should be a father-centred fellowship, with request to Jesus for a brother-centred fellowship. In fact, I'm not too chuffed with any set entrance-prayer for sinners. Nevertheless, a Sinners Prayer can, like the ancient catechisms, offer good guide value, in that it can systematically cover a few core ideas, such as...

- the unconverted being outside of the new covenant (*sinners*), but invited to enter;

- appreciation that God's son has made possible Christian life before death, and everlasting life after death;

- acceptance of God's offer to enter new life through Jesus;

- commitment to the idea that welcoming Jesus, is the ticket through his door, beginning spiritual life with him;

- commitment to live in the light of the new relationship as a family member.

But Sinners Prayers can also throw in a lot of church-speak, mere gibberish to converts, and cringe language that can turn them off. Viola and Barna put one Sinners Prayer like this: "Lord Jesus, I need you. Thank you for dying on the cross for my sins. I open the door of my life and receive you as my saviour and lord. Thank you for forgiving my sins and giving me eternal life. Take control of the throne of my life. Make me the kind of person you want me to be" (*Pagan Christianity?* 2008:189-90). Like me, Viola and Barna neither liked Sinners Prayers, nor pedobaptism, though perhaps they knocked the church overmuch. Unlike them, I am not emergent. Tradition is not always bad. Indeed, I traditionally wash every morning, and that keeps me from smelling like a farm animal.[79]

---

[78] Two points here. 1# sinners before conversion are evangelistically sinners, but converts who sin are pastorally sinners. 2# biblically, as opposed to ecclesiastically, all Christians are saints, for biblically the word simply means those within Christ's kingdom, in that sense *holy.*

[79] https://www.firstthings.com/blogs/firstthoughts/2010/02/emerging-from-emergent-church-evangelicalism

In my books, addressing Jesus is fine in the first bit of Viola and Barna. Converts inform him of things (their need of him; their openness to him) and thank him for things (for his death in their place, and the true life that brought them). However, moving to request—the last two sentences—it's the father—though as *God*, and having clear blue water between him and Jesus—who should be asked, not the son, nor the spirit. Theologically, it's a bit of a needlessly messy start to Christian life.

To rejig their example above, I'd have something like: "God, I need you. Thank you that Jesus, your son, died so that I, and others, could live with you. I submit to your will for me. Please, accept me into your heavenly family, save me from sin, and show me more and more of spiritual life. Thank you, both for forgiving me for not having gone your way, and for now giving me eternal life, making me new. Please help me to live more and more as a child of yours, and to call you father. Thank you father."

As said, for entrance-prayer, a set formula might be of some help, but biblically none is set, so none is required.[80] We can read in the Bible of some prayers for forgiveness: "God, have mercy on me, a sinner", and, "lord, remember me when you come into your kingdom." Both predated Christianity. Whether these are relevant to us, I leave you to decide. As far as I'm concerned, I take it as vital that prayer itself, as spoken within the heart about welcome of God's son, is vital to entering Christ's kingdom, the new orb of the spirit. And make no mistake about it, he will have been calling us, but welcome must be mutual to enter.

I do not deny that for some, the prayer conversation might begin without any formal words of welcome. I have in mind a doorstep journey, in which having hesitated perhaps years on the doorstep, the actual point of entrance might be impossible for us to pinpoint. But we suddenly realise that we have been in for a while. Similarly, friendship might spark at first contact, or friendship might form in such a way that we cannot pinpoint an exact time or place.

---

[80] In fact even such prayer formally follows the dynamics of conversion. The sinner had by the spirit become a saint simultaneously upon welcome of Jesus, so any Sinners Prayer is a formal re-enactment of prior entrance.

But once we're within Christ's kingdom, we really should see our primary relationship as being with God the father, God the son, and God the spirit. A quick look at Mt.28:19 might help: "...disciple all nations; immersing [disciples] into the name of the Father, and of the Son, and of the Holy Spirit" (Julia Smith Translation—slightly adjusted). Julia at least saw that here it's not about a water-baptism formula. In fact there is no biblical water-baptism formula, period. But in fact we can go deeper. It's not even about a conversion point.

Besides *into*, the Greek εις/*eis* can mean *in/with reference to*. Christian *water-baptism/immersion*, is a postconversional act *with reference to* the united name of the father, son, and spirit. Converts share the name *Yahweh*, and I'd guess that might have been seen in Matthew's days, but it may take many years for us to ponder the puzzle of one name, core identity, three persons. The text is about exploring the one name society, the three persons. [81] And it's also about our relationship with the church, ourself, the world, and the universe.

Subpar prayer-songs

Having brought some chapters together from other of my writings, I see that a number of points made here, are repeated in the next chapter. Harmonising the two would take quite some pain for small gain, and I have opted to leave them as they are. After all, repetition can be helpful. Here I'll spend some time introducing how our songs interact with the biblical understanding of God as trinity. That's partly because—certainly in my circles—we often sing many prayer-songs. Songs carry messages/narratives, and bypassing our critical facilities, they can worm their way in, whether for weal or for woe.

Sadly it is true that Christian songs can help or harm the biblical revelation of the trinity—and prayer—and are not uncommonly a

---

[81]   In *Mere Christianity*, C S Lewis used geometry to illustrate: distance (1D), space (2D), depth (3D). A two-dimensional square (personhood) is made up of four one dimensional lines (sub-personhood), but a cube (three dimensional) is made up of six squares (super-personhood, societal). I guess that one could illustrate by a three-line triangle, and a four-triangle pyramid. The one dimensional cannot comprehend the two dimensional. Neither can the two dimensional comprehend the three dimensional.

mixture of help and harm. The discrimination which Paul recommended for prophecy should also be used for songs (1 Ths.5:21). We should test all songs, and hold to the good. Or, I should say, to the good parts, and correct the other parts.[82] Some good Christians lack trinitarianism, both in head and in heart; some good Christians lack trinitarianism in their very blood. And all mere Churchians might have trinitarianism in the head, but will certainly lack it in the heart. Very many good Christian songwriters simply lack it in their blood—sadly it shows.

Take Pete Sanchez Jr. In 1977, he wrote a worship-song based on the KJV of Ps.97:9: "For thou, LORD, art high above all the earth: thou art exalted far above all gods." Sanchez altered that to, "For thou O Lord art high above all the earth / Thou art exalted far above all gods." Note first that the KJV *LORD*, used Tyndale's main method of fully capitalising the word *lord* when used as code for God's name, Yahweh.[83] If the KJV had properly used God's name in the first place, its text would be: "For thou, Yahweh, art high above all the earth: thou art exalted far above all gods."

Sanchez decreased the visual *LORD*, to *Lord*. Now to Christian eyes, that's very likely to look like Yeshua, rather than like Yahweh. For we're used to the Christian emphasis, that "Jesus is the Lord" (KJV:

---

82   Copyright law works against correction. If there was a global database for Christian songs, it could allow public input, starting with reasoned proposals for changes. It could allow anyone to use the adjusted lyrics, until the copyright holder had assessed them. The copyright holder could then either issue their reasons to reject the changes (red response)—allowing others to join the conversation—or in a spirit of mild disagreement, allow folk to use either the default or alternative lyrics (amber response), or amend the default version to reflect the proposals (green response). This process should not channel royalties away from the copyright holder—since that could motivate a red response—and might increase their royalties, since enhancements should encourage more throughput—this could incentivise reflection. This didactic approach would also tend to improve lyricology levels across the board.

83   Tyndale used an earlier handle on God's name, doing the best he could.

1 Cor.12:3). So, who is the Lord? Jesus is the Lord! But that's not who *the psalmist* was on about, and Yahweh is greater than Yeshua.[84]

Admittedly, Sanchez didn't sink the ship, since he didn't exactly say that he wrote it about Jesus, even though it looks as if he did. But lest heeding the psalmist we still sing it as a Yahweh-trinity song, along came a certain David Hodges, as good a patripassian as ever you could wish to meet, and tacked on, "your name is Jesus...your name is father", thus saying that the son of the father is also the father of the son. What a stroke of genius![85]

Well if you wish, just go ahead and take it from David that Jesus, dying on the cross, was the father being crucified, and that Sanchez' *Lord*, is Jesus our father. But boy, I despair at times at how easily some jokers can take centre stage, then make their personal fortunes by robbing singers of the knowledge of God.[86]

As I've said, there is a deific trinity, and that trinity is a trinity of three prime distinctions, personhood distinctions introduced to us as the father, the son, and the spirit: eternal deity; eternal society. But most Bible versions are fuzzy on this, thus misleading.[87] Fuzzy translators encourage writers like Pete and David to carelessly mangle God's word. We shouldn't expect them to give good theology if they haven't got it into their heads, let alone their hearts, and the Bibles in their hands mislead. Goodness in; goodness out. Garbage in; garbage out. Maybe that's why they've let us down. And we can lose their names as easily as two leaves in an autumn forest.

---

[84] And that's whether or not *Yahweh* is used as the trinity. In fact, the trinity is greater than one member, even the father (Jhn.14:28).

[85] https://genius.com/David-hodges-i-exalt-thee-your-name-lyrics

[86] As for these guys, I know neither their motivations nor their bank accounts, only the outcome.

[87] I've graded Bible versions on this and on several different points (*The Word's Gone Global* (2017)). Only the LEB/NJB/NOG/NWT/WEB consistently put God's name as a name in the OT. If they had been the only five I tested, and taking all the other tests and adjusting totals to ensure that none failed, their overall comparative grades would be: NJB/NOG (A+); LEB (A-); WEB (D+); NWT (D-).

So at this point, why not look at how we should, and should not, read the Old Testament and the New Testament, in order to see what the trinity is, and what it is not?[88] For shouldn't we enjoy a *trinitarian* prayer life? Fuzzy Bible translators and scholars have played their part in the West's slow slide into a form of Sabellianism, reflecting and reinforcing that slide.[89]

Sabellius? C3 Sabellius was a Christian leader who held that God as son, was simply a *mode*.[90] Not a distinct person, but an actor's mask, worn by God, the Eternal Person who sometimes pretended to be the spirit he sent to do things, and who sometimes acted as the eternal father—the sender. Nowadays, this idea is well reflected by such as Hillsong's line, "You alone are God, Jesus." Wrong, Mr Morgan, emphatically wrong. Yet it's happily swallowed hook line and sinker by many singers, who, singing below trinitarian values, in their hearts simply do not recognise the father and spirit as being distinct *persons*, so ignore them as persons, and offer their royalties upon the altar of Reuben & Co.

Now Sabellius was a singer, too, and would probably have welcomed that song, and many more from the same stable. He might have

---

88   Other writings have sometimes been caught up between *Genesis* and
      Revelation, and are still prized by various denominations. Indeed, until 1885
      the KJV had several such interesting writings (eg *Tobit*, and *Bel and the
      Dragon*). Though of dated scholarship, after Leipzig in 1519, Martin Luther,
      though still discarding some core elements of Roman Catholicism, held that
      such writings were still helpful to read—a position Jerome had held. Indeed
      they can be quite fun, if read with a pinch of salt and not as doctrinal
      platforms.

89   I heard from at least one NIV translator who favoured God's name as a name,
      but said he had to comply with translation policy.

90   A trinity of one person, not a trinity of persons. Some say he's not a problem,
      since he was officially anathematised by the church's damnatory clauses.
      Damned by the church he might have been, but he still sings to us. Actually I
      deny such councils and their verdicts any canonical ultimately, and I deny that
      we humans have the authority to ultimately damn. Both, I believe, are God's
      prerogative. That councils have had authority to exclude (anathematise) *from
      their church network*, I do not deny, but Sabellius could welcome Jesus without
      understanding deity.

explained that Jesus *alone* is God, in the sense that since there is only one *person* who is God, we might as well call him by his incarnational mode, as by his father or spirit mode. Bible translations often side with the Sabellian slide.[91] Actually, it is somewhat invidious to bang on about Hillsong, since many of the songs born in our generations, show such painful fallacy.

The translation convention of substituting, in the OT, God's name by *the LORD*, sometimes even without explanation, is part of the problem. [92] The *International Children's Bible*'s *lord*, ignores both God's name—Yahweh—and Tyndale's visual method—the LORD. Dare I say that for a children's Bible, it shows a rather childish understanding, sadly all too common among adults? God's name deserves a SHOUT! Usually song lyrics follow the ICB convention, even if they're cut-and-paste from an adult Bible version. But if ever we are to visualise the trinity in sung and spoken prayer, we must first learn the doctrine, then saturate it into our spiritual DNA, making it 'ours'. Name it, then claim it.

Various factors have suppressed God's name, and thus God's ID. The ethno-Jewish [93] people put up a hedge around God's name— seemingly for safety's sake. Their Greek translation adopted that hedge by the Greek term for *lord/sir*. However, it was often put in what's called an anarthrous way, which means lacking our term, *the*.

For instance, translating a psalmist's words into the Greek, we (in English) read of one coming "in the name of lord"—κυριος/*kurios* (Ps.117:26). Here the Hebrew has *Yahweh* (Ps.118:26—"in the name of Yahweh").[94] Likewise in Lk.13:35, the literal approximation of the Greek

---

[91]   MEVV Grades: LEB (A+); ERV (D+); NABRE/NLT (D); CEB/CEV/NCV/NIV/NKJV/NRSV (D-).

[92]   The NIV preface explained its policy in 1984, then inexcusably dropped its explanation.

[93]   The term *Israelite*, and historically sub-section term *Jew*, were theologically loaded. Code words, so to speak. It is useful to differentiate the mere ethnic chaff from the spiritual wheat. Theologically every Christian, whether ethnically Jewish or not, is spiritually Jewish, indeed a true child of Abraham, tracking back to the root of God's redemptive plan.

[94]   The Greek text is sometimes located a bit differently.

---

text says, "in the name of lord". That's since been smoothed over to "in the name of the lord" (KJV). Sadly, adding a definite article (*the*) has replaced code for God's name, by a job description.

If in the sixties I'd asked, "Is Lord in Hawaii?" I'd more likely have been asking about Mr Jack Lord by name, than about *the* lord of Hawaii. Had a Hebrew prophet asked it millennia earlier, they would probably have been asking whether Yahweh was there. With Lk.13:35, and in many similar texts throughout the Bible, to buy better English, we've unwittingly sold out God's name. The ancient OT translators preferred to buy better theology, by selling out good Greek. Sadly, that's the state of play.

But if a previous generation has sold the family silver, can the next generation redeem it? Can we buy back God's name? Today, modalism is draining the concept, *trinity*, into an unbiblical concept of being *Jesus*. Few high quality Bibles even tell us clearly about Yahweh. Some Christians, like an ancient pharaoh, nowadays respond with, "Who is Yahweh...? I do not know Yahweh..." (Ex.5:2). We must see that Yahweh is more than Yeshua. God must not be nebulous to us. Names can help us to understand.

Unless it's sunk into our blood—from head to heart—it's easy to miss out on this. Even Chris Idle (Reform 2013) cited Zp.3:16 as being about the *lord* (not LORD) singing, then related it to *Jesus* instead of to Yahweh—whether or not as trinity.[95] Nick Page showed a similar gaffe. It's so easily done. Following some brilliant points about worship not being worship *songs*, and about worship *times* (it's bowing our 24/7 lives to deity), Page defined worship as "showing God how much we value him", restating this as "showing Jesus what we think of him" (Page 24), agreeing with the Redmans that the focus of worship "should be Jesus.... It's really all about him" (Page 44). No, Nick, it isn't! God is not Jesus—God is a trinity.[96]

---

[95]   www.reform.org.uk (2013). Idle wrote as a lyricist: eg see his *How Sure the Scriptures Are!*.

[96]   Jhn.1:1,18, Rm.9:5, Tts.2:13, and 2 Pt.1:1, say that Jesus is deity. MEVV Grades:

Dave Allen's *There is a River*, referring to C18/9 Edward Irving's orthodoxy, says that Irving's controversial christology "did not, however, lead him into 'Jesusism'—that rather sentimental attachment to Christ sometimes found in charismatic circles that leads to a tendency to neglect other members of the trinity" (2004:102).[97] I think Allen was right about contrasting the Charismatic Irving, to today's Charismatics. Some, in sentimental attachment to Jesus, thoughtlessly overlook both father and spirit. Audibly misshaping God's name to *the LORD*, then visually misshaping God's name into *the lord*, can lead to crucifying the trinity, so to speak.

And in singing, the term *lord* has a tendency to switch meaning, becoming nonsense. That is, unless Sabellius was right, and C S Lewis—who said that saying that God is a person, is heresy—was wrong.[98] How often are songs simply introduced from the front, as if the congregation only needs to pick up the tune? As if prior thinking is pointless? Surely congregations should see the full lyrics, and give their feedback, before being invited to sing.[99] I don't know about you, but I like to see the map before beginning the journey. It's a thing of orientation, perhaps of adjusting the map, or even of cancelling the journey. Each song is a journey.

NLT (A+); NRSV (A); ERV/NIV (B+); NCV (B); CEB (C+); CEV/LEB (C); NABRE/NKJV (D-). But the emphatic biblical emphasis for the term *God* (*Theos*), either speaks of the father, or of the corporate trinity. Sad to say, the error of the Witnesses beats the truth of many Christians.

[97] Strictly speaking, Christ is not a member of the trinity at all, but a *mode* of a member of the trinity, namely God the son as a human being.

[98] In fact Lewis wasn't quite right on this, in that the term God, can be biblically used either for the trinity, or to highlight the father.

[99] I'm pleased to see some uncommonly good sense from the Gettys: "If you are using a new song, teach it. Email the congregation in advance if you can..." (Getty & Getty 119). Seemingly blind to the idea that Christian songs may be hazardous to Christian health, they simply assumed that any new Christian song will be fine but should be taught. The idea of us singing a new song *modified* (if subpar), or even *not* singing it at all (if subversive), seemed to pass them by as an idle wind to be regarded not. No, I say, email the congregation *and* invite discussion.

Okay, first up, imagine meeting a new prayer-song to the *lord*. Simple—or it should be. But I'd begin uncertainly, like Saul's "Who are you, lord?" Visualising, I have often sung heartily to the father, only to painfully discover midway that the song's *meant* to be about his son, or *vice versa*, or that the lyricist simply hadn't a clue.[100]

Imagine Jacob putting a wedding ring on Leah, then lifting the veil. That confusion, what I call misvisualisation, can lead to blushes. As a singer, I hit choppy lyrics. I stumble, dazed, shell-shocked, having sung my song to the wrong person. Hey, my brother is not really my father, but the songwriter, too busy making their first million or so, hadn't the foggiest. Nowadays, I'd rather silently scroll through an unfamiliar prayer-song, checking out at least who it's to, before I commit to singing it.

Alas, that can mean that by the time I've understood it to be fine, it has finished and folk are sitting down or singing a new song. Ah, *c'est la vie*. In my opinion, each song could alongside its title, indicate its target audience (its visualisation). In *Singing's Gone Global*, I have abbreviations, such as TD3—for songs sung to the spirit—and AD—for singing to each other.[101] Some songs defy my system!

Here's one such confusing prayer-song. It's Carman's *Lord of All* (2008), and begins, "Lord, you are wonderful". So sit back and sing it as a prayer. But nope, it toggles between singing to deity and to each other—what I call a hiccup. I guess that Carman was a bit clueless about what prayer actually is.[102] Anyway, at least we know that the prayer bits are to *the lord*. But is that *lord*, as in Yahweh (Ps.97:5), or *lord*, as in Yeshua (Ac.10:36; Rm.10:12)?

Well, without prior help, you might begin singing to Jesus, and I might begin singing to his father. Indeed *lord of all*, without further

---

[100]   Those unfazed include clear unitarians and fuzzy trinitarians.

[101]   TD being Theo-Directional (ie to Theos, Deity); 3 being the third person of the trinity, the Holy Spirit. AD is Anthro-Directional, anthro (Anglicised Greek) saying that it's sung between human beings. AD songs include *Be Bold, Be Strong*, which has often bemused me when singers shut their eyes *to sing* to fellow Christians—who would shut their eyes *to speak* it?

[102]   Incidentally a polydirectional song—bits to Jesus, and bits about Jesus.

context, might refer to either Yahweh or to Yeshua.[103] Well "Coz/That Jesus Christ is", suggests to me that we are singing *about* Jesus, so, I presume, not *to* Jesus. So I could guess that by *lord*, we're meant to visualise the father, bobbing in a bit to him about his son: that "Jesus Christ is lord of all." But overall the song tells us both that the "lord of all" is Jesus, and that we're singing *to* the lord of all. So at this point it thus looks to me that we're supposed to be singing *to* Jesus, weirdly telling him about...*another* Jesus! "[Jesus] you are wonderful...Jesus Christ is lord of all."

Come on Carman, try "[Jesus] you are wonderful...you my lord, are lord of all." That makes some sense. If I said, "Carman, you're wonderful, and Carman is a great guy", might Carman not wonder if I'm mentioning *another* Carman? As he sung it through, Carman failed to fix his eyes on Jesus: "*you* are wonderful...lift up *your* eyes" (hiccup), falls into the folly of degrading prayer.

Lincoln Brewster *All I Really Want* (2002) also begins with *Lord*. Its chorus begins "God I praise thee".[104] Now that seems clear—at least if you've ever met the KJV—until we see that "Jesus saviour friend of sinners" is probably the only person being sung to—as if he *is* God, is *alone* God. Neither father nor spirit are wanted as God, *only* Jesus, please. But fine, we're all Sabellians here, are we not Lincoln?

These kind of songs tend to use the term *lord*, in a sense of being one person who toggles between the terms *father, son,* and *spirit.* That idea is sometimes called modalism. According to Robert Letham, "...most Western Christians are practical modalists" (*The Holy Trinity,* 2004:212). Those who understand and welcome modalism, at least tend to be consistent in their belief. With a knowing smile they say that alleged trinitarians, by singing Jesus-only songs, are devotionally closet modalists, needing to come out.

Speaking about another point, Chris Idle said that it seemed "to rule out hymns by Unitarians, of which we sing not a few" (Reform 2013). He

---

103   Yahweh, the *lord of all the earth*; Jesus, the *lord of all Christians*—where *lord of all* means all the redeemed, whether ethnically Jewish or Gentile.

104   Grammatically, *thee*, spoken to God nowadays, implies that he is one *person*. But it would fit, if only it was to the father, and only to him.

implied, and I agree, that many of our songs are covert unitarianism. But we sing 'em anyway. Hey, if the emoticons are good, why fuss about mere words? All you gotta do is thank the father for dying on the cross and the spirit for sending Jesus, and smile that smile! Jesus Onlyism, Pentecostal Oneness teaching, is nontrinitarian/unitarian,[105] in the sense that it holds that deity is one person who plays three different parts (father, brother, and helper) and whose name we can simplify as *Jesus*. Jesus is all I need and all that thrills my soul is Jesus. True or false? Totally false. Let's not forget the trinity. Let's forget or correct songs that cause such forgetfulness.

I love Mark Altrogge's *I Stand in Awe* (1987).[106] As worship to Yahweh, the Eternal Society, the Land of Trinity, it exudes a sense of the mountain descending upon us, a weight of glory. Imperilled, we cry for mercy. As Malacandra might say, in our best thoughts there are still such things mingled which, if angels thought them, their light would perish (see C S Lewis' *Voyage to Venus*, 1971:181). My spiritual diet would put any healthy angel to shame—I am human, woe is me.

Altrogge's original song, if sung rightly, is sung-worship at its highest. Years later, he gutted it into a Jesus-song.[107] I wholeheartedly sang stanza 1 to Yahweh, feeling dwarfed by awe. Then his new stanza 2 jumped up and crucified my vision, blinded my mental direction. It was like Leonardo da Vinci had become Leonardo da Vandal a few years later, by painting a Hitler mo onto his Mona Lisa! Beware of the songs you sing. Be aware of the songs you sing. Enjoy if you may.

---

[105] C17 Unitarianism was more into Dynamic Modalism, the idea that the human Jesus was adopted by God.

[106] *You are beautiful beyond description / Too marvellous for words / Too wonderful for comprehension / Like nothing ever seen or heard / Who can grasp your infinite wisdom / Who can fathom the depths of your love / You are beautiful beyond description / Majesty, enthroned above / And..I stand in awe of you / Holy god to whom all praise is due...* Though personally, for singing I'd tweak *Holy god*, to *Holy One*. There is no holy god, but God is holy.

[107] The crucifying second stanza includes: *You are beautiful beyond description, Lamb of God, who died for me.*

Chapter 04   <u>Prayer and the Trinity</u>

<u>Sabellius and prayer</u>

This chapter continues something of the conversation begun in the last chapter, but I'd like to bring the spirit into it. Let's focus more on trinity dynamics for us. If you are a Christian, you are in a relationship with the trinity. But is it a by-the-way, or an intimate, interactive relationship? Are you aware of the trinity *each day*? Do you talk with each member *each day*? If not, why not? Could you be too Jesus-focused? Is that possible? Yes it is. Is that bad? Yes it is.

Ask yourself whether songs are your teachers. According to some song teachers, you shouldn't try to look beyond Jesus, for there is no beyond. The thing is, I simply won't sing their songs. I am a decided trinitarian. In fact, many Christians have gotten past the Jesus-only stage, and are binitarians, fellowshipping with the father and the son. Now, as to the third person of the trinity, I freely admit that the spirit is somewhat hidden in Scripture. For instance, while the first and second persons have intrafamily identities, namely *father* and *son*, and to us *father* and *brother*, the spirit lacks such a family designation, though some try to squeeze him into a family mould.

I suspect that there are reasons for this obscurity, such as us now having a *family* relationship with deity in terms of our eternal father and brother in heaven, and also having a here and now *missional* relationship with the spirit—he is the paraclete, the helper in mission. John's Gospel works on the picture that the father and son are now 'in heaven' overseeing, while we and the spirit are 'on earth' working. In short, that we thus have a 'vertical' and a 'horizontal' link with deity. Both a life to live and a job to do.

There might also be an apocalyptic reason for his hiddenness, along the lines that two 'packets' have been opened, and a hidden 'packet' remains. Like *Revelation*, this can remind us that there is so much more to deity beyond the sunset. Still round the corner there may wait, a new door, or a secret gate, and though we oft have passed them by, a day will come when by and by, we'll take the hidden paths that run, west of the moon, east of the sun. Ah, do we not walk in divine poetry? Yet hidden though he be, the spirit should be an ever present part of our relational lives. Is he?

So, back to the spirit, and to the question about trinitarian fellowship. Jesus never casts out either the spirit, or the father. But do we and our songwriters? And I'm going to reflect a fair bit more on what some songwriters believe and teach. I admit that it's a bee in my bonnet, buzzes around in my books, and gets swatted down. But here we go again. "Only Jesus can satisfy your soul, only Jesus brings redemption, only Jesus satisfies, Jesus only is our message, Jesus only will we see, Jesus all in all we sing, Jesus only is our saviour, Jesus only is our healer, only Jesus can our every sorrow know; he alone can truly help us." This is a simple string, pulled from a number of unitarian-friendly songs. The only trinitarianism glimmer in their fog is one which has us ask Jesus to fill us with the spirit.[108]

Are the father and the spirit redundant and insignificant to us, complications we can well do without? Does this reflect the picture in *John* of Jesus having ascended to the father, and the spirit in turn having descended to engage in the work of Christian salvation, being Jesus' special agent on earth? We should flesh out trinitarianism, relating to the father, the spirit, and to God the son noncarnate, to whom Jesus—God the son incarnate—is as a ray of light, a permanent projection into creation. This fellowship, this natterland, protects us from Jesus Onlyism/Oneness, and is biblical. So for all his hiddenness, let's not sidestep the spirit. Jesus didn't. Like Moses, he worked by God's finger, the Holy Spirit (Lk.11:20//Mt.12:28).

Unitarianism pervades our prayer-songs. The influence of Sabellius, a unitarian heretic in early church history, still pervades church prayer. I sometimes fear that we misunderstand prayer, almost as much as we misunderstand trinitarianism. "Most folk pray how I pray, so my way's OK", can equally be said in J-Witnesses and

---

108   Though it was wrong to ask Jesus, instead of the father.

Mormon circles. Parochial ways can be globally wrong. Whatever the ads say, ten million cats *can* be wrong. Martin Luther's big revelation was that assurance of forgiveness comes through trusting that God welcomes all who directly come to him through Christ. It was a minority report. I believe it, but many still think that assurance of having been redeemed, is risible, and merely hope that they will be redeemed. [109] Global majorities can be wrong. Christian songs are often prayers. Belief shapes, and is shaped by, prayer. Let's look more generally at prayer, sorting some things out at source.

Prayer is talking in God's direction, hence my expression, *theo*directional, or *God*ward. "You are praiseworthy, God", is theodirectional. "God is praiseworthy", is anthrodirectional—manward—and if said/sung by you to yourself, is egodirectional. [110] Prayer, if based on biblical belief, will form a virtuous outward spiral, getting better and wider. Prayer, if based on unbiblical belief, will form a vicious spiral, getting worse and worse. What relates to prayer relates to deity, and what relates to deity matters. Laziness of mind impedes proper thinking. To love deity with our mind, is a moral duty, and leads to joy. Without the mind, we can be happy and clappy, but it will be excitement without exploration.

Of course, attention to the form of prayer should not distract from the overriding importance of meaningful content in prayer. Even bad theologians can pray faith prayers, and see mountains of problems removed. But who would argue that the less biblical we are, the better we can pray, or that blessed are the heretics, for they shall not obtain truth? Even as we can have both assurance of salvation and holiness in salvation—as John Bunyan taught—why can't we have great theology and great faith-prayer? Why accept antibiblical prayers which sustain, and spread, bad theology? After all, "all praying presupposes an underlying theology; conversely, our theology will have

---

[109] Some fear that, given too much too soon, the God-given will not live up to the holy gift—why strive for the eaten carrot? So, keep the donkey moving by fixing the carrot in front and uneatable—be holy or starve?

[110] The Greek word *egō*, simply means 'self'. In itself it isn't bad, though an egocentric egotist is bad. We should increase in Christ, as he should increase in us.

---

a decisive influence on our praying.... It is also true to say, that our praying (or lack of praying), will also influence our theology" (Carson 1992:95).

Petitionary prayer

Good theology will see that when it comes to asking deity, it's a case of asking the father. Trinitarianism underlines a definite structure within deity. But should any Tom, Diane, or Harry, ask God the father? Do you believe that you were born a Christian, or born anew a Christian? Does it matter, either way, for petitionary prayer?

I believe that it does matter, for being born to parents in Christ's family, isn't the same as being born into Christ's family. The first is parental choice; the latter is offspring choice. Unless children have chosen Christ, they should not be taught to pray to God as father in Jesus' name, because they are not in Christ, his father is not their father, and they have neither Christ's authority nor his mission.[111]

If they have been born into Christ's family, it's another matter.[112] Dual citizenship comes with personal faith-welcome. But prior to that, they should at most pray to God-as-God (Common Level), not to God-as-individual-father (Christian Level). Throughout human history, all of us—unless born into God's family—have lacked God as our individual father. God-as-corporate-father, *Yahweh* to his former people (Sinai Level), was *Elohim* or an elohim, outside the covenant.[113]

Only in Christ's family are we Christians. As Christians, our primary biblical pattern is asking the father in his son's *name*. That is, asking

---

[111]   In a similar line, I'd allow water-baptism and the eucharist to all converts—irrespective of age—but otherwise disallow them—irrespective of age. And likewise, *contra* the spirit of the age, human interpersonal sex is only permissible within marriage. Democratisation—as the idea of all being open to all—can go too far, in somatic, and in social, and in spiritual, life. And when it does so, it becomes demonic, not to say, foolish.

[112]   Our daughter was born into it at around year 5. I would have been happy for her to have been water-baptised at that time.

[113]   He was the corporate father to his covenant people, not individual father to its individuals. Outside of covenant, he was merely God, and sometimes called a god.

in the authority and in the identity of the messiah. To ask the father in the father's authority and identity, doesn't quite cut it. Yet some unbiblically pray, "father, we ask *in your name*". No they don't. Christian petitionary prayer is based on some understanding of the mission and person of Jesus.[114]

God the son became a human being, and walked with man, as 'Jesus'. In the mortal shadow of the cross, he taught his apostles about direct access with the father, based on his (Jesus') own soon to be authority.[115] *In his name*, served as a way of saying, *in his mission*. This special relationship of working family, which we are to enjoy with the father, is clouded if we make petitions *to* Jesus (Jhn.16:26-8).

Roman Catholicism makes similar mistakes, when asking Mary to help out.[116] In fact to be *in Jesus' name*, petitionary prayer, whether

---

[114] Some object that petitionary prayer is a philosophical contradiction. If God is all knowing, he need not be informed, and if he is all goodness, he need not be asked to do good. If your neighbour loves cats and knows you're going on holiday and leaving your cat in your garden, why ask them to feed the cat? In the case of the human neighbour, one might say it's courtesy. In the case of God, one might say that although he will work out his cosmic plan, he allows us to interact with parochial issues, in order to mature our focus on the spiritual. He wishes us to invoke him into our lives, helping us mature. Petitionary prayer can also be to attune our hearts to godliness, to think as God thinks, so it's *us* being involved, not simply prayer aimed at God being involved. Prayers that end "for your sake", overlook that requests are for *our* sake. Please heal me for *my* sake, and heal them for *Jesus'* sake!? Give me a break! Jesus gave himself for us—for *our* sake (Jhn.17:19).

[115] Mt.28:19: all authority was given to him after his death (Php.2:9). That was not based on his deity-link, but on the new type of humanity he had begun, as the first in time and in rank of the new order: Eph.2:15. It was the incarnational lordship and authority of God the son.

[116] RCs sometimes say that asking *saints* (they mean spiritual postmortal VIPs) to intercede, is no more daring than asking a Christian friend to do so, and indeed that heavenly saints are more likely to influence God. Fair doos. I'd say that if you ask an undeceased Christian to pray for you (each is biblically a saint and a priest), then you should still ask God direct. Don't cop out.

sung or spoken, doesn't really require us to say "in Jesus' name", or "in the name of your son", or any such suffix. A simple, "father, please do A, B, and C. Thank you", is fine. It simply needs to be from those in Jesus' family, asking for what is in his will.[117] And petitionary prayer that's synched to Jesus' mission, if it's needed for that mission, will *probably* be in God's will (father and son are one in will: Jhn.10:30),[118] and will therefore probably be granted. It boils down to meeting God's criteria.

I say 'probably', because even here mission is part of a bigger picture.[119] God can allow obstacles to us doing mission, in order to work on us or on others. Paul had wished to visit the Thessalonians (1 Ths.2:18), but God had allowed Satan to stop Paul for a while, perhaps both to build up Paul, and to build up the Thessalonians. That's God's strategic will. Even his will, in the sense of his desire, has intrinsic limits. For instance, he *wills* all of us to be saved, yet allows our rejection. Love will woo, but will not force, our heart.

Similarly, if you ask a deceased saint, you should still ask God direct. My main point is that if you are a Christian, you too are a saint and a priest, and should not cop out of asking direct. Besides, you should know that you're in God's family, and that you don't need anyone else to get him to hear you. Even as God invites our prayer participation, so we may invite others to participate in our prayers: it is a certain honour to be asked. But within a context of our active priesthood, meditations on very spiritual persons, and on their mediations, can help our prayers (Jas.5:17-8). Perhaps God intends that Christians on Earth's stage—since they can gain from mutual support and maturation and in a way or ways in which perhaps the heavenly audience cannot—should share each other's needs in this way.

[117]   God's will can be fluid, adjustable, negotiable, reactive to human choice. While he can have a set mission into which we fit and which fits us, we can have additional wishes which we may put to him, and which though not strictly necessary, he may grant.

[118]   Had John used the masculine gender *one*, he would have implied one person. He used the neuter gender *one*, probably implying will, plan. Sadly I recall one point-scoring Sabellian lady in an Elim house group (Leeds), strongly assume the former, thus denying the trinity—ironically she was applauded.

[119]   This is not death by a thousand cuts, but merely fitting a biblical text into the biblical matrix, cutting away the dross.

Still, we hope that our requests are in Christ's mission, so will be granted. Or at least that they are not opposed to it, so might be granted. I have heard many folk bang on in prayer about why God should grant their requests, as if they're trying to convince him. If the things we ask are in Christ's mission, do we need to tell his father that they are? If they are not, should we try to deceive him? A *please* and *thank you*, should suffice. But that said, adding reasons in prayer can help *us* to work out God's missional will, and in a public meeting, to explain to others our requests to God.

Incidentally, here's a chart about who and in whose *name* to ask.

Person asked	**Father**	**Son**	**Spirit**
Bless me	Yes	No	Maybe
Bless us	Yes	No	No
In the father's name	No	No	No
In Jesus' name	Yes	No	No

Ultimacy of the father

Ultimately the father is lord (*Jude* 1:4), and in essence he is spirit (*Jhn.*4:24). And by that, Jesus meant that he belongs essentially to the realm of spirit beyond the realm of creation, not that his father was *a* spirit among spirits, or *the* spirit. It is from that realm that God the son had become one with us, Emmanuel.

I will get onto prayer to *the* spirit—the third person of deity—but suffice it for now to say that although he is the perfect paraclete (helper) on earth, we're not told to ask of him, and if anything should see him as helping us ask the father. As regards praying to the lord, in our state of decaying trinitarianism, while we seek to rebuild trinitarianism, is calling God *lord* not best dropped, confining the term *lord*, to Jesus? I think it is.

Prayers that address the father and the son as lord, can easily start with the father as lord, then unconsciously move to Jesus (the Christian focus of strategic lordship), while still vaguely picturing one *person* (the lord!) being spoken to. It can be quite confusing to listen to. This is Oneness, something the Athanasian Creed's bit about "confusing the persons", warned us against.

For example: "*Lord*, thank you for sending your son. And lord, *you* said, 'if I your *lord* and teacher have washed your feet....'" No, their rabbi-brother, not God who sent him, washed their feet. Such prayers encourage the heresy in numerous songs that we are children of Jesus, or even of the spirit. Yes, if you search the scriptures you *can* find that Jesus called his non-Christian disciples his children. Yes, in the same sense that disciples might be *children of John*, or of Paul. It was a rabbinical picture for disciple-to-teacher, not a trinitarian use expressing eternal parentage. Relationally, the biblically highlighted position is trinitarian: we are children of the father, brothers and sisters of Jesus, and work with the Holy Spirit our helper.[120]

Athanasian soteriology might be a bit iffy,[121] but its theology is sound. Here, slightly reworded, is part of the Athanasian Creed:

> ...we worship...God in trinity, and trinity in unity, neither confusing the persons, nor dividing the substance.[122] For there is one person of the Father, another of the Son, and another of the Holy Spirit. But the deity of the Father, of the Son, and of the Holy Spirit, is all one, the glory equal, the majesty co-eternal. Such as the Father is, such is the Son, and such is the Holy Spirit. The Father uncreated, the Son uncreated, and the Holy Spirit uncreated. The Father beyond our full comprehension, the Son beyond our full comprehension, and the Holy Spirit beyond our full comprehension. The Father eternal, the Son eternal, and the Holy Spirit eternal. And yet they are not three eternals, but one eternal. As also there are not three beyond our full comprehension, nor three uncreateds, but one uncreated, and one beyond our full comprehension. So likewise the Father is almighty, the Son almighty, and the Holy Spirit almighty. And yet they are not three almighties, but one almighty. So the Father is deity, the Son is deity, and the Holy

---

[120] See Rm.8:17; Heb.2:11. Mk.10:24's rabbinic relationship does not refute my point. Likewise Paul and John also called *disciples* their children, but as regards God's family, all are brothers and sisters.

[121] I allude to its damnatory clauses.

[122] For example, not saying only one is lord, only one is saviour, only one is deity.

Spirit is deity. And yet they are not three deities, but one deity. So likewise the Father is lord, the Son lord, and the Holy Spirit lord. ...yet not three lords, but one lord.

This is an early systematic theology of triunity, of oneness relative to *society*, and threeness relative to *persons*, and an implicit recognition that we are dealing with patterns of understanding which we can at most comprehend in part (1 Cor.13:9-10). Not each a lord, but each being lord; not each a god/deity, but each being deity in substance/ ουσια. Singing "In the name of the father, in the name of the son, in the name of the spirit", as Paul Baloche mixed in with some polytheism, can suggest three names, rather than the one threefold name of Mt.28:19. Trinitarianism is best.

Nor is the OT a justification for calling Jesus *lord*, for the English rendering of *Yahweh* as *the LORD* is not inspired by deity, though Intertestamental Jewish Religion (IJR) superstitiously used lordship terms to avoid God's name. Even for the sake of argument granting OT justification, the NT position remains clear: it is Jesus who for us has been given the function of lordship (Php.2:9-11; 1 Cor.8:5-6), and the spirit is delegated central command, lordship, on the ground.

While arguably overkill, if we never call the father *lord*, and never ask the *lord* for anything, it can enrich our trinitarianism.[123] This seems to have been Paul's rule of thumb.[124] The Athanasian Creed makes valid points on ontology, relates to each person each area of definition, and implies (without investigating differences of our interaction to each by the different

---

[123] The common "lord have mercy", *kurie eleēson* (a.k.a. *kurie eleison*) would be better as *patēr eleēson* (father have mercy), although we might still think it strange asking for mercy from one who *has* had mercy on us by making eternal life, which Christians have, available. Did a penitential sense of distance inspire this phrase, now embedded in the church courtesy of the East? But then, it is weak on the idea of aorist mercy.

[124] For example, in *Romans* there are 38 justified Greek NT references to *lord* (*kurios*). 9 are citations of the OT, put the Septuagint way as *lord* (4:8; 9:28-9; 10:16; 11:3,34; 12:19; 14:11; 15:11). 16 are new references clearly to Jesus (1:4,7; 4:24; 5:1,11,21; 6:23; 7:25; 8:39; 10:9; 13:14; 14:9; 15:6,30; 16:18,20). The remaining 13 are probably about Jesus (10:12-3; 12:11; 14:4,6,8,14; 16:2,8,11-3,22).

basic titles of father, son, and spirit) the ABC of a triangle. All lyricists should have a dust free copy on their desks.

Adding back the spirit

The Director said to Jane: "You are offended by the masculine itself: the loud, irruptive, possessive thing—the gold lion, the bearded bull—which breaks through hedges and scatters the little kingdom of your primness.... The male you could have escaped, for it exists only on the biological level. But the masculine none of us can escape. What is above and beyond all things is so masculine that we are all feminine in relation to it." (Lewis 1983:315)

Before moving on, let's scotch the ridiculous idea—though it can sell some books—that the spirit is a she, and maybe somehow the father's wife, his son's mother, and our mother. Language often has non-sexual gender, and they who blindly jump from general language to claim revelation, can confuse themselves and others. In English, we speak of a ship as a she, even if *she* is a *man*-of-war. Nowadays some toilets are actually called Female,[125] but so far we haven't descended to the folly of calling ships, females!

When it comes to *spirit/wind/breath*, "the origins of the word 'spirit' in both Hebrew (rûaḥ) and Greek (pneuma) are similar, stemming from associations with 'breath' and 'wind', which were connected by ancient cultures to unseen spiritual forces, hence 'spirit'" (Elwell 1985:521). In fact, in almost half the OT uses of *ruach*, the meaning is *wind/breath*, not *spirit*. Are wind and breath, feminine, let alone females? But if we insist that *ruach* proves the spirit to be a *she*, we must equally insist that *pneuma* proves the spirit to be an *it*. Yes, a nongendered *it*, since pneuma is not a Greek feminine gender, but is a Greek neuter gender. In fact in the expression, *spirit of Yahweh*, *ruach* is put 15% of the time in the masculine, violating grammar to make a gender point (Carson 1998:95).[126]

---

[125]   They will doubtless give birth to baby male and female toilets. Likewise, toilets called Disabled are presumably out of commission.

[126]   Badly, Carson put "Spirit of the Lord": *adonai* is possible only in Is.61:1.

Some translators have woodenly followed language genderisation, while others have seen past the wood of nominal genders, to the trees of true theological meaning. Thus for Jhn.1:32, the 1582 Roman Catholic Rheims NT, referring to the spirit, says that "he remained upon him", whereas the 1611 KJV (Geneva likewise) says that "it abode upon him". The Greek text doesn't prefer either the optional *he* or *it*.

For Rm.8:16, the Greek text has the personal neuter pronoun—thus αυτο/*auto*, in line with the neuter noun, pneuma. A wooden translation of the pronoun would be *itself*, not *himself*. The Rheims has "the Spirit himself"; the KJV has "the Spirit itself". And confusingly the RSV/ESV, have *himself* here, but *it* in Jhn.1:32.

Needless to say, the Witnesses' NWT translates the spirit as an *it*— where it can. Yet even it has given way when forced to do so by John. For on this point, John actually broke with wooden grammar, in order to underline the personhood and also, I guess, the masculine quality of the spirit rather than following the feminine of ruach. It was as if in English, speaking of a castle, we said something like, "When Harlech Castle was built, he was built against the Welsh."

Now that would grate. Now when it comes to Jhn.15:26 and 16:8, grammar dictated the neuter term *itself* (εκεινo). But in defiance, John—who I presume followed Jesus on this—wrote the masculine form εκεινoς/*ekeinos* (*he*): not the neuter εκεινo/*ekeino* (*it*), nor the feminine εκεινη/*ekeinē* (*she*). Now if Jesus believed that the spirit was a she, then why, given half a chance to say so, did he say he?

Now this does not preclude a feminine side, so to speak, but it does, in defiance of grammar, focus on his masculine personhood. Following Elaine Storkey, I am a Christian Feminist. But when even the man Paul could speak of his feminine side, why should we feel a need to assert that God is a she, or that the spirit at least is a she, as if trying desperately to squeeze in a she into our mould? Deity is the source of both these nonbiological genders—which can connect to biological sexes. But biblically, his masculine side is predominant to us by his design. Let's move on.

Old Sabellius has many songwriters busy recruiting new singers for his old song. Now I personally do not like knocking devotional songs simply for having a tinge of unitarianism, but I fear that the cumulative effect of many such songs can undermine what I hold to be core biblical teaching—and prayer.

Take a different example, where wilfully or not, the trinity has taken back seat in our minds. First, we all know that Jesus is the *only* saviour, right? Thus the KJV rightly says "To the only wise god our saviour, be glory and majesty, dominion and power, both now and ever. Amen" (*Jude* 25). But the NIV reads "to the only god our saviour be glory, majesty, power and authority, through Jesus Christ our lord, before all ages, now and forevermore! Amen." We thus side with Gail Riplinger[127] and dismiss the NIV for moving the text away from its witness to Christ's deity, since as Gail said about Jude's text, "our Savior is Jesus; therefore Jesus is God" (*New Age Bible Versions*, 1994:371).

That at least is clear, isn't it? But alas, besides overlooking some good textual evidence, Gail overlooked the simple fact that the beloved KJV speaks of "God our saviour, and Lord Jesus Christ" (1 Tm.1:1), [128] as different persons. In short, Jesus is not our *only* saviour in a wider trinitarian setting. So that being the case, why insist that *Jude* 25 calls *him* saviour, unless it's clear that that's what Jude called him *in that context*? Was Gail overlooking the Athanasian Creed, and even the Bible, in order to follow her beef and her milch cow? In different ways and for different reasons, we can easily drop into unitarianism. And is the Holy Spirit not saviour, too? All three are saviour, since all three share that *name*.

Whatever our hobbyhorses, it's helpful to see that "the theology of the NT revelation is Father, Son and Holy Spirit, one god.... In every activity of each of these three 'persons' of deity it is always...God who acts; the NT principle was subsequently formulated in Catholic theology by means of the formula: *opera trinitatis ad extra sunt indivisa* [that is, the works of the trinity are entirely undivided.] That is to say, the *personæ* [that is, persons,] must not be rigidly separated from one another and identified with particular divine functions (for example creating, redeeming, sanctifying), for all the *personæ* act in every divine work" (Richardson 123).

---

[127]   Mentioned much more in my *The Word's Gone Global*.

[128]   The *Geneva* had better grammar on this: "And of our Lord Jesus Christ".

That said, we needn't discount, say, John's picture of the father and son 'in heaven', and the spirit walking with us on or beyond Earth. There's an emphasis on a particular person, though the father and son walk with us by the spirit. And that walk is salvific. Let's add back the Holy Spirit as saviour and sharing life with us in general.

We should question *Jesus-only* statements, and ask in what ways, *if any*, the father and spirit might be involved. For example, we might say that Jesus saves. Yet in such salvation, the father secures, the son—as Jesus—procured, and the spirit cures. We should bear the trinity in mind, and in heart. How do we do this with the spirit, with him whom C S Lewis said we might find "rather vaguer or more shadowy in [our minds] than the other two" (Lewis 2002:4.4.175)? Easy, by minds and hearts fed by God's word and by proper songs and general teaching, that's how.

Let's spend some time in looking at a seldom covered area of theology, called pneumatology. I'll look at how the spirit should be incorporated into our devotional prayer-life. I believe that binitarian movement away from Jesus Onlyism, whether towards the father, or towards the spirit, is gain. I believe that incorporating the spirit into our daily thinking, will make it more obvious to incorporate the father, whereas broadening from fellowship with father and son is less obvious. How do we relate with this shadowy figure? I'll get there.

The father first[129]

But our primary relationship is with the father. And *relationship* can mean fixed, static relationships. For example, Earth to Sun is satellite planet to host star; and a daughter remains a daughter until death

---

[129] In so far as we don't pick this up, Jesus has failed! The title of an old favourite book of mine, Thomas Smail's, *The Forgotten Father*, says it all. Reasons we ignore the father:

  1 bad traditional teaching that's never been ironed out;

  2 the father seeming unapproachable (Heb.12:28-9), while Jesus, being incarnate, seeming approachable (Heb.2:17). Romanism perhaps implies that Mary is even more approachable;

  3 1 Jhn.1:3.

parts.[130] But relationship can also mean *vibes*. For example, in the relationship of employer to employee (impersonal idea), there could be a bad or a good relationship (in the sense of *vibes*). The two people could swap job roles (static-relationship change) and retain their bad or good relationship, their dynamic relationship. This sense of *vibes* is sometimes called *fellowship*, or *koinonia*. Christianity is about beginning fixed family relationship in the first sense (Mt.28:19), then building loving dynamic relationship (fellowship) in the second sense (1 Jhn.1:3; Php.2:1). Likewise converts are holy, but sanctification is built up dynamically.

Many evangelical Christians begin fellowship only with Jesus—as I did way back in the sixties—time flies. That's fine, and since he is the 'door' it's understandable, since we meet the entrance door before we meet the room. Some, seeking first he whom he is the way *to*, walk straight through the door without looking at it, first meeting the father (Jhn.16:27), later turn around and meet Jesus, and later move from binitarian fellowship into trinitarian fellowship (Jhn.14:16). A few might (I do not know) even meet first the one guiding them towards the door, before arriving at the door.

The spirit is at work around and about and within us. [131] For Christians, he is in fact a work colleague, whether or not we know it. [132] That's a fixed relationship. But a dynamic relationship—fellowship—is Christian too. When we sit down after a day's spiritual work and put our feet up, he's with us in the next chair, so to speak. But first, to say again, the father is first.

Jesus is the way—not the destination, not the navigator. The trinity distinctions includes a structure of authority. Mt.12:28 makes it clear

---

[130]   There are no families or spousal reunions in heaven—the redeemed are equal family.

[131]   Jhn.7:39 meant, given in/descended for, a certain role. Jhn.5:17 says that God the father had always worked even on Sabbaths, but doesn't tell us *how* he had worked. It was understood that he worked by the Holy Spirit.

[132]   I suspect that 1 Cor.3:9 probably implies human co-workers under God, and that 2 Cor.6:1 probably implies working alongside God, which in turn would be with the spirit whom he has sent.

that the spirit was working alongside Jesus, indeed had worked since creation. He would soon, in a new covenant way, represent Jesus working alongside the disciples (Jhn.14:15-31): *Acts* selectively sketched Jesus' continuing mission of illumination and intervention (Ac.1:1)—by the spirit. Christians, alongside the spirit, would be witnesses together (Jhn.15:26-7), and the very fact that he was manifestly with them was manifest evidence that they—unlike for example the Jewish Sanhedrin—were those who were obeying God (Ac.5:32).[133]

The issue of whether the spirit was sent primarily by the father, or equally by the father and the son, helped create needless division between East and West.[134] This was within the bigger issue, of course, of whether the Western side of the church—represented by Rome—had more authority than the Eastern side—represented by Constantinople—or parity. That great schism has somewhat healed.

---

[133] Does not Ac.5:32 mean the obedience of accepting Christ, from which flows obedience in Christ?

[134] More can be said. Source or sender? If the Nicene Creed simply meant mission, East and West could be fairly happy. But if speaking of ontology, the Filioque Clause sounded like father and son were equal sources of the spirit. The West failed in consultation and humility, and unilaterally demanded that the East accept into the Nicene Creed the clause 'and from the Son'. The East rightly objected to unilateral and ambiguous changes to the creed, and rejected as heresies the ideas of authoritative papal primacy, and of any father/son equivalence which undermined the uniqueness of the father as the sole or primary Fount. Perhaps a better balance of Augustine (West), would have fitted well with the Cappadocian position (East), that the spirit proceeded "'out of the Father through the Son'" (Young 1991:64).

The West thought that even in its *eternity* sense—which it didn't mean—it fitted with biblical teaching on the trinity. While believing the filioque theology, Pope Leo 3 peacefully attempted to restore the original creedal form, but failed. In 1054 came the so-called Great Schism between East and West, each side cutting the other off, excommunications withdrawn in 1965 by RC and Orthodox leaders, though the Schism remains.

Jhn.15:26 speaks in a temporal sense of mission: was the son co-equal, or secondary, sender? Who has primarily sent us? Are father and son of equal *weight*? Indeed was the sending not a standing back and letting the spirit move into his field of global operation?

But as regards the spirit, God's son was involved in the sending, and his cross was crucial, but he had come in his father's *name*: (Jhn.5:43; 10:25), so the father was first. Incidentally, baptism was *into*, or *relative to*, the one name, showing a joint lordship of the trinity (Mt.28:19): the spirit is joint-lord. Yet, as usual, the father was mentioned first. And we are told that when the son has sorted out cosmic authority once and for all, he will hand it over to, you guessed it, the father (1 Cor.15:28).

<u>Distinctive plurality</u>

I've implied that workmates can become mates (likewise mates can become workmates), and that the spirit is a workmate. Both types of fellowship involve knowing someone differently. In both these ways we can fellowship with deity. I think that fellowship with the spirit is a norm (2 Cor.13:13/4; Php.2:1), even if, as some think, these verses mean fellowship produced among Christians by the spirit.

Besides meaning joint-lordship, I think that Mt.28:19 also symbolises disciples' immersion into *companionship* with the trinity. Remember, the Athanasian Creed hammered home that the global church should worship the trinity, the eternal society, and that alongside the father and son, the spirit shared deity, glory, being, eternality, transcendence, and lordship. But remember also that each trinity member is distinct, so that our relationship to each varies. As said, it's the ABC of a triangle, not, I may add, an AAA of eternal cloning.

Today in church, someone thanked God for sending, the lord for having come, and the spirit for living with us. Now that's trinitarianism: three persons, one society. On the other hand, I've heard on other days some thank *God* for coming and dying, and that by his wounds we are healed. Hey, God is unscarred and unmarred.

Tertullian of Carthage was exasperated by this confusion of persons, often expressed as crucifying the father—that's patripassianism (*patrem crucifixit*). Unitarianism posits one person expressed in three ways, or can affirm the personhood of spirit and/or son but deny their deity. Songs can work with or against trinitarianism. There are many types of singing to/about deity, some of a very high standard. In what ways can we sing to, or about, the spirit, as being an eternal individual within the eternal society? Let's explore.

Chapter 05 <u>Prayer and the Spirit</u>

I have long written on this question. As far back as 30th June 1989, I had a letter from Rev. Keith W Munday (AoG), Rushden, Northants. He kindly spoke of my "most interesting observations on meditation and music. They were most appreciated. I liked the thought of 'perceived reply' in meditation and I think this is quite valid when we are truly in the Spirit.... I have been exercised on...the thought of trinitarian worship...wondering if we have given sufficient thought to the Holy Spirit.... The essence of your thoughts is so rich I am still enjoying them. I hope you will not mind if I quote some in subsequent writings! With every good wish, Yours in Christ, Keith W Munday." May you too enjoy.

<u>Improper prayer</u>

<u>Request</u>

"Spirit of faith, come down", prayed Charles Wesley. Let's skip the obvious question about whether he's already come down. Let's simply ask whether we should ever ask the spirit, our personal paraclete and guide, for what we'd like. I probably didn't even think about this question, until I heard Yonggi Cho (Korea) in 1976. He took the line that besides being personal, the spirit, as *allon paraklēton* (Jhn.14:16), was our onboard helper (*paraklēton*) and exactly like (*allon*) the one he succeeded as helper.

Cho overlooked that he was using *Classical* rather than *Common* Greek, and assumed that since the disciples were to ask Jesus (paraclete 1) for things before the cross, it followed that disciples are to ask the spirit (paraclete 2) for things after cross. At the time Cho seemed to me both challenging and persuasive, and for some time I followed his thinking, tentatively expanding the ways in which I spoke to/with the spirit. I still do talk with the spirit, and we should definitely have him in mind. I stand profoundly indebted to Cho.

Nevertheless, I've come to see that asking the spirit for things, faces a huge problem. After all, Jesus said that requests were to move above the paraclete level by the cross, and were to be put directly to the father (Jhn.16:23-4; see Mt.6:9-10/Lk.11:2-4): the disciples were upgraded. Sure, a few other NT writings mention subsequent requests to Jesus, though they are linked to terminal matters rather than run-of-the-mill requests (eg Stephen's dying vision, and John's eschatological vision).[135]

Jesus passed the role of helper/paraclete to the spirit. But was that why Jesus wouldn't take on board further requests? To go Cho's route, fails to account for Jesus' explanation that there was dawning a new contact with the father (which proved Jesus' success as The Way). It was that doorway to the father, which would preclude requests to any paraclete. So, on the one hand, Jesus didn't say, "Ask your new guide." And on the other hand, he implied, "don't ask your guide."

Nor do I think that Jesus, missioning as a human being, ever asked the spirit for things, though they missionised together—and as a paradigm for us—as co-workers. Had he wished to teach that idea, would he not have taught it? Generally requests should go to neither the lord, nor to the spirit, but to God.

This rule puts into perspective our principal relationship (Jhn.20:17), and seems to me to make sense of requesting "in Jesus' name."[136] Requesting the father, also helps avoid the errors of either picturing it as a toss-up as to which of three equals should be asked (that is, father, son, or spirit),[137] or of picturing Jesus as greater than both the father and

---

[135] For Paul the trinity is *lord*, though its manifestation in Jesus' lordship is stressed. Thus 2 Cor.12:8 appears in context to indicate Jesus, though Paul's case was extreme, perhaps potentially terminal. In extremity he either justifiably or unjustifiably asked the lord direct (was he rebuffed?), or asked God directly, therefore the lord indirectly in line with Jhn.14:14/16:23-4.

[136] When seeking our father's help, it reminds us of our filial relationship (and thus servanthood), and is God's signature behind our commands. To ask Jesus "in Jesus' name" is thoughtless, nor does a royal petition such as asking the king "in the king's name" cover the strangeness of such speech, nor is it Scripture's meaning.

[137] A view called Tritheism—that is, three independent gods.

spirit, or even of picturing 'Jesus' as another name for the father,[138] and thus presumably for the spirit too.

Footnote 135 raised the idea that Paul, in line with John, asked the lord indirectly, not directly. Were they in line with Jesus? Looking forward to his crucifixion, Jesus was explaining about a changeover to new times (Jhn.14:28). Before he died, his disciples still looked to him for help as their thaumaturge (wonderworker) and rabbi (teacher/mentor). But, in the mortal shadow of the cross, he knew that they would soon have the direct access he had always enjoyed: a relational upgrade of truly epic proportions.

I do not know whether Jhn.16:23a means that they soon wouldn't need to ask him *for* things (NLT), or *about* things (ERV). I do know that 16:23b means that immediately they had welcomed his resurrection—and thus were spiritually born into his family—their requests were to go directly to their then heavenly father, who to him also—as a human being—was God and father. Direct contact was all part of the spirit's new covenant role (Jhn.7:39). It is by the spirit that we touch base with Abba. So to ask Jesus, is technically to deny the cross. The rule of thumb is that the father is God, Jesus is lord, and we ask God, not the lord!

But what of Jhn.14:14? Some would say that it only applied before the cross. After all, since the verse immediately before and after, had a pre-crucifixion setting, weren't the disciples simply being asked for any last requests before he died? Others might say that the text isn't a problem anyway—simply go with the KJV/NKJV. But have scribes complicated, or simplified, the text?

Even with the complicating word 'me', that's found in the Nestle-Aland/UBS text (also known as the NU or CT), but not found in the Greek text used by the KJV, if Jesus will respond *indirectly* by the spirit (though the text says *directly*), need we say more than that Jesus is *indirectly* asked (though the text says *directly*)? That is, we are to ask the father directly, and it's the spirit who directly responds, but indirectly it's as if Jesus is asked and answers.

---

[138]   A view called Modalism in the sense of God being one person who acts like three.

You may ask why Jesus would have spoken in direct terms, if he were an indirect party. Good question. I suspect the answer is that he was soon to become the essential hub between the one asked (the father) and the one answering (the spirit). He flagged himself up as the coordinating motif, the mediator to be. After all, it's the Holy Spirit who directly does things, not Jesus. Even in his earlier miracles, it wasn't Jesus working by his deity, but Jesus, a man working by the spirit (Mt.12:28)—a pattern we can follow.

Let's not be wooden. Even in Western society, a building contractor can say that they will build you a house. This doesn't mean that they will directly build every part of it. It means that indirectly, a dozen or so people of different skills (bricks, electrics, plumbing, etc) will be hired by the contractor to do the work. What literalist would sue contractors for not doing it all by themselves *as promised*? That would be the literalism that caught out poor old Shylock.

So we should neither hold Jesus to be the one directly asked, nor the one who directly responds. Yeshua is the middleman in the context of his mission and of us working as agents. You can go year on year without ever having a biblical reason to ask Jesus or the spirit to do anything: I've gone about five decades without asking the lord for anything, and I see no reason to change.

He taught us to pray, *our father*. He did not teach us to pray, *our paraclete*, or, *our brother*. Take Paul: access to the father, through Jesus, in/by the spirit (Eph.2:18). In *Ephesians*, the one able to do superabundantly (3:20) is not Jesus, as is so often assumed, but the father (14), unto whom is glory *in Christ Jesus* (21). Throughout his letters, Paul confirmed Jesus' teachings on prayer.

So, unless my feelings exceed my lord's authority, I cannot justify directly asking the spirit. Besides the texts which preclude asking Jesus, and which prefer asking the father, there's Rm.8 to consider. That seems to me to exclude asking the spirit. For according to Paul, the spirit is the one who points us to the father (15), and confirms us to be children of God, heirs alongside Jesus (16-7). And the killer text is v27: the omnipresent spirit is the one pictured as on earth *guiding* our requests, rather than being in heaven *receiving* our requests. Pictures make valid points.

In point of fact, I think that some hallowed old hymns, because they pointedly asked the spirit for things, are heretical old hymns, howbeit coated now with the gentle dust of tradition. For example, Baptist James Edwin Orr's *Search Me, O God* (1936): "O Holy Ghost...send a revival". Fifty years on, we had Pentecostal Chris Bowater's *Holy Spirit, We Welcome You* (1986): "let the breeze of your presence blow / that your children here might truly know / how to move in the Spirit's flow". Wow, in three lines Chris—at college my music teacher—petitioned the spirit, *instead* of the father; called the spirit—instead of the father—our *father*; and told the spirit about *another* spirit. Quite a lot squeezed into three lines![139]

Proper prayer

Gratitude

"Thank you spirit", sang Rebecca St. James. Being pleased for what he has been done, we should thank our helper,[140] even though he acts according to his nature—that is, does what he is without making a conscious choice "to love or not to love."[141] Giving thanks doesn't make him happy, brighten his day, or in any way reward him. The expression of gratitude increases *our* sense of connection. This helps us become more like Jesus, so pleases the father who delights in our wellbeing. Interestingly, when facing his death, Jesus gave thanks.

---

[139] Similarly *Fresh Wind* (Hillsong: 2021), which sings to the spirit (biblical), asking him (unbiblical) to pour out his spirit (ungrammatical—as if one spirit is asked to pour out another spirit), and by poor lyricology encouraging the idea that we are his sons/daughters: did Ac.2:17 flash through the Hillsong psyche? For good measure, Hillsong throws in a KJV *ghost*, and the unexplained idea of the spirit breathing on us (not justified by Jhn.20:22, incidentally). But it'll sell, which is after all what counts.

[140] The spirit as saviour is "as essential to our salvation as the father, as essential as Jesus" (Carson 1986:150).

[141] Consonance, rather than compulsion or choice, best explains why he acts as he does: he does what he is; he acts naturally. I deem it daft to thank deity for being deity—as if he could be anything else and chose to be so to help us out! You may as well thank someone for having been born, though you might be grateful that they have been. But for what he does for us, thanks is fitting.

The very term *eucharist* means thankfulness. Jesus was pleased to help us. Recognise both deity's givingness, and his needlessness. Recognise God the father's lovingness, at the cost of giving his one-of-a-kind, son.[142] And God the son's lovingness, in wholeheartedly welcoming his father's plan that he should become Jesus to die for us—like you sticking your arm into a fire—and to rise as the first of the new humanity.[143] And God the spirit's lovingness, in willingly taking on board the new covenant role of being paraclete to us—even we of humanity which rebelled and crucified the lord—and for lovingly guiding us, even though we often give him grief. In poor human analogy, could *you* love someone who you knew had butchered your best friend? If there is eternal pain within the trinity, that pain is shared by the spirit. Yet he loves us.

When the perfect comes, *thanks* will probably be swallowed up in *praise*. In other words, we'll no longer focus on the acts done, so much as revelling in the praiseworthiness of the doer. His acts show his graciousness, which is of course praiseworthy. Put it another way. Picture someone who has never given money to you, because you have never needed extra money, but whom you know has given unstintingly to many many poor people in dire straits, without seeking payback. You might not thank them for generosity, but you could praise them for their generousness. But for now we thank one to whom we are in debt, a debt beyond an iota of repayment.

Each day the spirit walks with us is gain to us, and worthy of thanks. Are we such nice people that we should imagine that he is privileged to walk with us? Are we so very wise that we don't need his guidance, his helping hand? Do we not need the transformation into messiah's likeness, which the spirit brings to our lives? Are we not at least

---

142   Most Bible versions fall short here. It's not *only, one and only*, and definitely not *begotten*. It is *unique, one-of-a-kind* (HCSB/ISV). For translation for the Gk. *monogenēs*, see the NET comment on Jhn.3:16. And 1 Clement 25:2

143   Jesus' death was proactive, not reactive. It was planned by the father (Ac.2:23) and, the son being no forced agent, by the son (Eph.2:15b), and so presumably by the spirit—a societal plan. Jesus understood the plan (Mt.16:21), and fully agreed (Jhn.10:30).

common beneficiaries of that greatest of individual miracles which he has done for us—conversion, birth into the messianic kingdom?

Thank you militates against human arrogance. In fact, even the little things God does for us are delivered by the spirit, though we often think they're directly by Jesus. The biblical big picture is one where God's son, having become Jesus, handed over to the spirit and 'left', never to return until the end of this age: *maranatha*.[144] Nowadays Jesus is only 'here' by his spirit, and if we invite Jesus to 'come', it should only be in an eschatological sense.

Say again: *how can Yeshua be here, and not here, at the same time?* Well, if you are reading and/or hearing my book, you are reading and/or hearing me. For where my book is, there am I also: I can be both with you and not with you. Similarly, where the spirit is, there is Jesus. Into situations in which the spirit is invoked, Jesus is invoked. When you see or hear the spirit, you see or hear Jesus. It boils down to a case of identification, representation. The Bible explains, but we are sometimes slow to understand. We often fail to thank the spirit, because we simply do not see that it's him at work with us.

<u>Praise</u>

"Sweet Holy Spirit, sweet heavenly dove", prayed Doris Akers. What really is *praise?* It is an expression of admiration:[145] a man might praise a painting or a young woman's beauty, without wishing to

---

[144]   Some think this word states an already fact: viz that our lord has come. IMO it states a future fact, our future vision—our lord shall come (Rv.22:20).

[145]   The distinction and link between praise and thanks can be illustrated thus: an artist freely gives me one of their fine pictures. I thank them for their generosity and praise their artistry (see Dennis & Rita Bennett's *The Holy Spirit and You*, 1974:ch18). Thanks is for doing, never for being. Hence it is daft to thank God for being God—it's not something he has done for us! "If you will thank me.. let it be for yourself alone. That the wish of giving happiness to you, might have added force to the other inducements which led me on, I shall not attempt to deny. But your family owes me nothing. Much as I respect them, I believe, I thought only of you", said Mr Darcy to Elizabeth, having raised Elizabeth's fallen sister (Austen 1980:299).

possess it or her.[146] Such admiration is healthy and (unless expression is imprudent or undermining) to let it flow is quite right—according to nature, as the ancient Greeks would have said.

One might almost say that praise harmonises logic and spirit, as both *head* and *heart* come together in praise.[147] Praise is a growth spiral of blessing! Indeed, stifling praise can cause internal injury. In praising the Supremely Praiseworthy, we are transformed by contemplating and accepting the source of all virtue.

Some overlook our benefit, and so might misunderstand why deity seeks our praise. He is not the Supreme Egotist,[148] and it is for our good that he encourages us to 'feast' on himself, so to speak. If he could create a more praiseworthy object for us to behold, then he would, and would command us to render to It our highest praise. After all, is it not clear that Levitical offerings made to him, were not food for him?

Praise to/of the spirit is obviously right, for even impersonal virtues are said to be worthy of praise (Php.4:8). Would it be right to praise a picture, a woman, a man, yet not the spirit?

<u>Worship</u>

"Holy Spirit, we welcome you", invited Chris Bowater.[149] What of *worship?* Since the spirit is a member of deity (and is rightly understood to

---

146   It's like *Obituary* (*The Rifleman*, S2.E4), where McCain explained to his son that looking at a pretty woman is "like looking at a sunset or a pretty picture painting. You can admire and appreciate them, without wanting to own them."

147   Strictly speaking, logic is probably to spirit, as Eve to Adam, both *from* and *spouse*—or, sadly, living apart. In *Star Trek: The Motion Picture* (1979), Spock finally realises that logic alone is lonely and incomplete. Loneliness logically implies a lack of something potentially available and needed by our nature—we are incomplete without other.

148   Though dated, C S Lewis' *Reflections on the Psalms* is helpful here.

149   Down sides: Chris' prayer-song included the ideas that we ask the spirit for things (misdirectionism), that the spirit is our father, and that the spirit should be told about some other spirit's flow.

be *lord*, 2 Cor.3:17; Heb.13:6),[150] we should worship him, ascribing to him the majesty of eternity which belongs to deity as deity: ultimate and supreme glory to the Most Holy (Is.6:3; Jhn.12:41; Ac.28:25-6).

In *John*, he is intentionally missing from references of the father and son being together (for example Jhn.14:20-4). This is perhaps to emphasise the truth that we are pictured as in heaven, simultaneously *with* both our brother and our father (Eph.2:6-7), and at the same time living in our world with our guide (Jhn.14:26; 16:7). That is, in a spiritual sense we have arrived, but in a mortal sense we still travel. Worship of the spirit is not ruled out.[151]

<u>Adoration</u>

"Spirit, we love you...and adore you", prayed Donna Adkins. [152] The trinity is *love*, so it follows that adoration of the spirit is a natural part of our walk with him (Gal.5:18,25). Moreover the spirit is closely linked to love (Gal.5:22; Rm.5:5). It stands to reason that the spirit doesn't walk with us simply in obedience to the father and son. No, he himself loves us by consonance, not by compulsion.

While the father is the one who invited us to come, and the son is he who blazed the trail to God's door, it's the spirit who guides us along the way. On this journey we wilfully stray many times into spiritual Bad Lands, but he stays with us (though free to leave) and suffers with us,[153] as did God's son who also came freely to save us into the journey of/to life, and the father in giving up his son.

---

[150] The corresponding verb of Heb.13:6 is used of Jesus (2:18), but it also applies to our helper (Gk. *allon paraklēton*) on earth (see Jhn.14-6). Carson held that *allon* is a pointer to worship, love, and (probably) thanks (Carson 1986:52).

[151] The KJV's expression *of himself* (Jhn.16:13) is simply an older way of saying 'off his own bat', or 'self-determination'. Many versions improve, and the NKJV is especially good.

[152] On the down side, she treated the three persons somewhat tritheistically.

[153] Him suffering is often denied by those who like me deny *patripassianism* (which in modalist hands means that the father was crucified), and by those who philosophically have moved from the extreme of passionate and fickle

Like the son (and the father), he loves us. He doesn't love us because of our *value*—we had no trade value, but have always had preciousness. But perhaps he loves us *into* value. Value is a tricky term. We can value beyond computation, the irreplaceable priceless love of parents, yet compute whether a replaceable computer is enough value to us, to buy it new parts. The spirit neither values us as items, nor for relationship, though he makes us useful (valuable) towards blessing others. He loves us because *he* is gracious and *we* need his love. So it is natural to love him, the loving spirit.

<u>Dedication</u>

Holy Spirit, I serve you? Yonggi Cho used to have a chair reserved for the Holy Spirit. That's never been my thing, but nor have I pastored a church, let alone an over half a million people church. I can see how it can be good pretence, a game of make believe in the order of C S Lewis' *Let's Pretend* (Lewis 2002:4.7). A good game, as long as we don't believe that the spirit literally sits in the chair, his feet (?) on the floor. But let the chair simply stand as metonymy for the spirit being with us in platform work, and all is fine. Cho's main point, I think, was his oversight by the spirit. And that too is fine, and better than fine. He taught that ideally we move from the spirit being merely our resident, to him being our president.

It is not so much a case of giving him everything, as being prepared to yield to him all that we have and are, and seeing that such is really his, anyway. A yieldedness of attitude. Abraham was asked to sacrifice his special son, the promised heir. Symbolically it was like transferring all his son's inheritance, along with the continuance of his own name, from Isaac to Yahweh, and allowing Yahweh to return that inheritance if he chose. Abraham was about to literally sacrifice

---

divinities, to the extreme of one dispassionate and staid deity—the emotionally unmoved mover of all. It may be that beyond time and space he cannot suffer, yet within time and space—the painting, the story, the creation—he can do so. Myopic deism denies that deity moves within creation.

PS: it helps to move away from the Jesus-is-God model. We need to be able to say that Jesus was crucified, without saying that God was crucified. Deity was not crucified, not even a member of deity, but a deific person *as incarnate*.

his miracle son, when Yahweh stepped in, showing him that it was faith and yieldedness he sought, and that he himself did not need literal human sacrifice (unlike some so-called deities of the day) and himself was the provider, not the receiver.

But though true dedication to deity is not boastful, sing along with Reuben Morgan if you must. But ask yourself, *do I really give the lord my heart and soul?*[154] Reality check, somebody? It's actually refreshing to admit that we don't totally yield, perhaps never have, and perhaps never will this side of eternity. Scripture speaks of us becoming more like Christ, the totally yielded one. It doesn't, I think, speak of us becoming fully like him in mortal years. Let dedication be tempered with modesty, and plain good sense. Granted our limitations, should we yield to the spirit? I'd certainly say yes. He is the tactical lord on earth. To yield to him is to yield to the lord, which in turn is to yield to God.

Apology[155]

God, remove the cobwebs from my life, prayed the church deacon, week in, week out; year in, year out. Eventually, as he sat down after asking for this yet again, another regular attendee jumped up and begged, *No father, please kill the spider.* The Heart of Worship (Michael Smith (2001)) flags up a common misconception of *worship*: we've sung our songs, done our *worship*, off home we go. Smith has us apologise for this God-dishonouring attitude. Well, it's a lesson some of us will need, but to sing it more than once implies that, like the church deacon, we haven't learnt the lesson! I shouldn't be coming back again: kill the spider and stop apologising.

Oh, apologies to arachnophiles, by the way. And certainly apologies to he who made spiders, not least because our inner spider creates more cobwebs than a cave full of Shelobs. Many of us are indeed troubled by the weekly cycle of cobwebs, the weekly backsliding. But

---

[154]   http://www.worshiptogether.com/songs/i-give-you-my-heart

[155]   Apology logically should relate to all the persons of deity: we find that water baptism, which is symbolic of our initial entrance into God, is *into*, or *relating to*, the corporate name of all three (Mt.28:19). Yet if apology is the main part of our talk with God, then are we living as he intends?

is Smith's lesson really one which, learnt one week, must be learnt again the next *ad infinitum*?

Let there be different apologies, for different sins. Then, if we really don't need to learn again what *it's all about*, let's sit out the song rather than negatively confessing. If it only applies to one in the church, let them sing solo! Singing Smith's song weekly, implies a weekly cycle away from, as well as return to, *the heart of worship*. At the very least we should be working our way through Shelob's Lair and towards the eucatastrophe, not merely cycling through life.

Just incidentally, Smith's song is also a unitarian song—*it's all about you Jesus*, so ruling out the father, the spirit, and the noncarnate son (the Logos). So he really has missed the heart of worship by a long chalk. But the really good bit, reminds us that apology can be the way forward. Anyway, this is all a bit general about apology. Ought you to apologise to the spirit for your sinfulness?

Hold on to your answer. First, are you a sinner or a saint? Scripture has at least two definitions of *sinner*. And as one psychology professor put it, "we are—all of us—disordered. We do not like to think of ourselves as disordered, and this too is a reflection of the fall" (Mark Yarhouse's *Understanding Gender Dysphoria*, 2015:40-1).

The first definition is of human beings outside God's family who are, and do, wrong by their very nature. It's far from saying that you must be a wicked person, so don't take the huff. But if this is you, you need to welcome God's welcome into his family: you are a sinner, loved by God. And he gives you an evangelical call, to at the deepest level (*repentance*) allow him through messiah to become your heavenly father. In fact, before conversion you can overlook the spirit, but if you are at conversion, he will not overlook you.

The second definition is of persons inside God's family who are, and do, wrong in spite of their new family nature. If this is you, you have welcomed God's welcome into his family: you are a saint, loved by your heavenly father. And he gives you a pastoral call to repent from daily sins (*decontaminate*) in order to live a life that best pleases both him and you. To you, on the one hand confession's not an issue to get strung up over—a truth a Joseph Prince might flog to death. But on the other hand, it is a serious issue. As Peter Gillquist put it, an obsession with confession is not called for, so much as you walking in God's light: God in the background will be decontaminating you.

Put another way, living well with Christ will make us more Christlike. We will understand our moral imperfection and our family belongingness. For saints, apology is as family members clearing the air. For saints, sin as the barrier to God has been overcome. The mega-apology of life-change conversion (*metanoia*), is followed by daily micro-apologies of a different sort, and for a different reason. Thus the paternoster speaks of being daily restored to good fellowship—forgiven as likewise we forgive, harmonised.[156]

I used to ask: *Is my heavenly ticket revoked whenever I sin against God, and only reinstated if I forgive those who sin against me?* No, we're not talking about ultimate hell/*hadēs* here. But being reluctant to forgive will degrade our daily family life with our father.

So it's important to keep the two types of sin listed above (the rebellion against family, and the rebellion within family), distinct in our minds, and to see that all Christians have passed from ultimate condemnation (*katakrima*: Rm.8:1), but not ultimately from condemnation—we too should condemn our sins. It is to saints that I put the question: Ought we to apologise to the spirit?

The *Our Father* (Paternoster) addresses the chief party aggrieved, namely our father to whom we should apologise for our daily sins. This is as kids, during family time, admitting to themselves and to their father, their disobedience.[157] In effect, it is also asking their father to help and heal them at the moral level—killing the spider.

Have I a biblical text? Well, perhaps Is.63:10 doesn't clearly specify the spirit—as being a person—since it would not have been so read by Isaiah's initial audience, to whom monotheism was taken to be

---

[156] For his ethno-Jewish readers, Matthew put this in the Jewish cultural way of something owed, a *debitum*/debt (Mt.6:12). God was their people's father; he is our personal father.

[157] When Jesus spoke about us not forgiving, I reckon it's an attitude of unforgiveness—rather than forgiving—that he meant. If it takes an apology (request) for God to forgive, it likewise is required for us to forgive. Resentment, bitterness, can hinder our fellowship with God.

monopersonal, not bipersonal. But wasn't Eph.4:30 written to those to whom the individuality of the Holy Spirit had been revealed? They would have seen that the person called the Holy Spirit, could be grieved. They were in a higher class than Isaiah. They could see that Isaiah's generality meant that grieving Yahweh was in fact grieving the eternal society of father, son, and spirit.

On balance it seems reasonable to me, even if it isn't biblically underlined, to also apologise to the spirit, whom our sins also sadden. After all, he walks with us from earth to heaven, so to speak. Apologies to each person whom we needlessly grieve, is good. When we misguide our guide, is it not courteous to apologise to him?

Chat and complaint

Chat is not explicit in Scripture, though arguably it's implicit in the Yeshuic Covenant, insofar as we who are identified in Christ are individually children in God's family. In God's home, mayn't we be homely, slippers on? The Bible teaches that in one sense, we are home (in True Canaan), yet in another sense are still travelling there (True Exodus): we combine the good we've got, with the ultimate still to come. The eucharist symbols of bread and wine, symbolise both the quick-baked bread, and the vicarious blood, that prefixed the exodus. These elements also symbolise the bread of travel (manna in the exodus) and the wine of arrival (the joy of the Promised Land).

We are travelling to his kingdom in heaven, and since we are travelling with the spirit, may we not chat with him as we walk the road? Well, it seems reasonable to me. Perhaps the big hurdle is moving mentally from mere formality with God, to family informality. This should be done with family awareness that our father is busy on a salvation job, which we should share in under his direction, and with his help, even as did his uniquely unique son.

As for complaint, that is well attested in Scripture.

On the one hand, it can be good. Habakkuk sat in his watchtower awaiting signs of invasion, and complained to Yahweh, first because Yahweh caused Babylon to invade evil Judah, and second that Babylon, being more evil, deserved invasion more. His honest complaints from a loyal heart, received honest answers: punishment in due order. Jeremiah, pressured into becoming a prophet (Jr.1:7-10), was given a task which turned him into the butt of every bad joke of the enemy within. The danger he prophesied didn't materialise straight away. Tormented in mind, he still couldn't bring himself to reject his prophethood, and still believed he would be vindicated (Jr.20:7-13). Our lord, dehydrated and dying, recalled words of dereliction (Ps.22:1): hallowed complaint.

On the other hand, complaint could flow from rebellious attitude, and Jesus warned a seemingly appreciative crowd, that they might fail to make the true Canaan, even as a generation that made it out of ancient Egypt, failed to make it into ancient Canaan. Alas, thinking themselves True Israel, they didn't see that they were living symbols of Global Israel. Seeking national renewal only, they deserted Yahweh, losing spiritual as well as national renewal. The term *gonguzō* (*I complain*) in Jhn.6:41,3, is also in Nb.14:29.[158]

Summary

It's a shame that the Witnesses dump the deity of the father's son. We thank Jesus that we're better than them, since we merely dump the deity of the son's father—"you alone are God, Jesus" (Hillsong). But where the song leader leads, we will follow, follow, we will follow on—all hail the god of good music. Besides, anything for a simple life, yes? And why on earth should God complicate our life? Yet facts are stubborn things, and our wishes, our inclinations, even the dictates of our passions, cannot alter the state of facts and evidence.

Singing can be a powerful way to avoid the trinity. I believe that instead of treating songs as canonical, it is better to build our trinitarianism from Scripture, and from its spinoff, systematic theology, which marshals biblical data under set headings, codifying

---

[158]   Ronald B Allen said that in the Torah, these Israelites were known as 'The Grumblers' (Allen 367). Nb.14 shows a radical rejection of Yahweh's leadership and plan. Seemingly Moses was then tested, and argued that the whole people did not deserve to die without seeing Canaan (Sinai Level loss). In Yahweh's plan, only rebels who had left Egypt with adult awareness of his power, would suffer his judgement within the wilderness. Like the Christian Level (Heb.6:4)?

them. [159] As to internalising it, our trinitarianism should also be devotional. I don't just sit and gaze at my marriage certificate; I live till death does us part with the woman as if she really is my spouse. We should see that God, as societal—deity—is tripersonal, triunity. So songs really should affirm, not disaffirm, this. And we should see that each person of deity can fellowship with us daily.

Jesus is the permanent temporal mode of the uncreated eternal second person of deity. And we may picture Jesus as the one who connects us to both the father and to the spirit. To look at various ways we can fellowship with them, having noted that co-operation is one way, I have looked at verbal, contemplative ways, particularly related to the Holy Spirit. I don't believe that you shouldn't ask him to help you, but I have highlighted that the biblical injunction is almost totally to ask the father—neither the lord, nor the spirit. Request aside, in many other ways the spirit may be talked to/with along the lines of thanks, praise, worship, love, commitment, apology, chat, and complaint.

---

[159]   Another sister discipline is sometimes called Biblical Theology, which uses the biblical terms and pays much attention to unfolding themes. Which sister we prefer will vary, but let's have them both.

Chapter 06   <u>Prayer and Authority</u>

<u>Authority commands</u>

We can talk till the cows come home about charismania and charismata, but it is hard to overlook the fact that, for the most part, we fall below the biblical pattern. To stamp out silly sparks, should we stamp out God's fire? Or should we fan into flame God's fire, and risk a few strange sparks? What of healing fire? Have we, or have we not, God's authority to heal?[160] Some circles load all such authority onto ecclesiastical priests, and have developed healing rites—sometimes powerless. Some circles, sometimes in a reformation wave of reaction, totally deny that we channel God's healing, other than as conversion—conversion *is* therapeutic. The latter sometime allow that within petitionary prayer, we may ask God to physically heal—*but don't place your hands on me!*

Interestingly, Jesus commanded, not prayed, in a lot of situations, where at most, Pentecostals are likely to pray, perhaps crossing holy fingers. There is I think, a challenging middle way between sacerdotal superstition, supreme scepticism, and simple silliness.

In the silliness camp one blogger, I guess plugging the Prosperity Gospel, agreed that Jesus never commanded a billion dollars or denarii, but then asserted that Jesus *commanded* moderate wealth. Far from it, the son of man who sometimes had nowhere to lay his head, was financially assisted by friends and generous patrons—and

---

[160]   Some load too much onto the idealism in the psalms. Eg Ps.103, which was not spoken to us, but even so it neither meant that the psalmist would never be physically diseased (3), nor that the psalmist would never physically die (4). I doubt that the psalmist meant that Yahweh healed all of their physical diseases, or had promised to do so under the Sinaitic covenant. Did the psalm speak of spiritual diseases leading to spiritual death?

some of that was creamed off by good old Judas. But he didn't preach rags or riches. What about Paul? His lifestyle toggled between raving with the rich in the Ritz, and bunking down with the beggars in the basement. And he was content with that (1 Tm.6:6). Some, keeping quiet about Jesus' low bank balance, say that Paul failed in faith to command financial blessings, so deserved poverty, and like Moses, failed to inherit the Promised Land. One wonders why these winners ever quote such a loser—or Jesus, for that matter. Let's move past commands for financial wellbeing. Let's look at Jesus, who went in for verbal commands.

Not all of what he did was by verbal commands, by any stretch of the imagination. For instance, there were his miracles of multiplication to bless the people.[161] These were works of the spirit, works for which Jesus neither prayed nor commanded, but simply believed and played a silent part like those he commanded to fill stone jars with water.

Wait a minute. Have I just likened Jesus to a servant role, akin to obediently filling water jars? Well, that can't be right, can it? Of course, even at Cana his passivity was on a higher level than theirs— he believed, they merely obeyed—and it was his miracle, not theirs, though it was not directly done by him. And that is my point. A doctor can tell a patient to take medication, but it is the medication that saves. The doctor is but an active conduit. Still, they deserve praise and thanks for their diagnosis and prescription.

But with the multiplication miracles, did not Jesus *actively* enrich, bless, the food? After all, doesn't Lk.9:16 say that he eulogised (ευλογω/ *eulogō*) them, *them* being the fish and the loaves? Well, maybe, but it also says that he looked up to the heavens. That expression often signalled thanks to God. Depending on context, the Greek *eulogō* can mean bestowing gain (blessing), or bestowing praise/thanks. Context is king, and not simply grammatical context.

A theological context here, was that under Sinai, looking up and eulogising could read as looking up and expressing gratitude. Neither Matthew nor Mark said what or who Jesus blessed/thanked. So,

---

[161] For various reasons, it is generally taken that the larger crowd was Jewish, and the smaller crowd Gentile.

should we interpret Luke's text as "blessed the food" (CEV), or as "gave thanks" (NIV)? John used a different word, ευχαριστω/*eucharistō* (Jhn.6:11). This word was more narrowly about bestowing thanks. To illustrate, it is a bit like Mark saying that I bought some cola, and John saying that I bought some Coke—or Pepsi.[162] In short, I think this was a case of Jesus knowing God's specific will, and thanking God who would bless, multiply, the food.[163]

There was a close relationship between giving thanks (*eucharistia*), and *eulogia*, which meant that when used as synonyms, one could prefer the narrower term. Thus, though Mt/Mk. use *eulogō* for the passover bread/body, and *eucharistō* for the passover wine/blood, Lk/1 Cor. use *eucharistō* for the passover bread/body, and a 'likewise' for the passover wine/blood. Indeed, the Majority Text seems to have switched from *eulogō* to *eucharistō* in Mt.26:26.[164] Translating into English, Tyndale went with 'thanks'.[165] The Geneva and Douay went with 'blessed', followed by the KJV, although had they been savvy enough to factor in the C1 norms of the setting, all these might have better translated as 'gave thanks [for]'—which is what some mean by the rather inelegant expression, 'bless God' (Heb.7:7).

Finally on this, we should note that well before Jesus, both Elijah and Elisha performed miracles of multiplication (1 Kg.17:8–16; 2 Kg.4:42-4). We are not looking at a miracle-type unique to Jesus. His miracles fitted the pattern of common humanity working with God by the spirit. We should also note that with this miracle, while Mk.8:6 records him giving thanks for the loaves (*eucharistō*), Mk.8:7 records Jesus blessing/giving thanks for the fish (*eulogō*).

For surely the fish fared the same way as the loaves? Would we not say that the 'unblessed' loaves were as blessed as the 'blessed' fish? It

---

[162] Perhaps Coke is preferred by the palate, and Pepsi for the afterglow, but hey, I usually just go for supermarket brands.

[163] Similarly, by saying that Jesus blessed the wine at Cana in Galilee, we are saying that God blessed the wine by the spirit and through Jesus.

[164] "..Jesus took the bread, and giving thanks, he broke it, and gave it to the disciples..." (EMTV).

[165] I have not bothered with which Greek tradition he used.

surely makes sense to see that *eucharistō*, overlapping in meaning with *eulogō* and so functioning as a synonym, showed Jesus as thanking God, who blessed the food.

However on numerous occasions, Jesus did have to speak words of command. That could have been in exorcisms (Mk.1:25; 9:25)—sometimes contested (Mk.5:8). It might have been commands to people (Mk.3:5), or to things (Mk.4:39). Commands could accompany positive faith-actions (Mk.1:41; 5:41). Or perhaps there were positive faith-actions without command (Mk.1:31; 6:41; 8:6). Others could receive through a positive faith-action (Mk.5:27; 8:23-5). Jesus could simply prophesy miracles (Mk.7:29).

Acts kicks off with Jesus' programme being continued by the church. Incidentally, it is better to ditch the silly saying that the Day of Pentecost was the birthday of the church. The church began with a woman on Resurrection Morning. Jesus had prophesied the church, but it is a community born into by spiritual birth (Jhn.3:3). And our being spiritually birthed (ie *from above*) is based on our welcome realisation that Jesus has risen from death—he is the appointed lord of the messianic community. Thus the 120 who had assembled on the Day of Pentecost, were already members of the church, though many would have different spiritual birthdays.[166] The Day of Pentecost was when the church was publicly floated, energised, and many who had been discussing Jesus, were added to it—stakeholders.

Let's look at apostolic miracles recorded by Luke in this, his second volume on the primitive church.[167] Many a time Jesus' followers had

---

[166]   Eg, the couple on the Emmaus Road became Christians at the point where they realised that after death, Jesus was with them. Some had to get over their doubt, before entering the community (Mt.28:17). But the Birthday idea wishes to believe that spirit-baptism is conversion.

[167]   *Primitive*, here, simply means the foundational. The canonical New Testament was not written by theologically primitive beginners, but was primary, foundational. I do not say that the *form*, the common clothing of the day, must be worn today, though we must hold to the body of teaching within the clothing. Bultmann, 'demythologising', went too far by deeming

to speak words of command. That could have been exorcism (Ac.16:18). It might have been a command to someone (Ac.9:34,40; 14:10). [168] Commands could accompany a positive faith-action (Ac.3:6-7). Or perhaps there was a positive faith-action without command (Ac.20:10; 28:5). [169] Others could receive through a positive faith-action (Ac.19:11). They could simply prophesy miracles (Ac.5:9; 13:11). [170]

They could pray and place hands on the sick (Ac.28:8). Here, prayer might have been preliminary, rather than petitionary, even as Jesus prayed before commanding Lazarus to come forth (Jhn.11:41-3). In *Acts*, general mention is made about *apostolic* hands, which could indicate the touch aspect of miracles (Ac.5:12; 14:3; 19:11-2), [171] but it might just have been a poetic way of saying, *through the apostles* (Ac.2:43). Even apostolic shadows could be the touch points of faith (Ac.5:15)—heady days. [172] While we might think first about Peter and Paul, let us also think Stephen and Phillip, as having been wonderworkers (Ac.6:8; 8:6). We read too of the church praying for Peter's release, and God's miraculous response via angelic power.

---

supernaturalism to be the clothing for an ethical body. Some, influenced by the idea that only Gen 1 Christianity had apostles and prophets, jobs transmuted into a Gen 2 clergy system, speak of the 'apostolic church' as past tense.

[168] I hold that verbalising, "In the name of Jesus", is sometimes needless but sometimes helpful. Here, perhaps Paul was wrong not to publicly say in whose authority he had worked his miracle, thereby causing confusion.

[169] There was revivification after Paul's positive faith-action. "Luke would not have devoted space to the raising up of someone who [had been] merely apparently dead" (Marshall 1992:326).

[170] He had also experienced a miracle of knowledge (5:4).

[171] And Barnabas too was an apostle (v14). Has there only been 12 apostles? Those who hold this usually allow that Judas was replaced, either by Matthias, or by Paul. Ditching this idea of *only 12* opens up the way to accept apostles today. Arguments for include Continuationism, and apostleship set as a pattern to propagate new churches (eg Eph.4:11-6): this underlines spiritual dynamics— let apostles add to the church. Arguments against include Cessationism, and criteria set as a pattern to fade-out apostleship (eg Ac.1:21-2): this underlines Scriptural authority—let not apostles add to the canon.

[172] I presume that dead cats would not revive under Peter's shadow, nor the lame who hobbled by without noticing him. Faith to receive can be key.

This is admittedly a rather short survey, and admittedly it only reports on some 'big' people in some big time. Did all accounts have all the data? Did prayer factor into more cases than that of Lazarus? Even with him, it was not a petitionary prayer, with Jesus then standing back to watch. Wait and see? No. As he approached the sea, Moses was roundly condemned for his wait and see approach. He should have seen that he had at hand all he needed for a faith-action (Ex.14:13-6). Jesus did not make that same mistake. Do we?

If we do, then what, we might ask, would have happened if Moses had not realised his mistake, and in faith moved on? The exodus was a big event. Of course, Yahweh can look for help in big issues, only to discover that he must do all the work himself (Is.59:16; 63:5)—which is a shame because we lose out. But arguably with the stakes so high, Yahweh would have simply adjusted his plan, stopped the Egyptian pursuit in its tracks, and gotten his people into Canaan by another route at another time. Even his plans for Moses were modified because Moses insisted he needed help—*here am I, send Aaron* (Ex.4:14)—and perhaps when later Moses had proved insufficient to lead his people into Canaan.[173]

In the world of smaller matters—I do not say unimportant matters—I suspect that many good interventions simply never happen. Many of the lame, the blind, the bound, the dead, simply never receive miraculous intervention.[174] Sometimes, that's because we did not intervene. And is this too hard to accept, too heavy a load for us to bear? Is it any harder to accept than the obvious fact that after Jesus'

---

[173] Some would reply that Yahweh merely pretended to interact with Moses, but had planned to use Aaron that way, and had decreed that Moses would protest. When so much appears to be random—or devolved sovereignty—pressing deific sovereignty to the exclusion of it being shared with those in his likeness, presents God as the ultimate pretender.

[174] There is an idea in *Miracles* (C S Lewis), that God has sovereign locations and times for miraculous interventions, and I agree. However, sometimes it's simply that we don't ask in faith (Jas.4:2-3). Confronted with a major epidemic felling his congregation like flies in Newtown, Sydney, John Alexander Dowie turned to Ac.10:38 in 1875, going public in 1882. God would shine more if our light shone brighter.

resurrection, Peter did not free either the Australian aborigines or the Inuit's by evangelism?

In heaven, many might say that we did not offer them needed food, shelter from the storm, a coat when theirs was threadbare, a healing hand, a visit when deserted.[175] But then, they might add that we simply weren't around, so they had to get on with what life handed out. In the storyline, Lazarus only got relief after his death.

Still sometimes we will be around, but not offer the helpless the help we could give, even the help we should give. They might have to make do without. They must learn to live with our weakness, as well as their own. Life can be tough. Life can suck. We might have to live with our weakness. I do not say that we should not seek to up our game. I do say that we should not beat ourselves up for not playing well. Let's look to Jesus, the supreme coach. Pray for help.

So too with evangelism. In my early Christian years, I was taught that if those I could have evangelised died unevangelised, ultimate hell would be their destiny, and ultimate responsibility would be mine—if I had been their last evangelist this side of hell. That was an abuse of Ezk.3:16–27, which was not about evangelism, still less about ultimate destinies. That was about urging ethnic Israelites/Jews back to their covenant loyalty, for Yahweh would purge his people before releasing them from Babylon.[176]

I hold that, at the higher end, the church has authority to act as Jesus acted—in general terms. Certainly as regards procuring atonement for whosoever will welcome God, the cross was a one-off act. But as regards wonderworking, the church should still be in the business. It

---

[175]   I have borrowed some imagery from Mt.25:31-46.

[176]   Think also of some physical purges under the Yeshuic Covenant (Ac.5:5,9; 1 Cor.11:30). Opportunities given to repent were not always taken up. Yet death is not *per se* an evil. Death is a door from/to. That we ought not to push anyone through for our selfish ends (by murdering: Gen.9:6), does not mean that we are wrong to push anyone through for societal ends (by killing: whether by judicial or military wisdom), nor that it is wrong for God, both sides of the door, to push/pull anyone through (by killing) according to his ultimate wisdom. Death ends our preface, but not our story. Premature death by God's design, neither implies their ultimate sadness nor joy.

seems to me that the same methods he used, followed by the primitive church, obtain for us today. Not all are gifted for the same tasks—I was never an evangelist—but through the body of Christ, through the church of God, some should be up to the faith level of commanding by words and by deed. Maybe not you; maybe not I. But maybe we *will* rise to such heights. Let's look at some ideas on how words of command are said by some to work.

Declare and decree

"Faith obtains! Faith possesses! Faith moves the hand of God! Faith captures the promises of God and makes them work![177] And real faith is always known by its confession. Faith is bold to speak. Faith is always eager to affirm its confidence in Christ, to say what God says, and to declare that the promise of God will come to pass" (Chant 53).[178] There are blessings in positive confession, especially in biblical confession, as it relates to God's individualised or church promises to us.

Now, I am not an apostle. I'm more of a hermit, really. Some, rightly or wrongly claiming to be Christian apostles or prophets, declare and decree that Christians should declare and decree—as if by God's command. And that filters down to ground level. Some link decree and declare to binding and loosing—more anon. If, as some argue, Christian apostles and prophets do not exist today, then such claimants are mistaken as to their titles.

Yet if they are mistaken on one point, are they mistaken on all? I believe that Christian apostles—and prophets—exist today. I also believe that even apostleship is no guarantee of perfect biblicality. Obviously, any biblical apostle would doubtless have a basically sound platform on which to build doubtable ideas—such as Leo Harris and his British Israelism. Even spirit-anointed teachers can disagree over doctrine. They should, of course, agree over a basically Christian platform, such as the basic kerygma (core preaching).

Granting, for the sake of argument, that someone might be an apostle, it is possible that they might on the one hand disagree with

---

[177]   I'd rather say *sees* here, than *makes*.

[178]   A *double-entendre*, on top of = victorious over [the (sinful) 'world'].

the 'decree and command' doctrine, but on the other hand agree with the 'positive confession' doctrine. Or perhaps hold to neither—I think of the great W F P Burton (Congo Evangelistic Mission). To claim true apostleship is not to claim perfect biblicality. We should not claim noncanonical[179] prophets or apostles, as infallible guides.

Listing to the range of things declared and decreed, can suggest that you are in a selectivity game, perhaps a game for mugs, binding us into the mentality of Promise Boxes. In the latter, a relevant card might come up and prove to be a genuine blessing to a given individual—what some, usually a bit weak on Greek, used to call a rhēma-word. Promise Boxes, and Prophetic Boxes, tend to exclude the negatives. But that's a bit like having Mount Gerizim without having Mount Ebal (Dt.11:29): both were within the Promised Land; both were needed for those whom Yahweh loved.

Such Boxes also tend to ignore biblical context and applicability. One *Women's Aglow* box I've seem, prefixed each encouragement with, "Lord you said"—missing Mt.16:23. Did he, and if so, did he say such to me? These cards obscure the distinction between Yahweh (LORD) and Yeshua (lord), besides obscuring whether such encouraging words were issued for a community application (whether Yahwistic or Yeshuic), and/or for individual application. And the next question could be, for *which* communities and/or persons? Sometimes these cards throw in some ideas which might or might not be biblical, but certainly sound dynamic, glowy. Similarly, when it comes to Decree and Declare, selectivity plays a big part, selecting out the negatives.

But why exclude the negatives, if they're biblical? If we do not declare and decree that God will make us as despised as Edom (Ob.2), is it because we see that it was never said to us, or because we prefer to keep what we like and chuck the rest? Do we declare and decree that Yahweh has left us among the dead, like the slain who lie in the grave (Ps.88:6)? Far nicer to declare and decree that Yahweh has plans to prosper us (Jr.29:11), a decree declared to the sinful Judahites (4) who would wait 70 years while they were punishment-purged (10) to have

---

[179]   Canonical apostles/prophets were they in Scripture who spoke from God.

---

the stuffing of idolatry knocked out of them. Should I decree and declare that I am a worm, and not a man? Well that's biblical, isn't it?

Will our decrees always pan out? Even God's decrees are not always enforced.[180] Especially outside of Christ, some postmodernists preach that gender is whatever you declare it to be for you, a construct of the human mind, not a discerning of something real beyond our minds. Declaration is not magic, whatever they believe, but it can be devilish, imposing its own decrees.[181]

So-called reification, the idea that we reify, make real, make our own *fiats*, is illusion. Some, unhappy to face God's decrees in the real world, seek to hide within their own illusions. And to a sinful world, many of God's decrees are treated with undeserved contempt. As mortals we can literally get away with murder (Dt.5:17). There is a big difference between authority to issue a decree, power to enforce it, and willingness not to enforce it. I will say more about human freewill. But first let me say that nowadays, some Christians are too easily jumping on the idea that our decrees will always be enforced, as if they carry their own enforcement power. But at least they factor in God and seek to align with him.

The internet proclaims that "when we decree, 'I am blessed' (inspired by Ps.112:1), we establish the blessing. When we decree, 'My home brims with wealth' (inspired by Ps.112:3), we establish our wealth. When we decree God's peace and unity in our family, then anything against peace and unity has no valid standing to come against us."[182]

What does that psalm say? "Praise Yahweh. Blessed are those who fear Yahweh, who find great delight in his commands" (NIV: Ps.112:1). If we contrast getbibleanswers.org to getbibletext.god, we see that the psalmist didn't say that people needed to verbally establish what Yahweh had blessed. It should also be noted that the Bible has many texts of tendency. As we might put it, "other things being equal, we will get A rather than B." Thus "teach your children right from wrong,

---

[180]   Eg, Jr.18:8,10.

[181]   Philosophical Foundations of a Transgender Worldview: Nominalism, Utilitarianism, and Pragmatism - The Gospel Coalition

[182]   https://www.getbibleanswers.org/command.html

and when they are grown they will still do right" (CEV: Pr.22:6), sounds clear enough, yet Ezekiel noted that good parents can have bad kids, and bad parents can have good kids (31).[183] Socially the proverb is true as a tendency, but not as an absolute, according to human freewill.

The proverbs are not promises, and reflect both the ideal and the real. Those who lived as good citizens in ancient Israel, if under a godly monarch, might reasonably have expected to enjoy the blessing of comfortable finances and success for their good work. Under a Mao Zedong, they would probably have been stripped of all human wealth for standing up against political correctness, then re-educated and forcibly squeezed into a correctivist mould. Under a bad king, godly Jeremiah lived awhile down a well, in the pits, and his home brimmed not with wealth. I no more dispute Psalm 112, than do many lament-psalms, psalms which speak about those who, because they reverenced[184] Yahweh, suffered significantly within their community. Would we stick with him through thick and thin?

Jeremiah surely feared Yahweh, yet like we in this woebegotten world, he had trouble by the bucketload (Jr.8:21; 20:14; Jhn.16:33), and has been dubbed the Weeping Prophet. Well, that's better than the Sleeping Prophet! Wisdom writings emphasise blessings deserved, but the psalms flag up that we don't always get our due deserts in this world. Though eventually "sunrise breaks through the darkness for good people" (MSG: Ps.112:4), "wisdom does not always seem to be beneficial. Adversity also comes on the path of the godly. 'Darkness' is a metaphor for adversity" (VanGemeren 25223-4/30250). *Hebrews* says that some who feared Yahweh, were mocked and mugged, destitutes in the desert, hunted and harried, holed up in caves or crevices, slain by

---

[183] Written under Sinai, this chapter used a mixture of things which have been always right everywhere throughout human history, and cultus things that were important covenant teaching practices, disobedience to which was sin. Such cultus sins died with their covenant (eg human male circumcision), though some remain contentious (eg sabbath observance). D A Carson's *Sabbath and the Lord's Day*, remains a basic read.

[184] "'Fear' (yir'â) denotes an attitude of submission and openness to divine instruction" VanGemeren 4429/30250.

---

swords or by stones, "...making their way as best they could on the cruel edges of the world" (MSG: 11:36-8).

Yet, they were, and we are, blessed, and spoken well of by God. Job was blessed by Yahweh, even when just having lost his farm, family, and fitness. Ironically his loss was because he was spoken well of by God. We can be blessed within, and we can enjoy the wonders of this world and beyond. Nevertheless, our outer world, like Job's, might not always contain the blessing we would like, and the true Promised Land will only bloom in the age to come.[185] Jesus went through many tears and traumas to reach spiritual maturity, in order to bless himself, and to enable him to bless others. Paul also went through such, also for the sake of others.

Our verbal decrees, based on texts we happen to like—even if they were targeted to bygone people under a bygone covenant—have neither authority nor power to change our outer world, though they might steady or stumble us. Nor should we think that we need to act (*speak into reality*), in order to establish what God has blessed, as if he dumps his blessings on the doorstep, leaving our words to carry them through the door. That we can bless ourselves, by declaring what God has decreed, is a given. Evangelism is a case in point—we declare the cross; glossolalia is another—we declare his praise. Those things are surely biblical.

But isn't Christian declaration and decreeing biblical, too? Doesn't God honour our faith-commands as an alternative to praying? Aren't we seated in heavenly places? Indeed, some will hold such commands to be verified by experience, along the lines of *I Decreed and Declared; it worked; QED it's proved*. Yet I fear that some will deem it falsified, along the lines of *I Decreed and Declared; it didn't work; it's disproved*.

It is not logical, but it is human to ditch God if promises one had believed had come from him, fail. For can God fail? Failure would therefore seem to render the idea, God, false. If we set people up for false expectation, we set them up for a false fall. God sometimes does things we declare and decree, not perhaps because we declare and

---

[185]   Joshua led God's people into the seed level of it; Jesus led his people into the stem level of it. The bloom will be everlasting.

decree, but because our faith is in line with his will. It does not vouchsafe that he will always do what we declare and decree. It does not mean that he will always honour our faith.

But as to biblical declarations, I wholeheartedly agree that not talking ourselves up or down, but rather talking within ourselves about what God has said about us, is a proper part of good biblical meditation, of biblical confession. If we are identified in Christ, we are sitting on top of the world, even if wobbly royalty. But many texts or snatches of texts, have been taken to build a framework for verbal declaring and decreeing. So, is it a biblical framework? Let's come to them. Laurel Davis has provided some timesaving teaching here, which I have piggybacked on below.[186] Here are some common texts which some suggest affirm their particular belief in verbal confession. I add some comment. To a large extent, Laurel and I have both sought to highlight that biblical context is king.

Job 22:28:[187] Here the TVB is perhaps most in line with D&D thinking: "You will pronounce something to be, and [El-Shaddai] will make it so." This text was spoken by the misguided, though well-intentioned, Eliphaz, who was rightly rebuked by Yahweh for being out of sync with him (Job 42:7). Since Eliphaz was shot down by God, why should we say that his words were prophetic, instead of pathetic? Why should we affirm the words of Job's friend, any more than we affirm the words of Job's wife to curse God and die (2:9)? Even if it was a prophetic word to this one person—even Caiaphas could truly prophesy—why say that it's a *principle* for us?

Is it not a weak foundation? In fact, as it stands it was merely an if/then. Eliphaz tried to say that if Job repented of his dire sins—in fact Job hadn't any dire sins to repent of!—then Job would get back to

---

[186]   See http://www.reluctantfirstlady.com/abracadabra/ and also her Part 2.

[187]   *Gâzar* (decree: KJV). Usually, if you read the word 'decree' in an English version, do not expect to find the root word *gâzar* behind it. And if you properly search through where *gâzar is* used, you'll find that it seldom carries the meaning of a legally binding decree. See 1 Kg.3:25-6; 2 Kg.6:4; 2 Chr.26:2; Est.2:1; Job 22:28; Ps.88:5; 136:13; Is.9:20; 53:8; Lm.3:54; Ezk.37:11; & Hab.3:17. Its primary meaning is division. Websites can blind with Hebrew, without knowing what they are on about.

normal life, where one could usually plan for the future with reasonable confidence, with reasonable expectation of some success. "You will succeed in all you do" (GNB)—walk in the light. With such blindness about Job, Eliphaz was hardly a prophet proclaiming under heavenly inspiration that the non-Christian Job—much less the rest of us—would get from heaven whatever he said he would get, and give to heaven whatever he said he would give. If I decree that you will get the job you applied for, and you get it, don't declare that you wouldn't have got it unless I had so decreed, unless you work for me.

Pr.6:2: Verse 2 follows verse 1 and precedes verse 3. Why do I state the obvious? Well, simply to underline the idea of the context of this short speech. Its advice is to be cautious about giving a promise to a fellow human being. It's not about speaking to heaven or hell. It's about practical citizenship, not spiritual warfare.

Pr.18:21: Wisdom teaches that what we say, can sometimes save lives, and sometimes end lives. I think of the WW2 slogan, "Careless Talk Costs Lives". It's better to live as those who speak of others honestly, rather than dishonestly. That's the proverb here.

Mk.11:23//Mt.21:21: The context speaks of an unhappy fig tree. Sure, it wasn't the ripe time to eat figs, but any fig tree in leaf was advertising that at least it had unripe figs—not tasty but eatable at a pinch. Jesus lingered at one particular tree, for it illustrated those who advertised what in fact they lacked: its cash value fell well below its face value; a giant gap between sale and substance.[188] As a pattern it would fit snugly with his cleansing of the temple. Well, he would put the temple-gone-wrong out of its misery, even as he would put the fig tree-gone-wrong out of its misery. Thus he would end that show. But it was the quickness of its demise—presumably within 24 hours—

---

[188] If there was no hidden message in the fig tree as such, merely an object lesson in faith, it would stand as unique, but Matthew's thematic account, and Mark's chronological account, ties it in with the corrupt temple, or perhaps even the idea that Sinai had never been designed for fruit (*this* mountain?), so corruption was inevitable. Perhaps as an indirect tie-in, Jr.24:1-8 spoke of a division between ethnic-Jews (ie Judahites). Jesus spoke similarly, lambasting a segment of the population for belying the mission of a global prayer centre (Mk.11:17).

which surprised his disciples, who were blind to the bigger picture. Jesus went on to talk about *their* faith.

He spoke either of faith in God (if the genitive is objective: the object of faith being God: Tyndale), or God's faith (if the genitive is subjunctive: Wycliffe—God's confidence?): Mk.11:22. The former is more likely, because it's a more general theme and Mt.21:21 speaks generally of faith. Either way, God-based faith is in line with God's will. With a God-based faith, they too could speak powerful words of command, whether for small or for large things, for fig trees or for mountains.

Mark's account was fuller. Words spoken in God's specific will, without wavering, would not work on their own, but would be worked by God—"it will be done for you" (NRSV: 23). Likewise with prayer, for while words of command can give, words of prayer can receive—"it shall be done unto you" (NMB: 24). And Yeshua reminded us that God finds it hard to hear bitter people (25). However, no fancy D&D mechanism, but a simple command (23).

Rm.4:17: "This promise was made to Abraham because he had faith in God, who raises the dead to life and creates new things" (CEV). Abraham believed in God. God could raise an infertile wife to fertility (Gen.17:17). God could create a new nation (ethnic Israel) from her. God had created mankind from dust (Gen.2:7). God could from old Canaanite stones in a river bed, create children of Abraham's faith (Mt.3:9).[189] Abraham, symbolically speaking, fathered a spiritual nation (Spiritual Israel) too, which so to speak came into existence through the 'Sarah' of ethnic Israel, illustrated as Yahweh's 'wife'.

The text also carries ideas of God's *fiats* (the *let there be*'s) of *Genesis* 1. But being in God's image (Gen.1:26) does not authorise us, nor empower us, to act as little divinities who speak their own little fiats, though we may rightly declare what God has decreed. Gen.9:6 makes it clear that in Adam, all human beings are *imago dei*. It is also clear

---

[189] I am surprised that some assume that Jesus meant *children of Jacob* (Israelites), or *children of Judah* (Jews). Beelining to the root/radix of the tree, Abraham (Rm.11:18), he bypassed both family lines. Ethno-Gentiles became children of Abraham (Gal.3:7). On Gen.2, incidentally, literalism need not be pressed.

that being in Adam neither authorises nor empowers anyone to decree and declare as if God.

At the higher level, the *imago christi*, we have a commitment (and command?) from messiah, to work miracles—a position called continuationism. Elijah's miracles were not based on his deity; Jesus' miracles were not based on his deity; Paul's miracles were not based on his deity. They were based on God's will through God's spirit. Jhn.14:12 adds to mere miracles, the greater work of leading others into the messianic community. That was something impossible for Jesus to do. But then, it was something utterly impossible to do before the cross. The cross created the community.

We can work miracles as Elijah, Yeshua, and Paul, did. But Paul did not teach that our declarations and decrees will create even one jot or tittle. Through trust, Abraham received Yahweh's promise. It was Yahweh, not Abraham, who spoke of realities that were yet to be.

2 Cor.4:13: "I kept my faith, even when I said, 'I am greatly afflicted'" (NRSV: Ps.116:10). This is a persecution setting, in which Paul said that he was like the ancient psalmist. (Incidentally, Paul used the LXX, which had this line as the first stanza of Ps.115.) What was the context? Both the psalmist and Paul experienced persecution because of their covenant faith in God, though took their woe in different directions. The psalmist spoke of suffering; Paul spoke of sermon. Because he believed the message, in spite of persecution he vocalised his belief, having the same spirit of loyalty to Yahweh as had had the psalmist—continuity. But his words were not about speaking words of command, but about the command to speak words about God.

In context, Paul made plenty of negative confession, mixed in with good contrast. The very real woes which we too can know, include affliction by the world—though not abandonment by God; knocking down by the world—though not knocking out by the world; suffering socially from the attitude which crucified Jesus, though revelling in his post-crucifixion life; condemnation by the world, but justification by God. It was not Paul's own social standing he sought to declare, but the spiritual wealth which, as a slave (5), he passed on to fellow Christians (12) and shared with them (14).

Some would shoot Paul down, reckoning that he *produced* the negative by *speaking* negative confessions, negatives in which he even seemed to rejoice! "Most make decrees daily. We decree and declare our lack of faith, our lack of money, our sickness, and our difficulties. All such decrees the devil uses to bring faith-killing doubt and destruction into our lives." [190] Did not Paul speak both praise and curse, contravening James? Let's go to James.

Jas.3:10: We should lament the ethical inconsistency of Christians following holy praises by unholy curses. But James was not advocating verbal commands, either to bless (loose) the kingdom of light, or to curse (bind) the kingdom of darkness. Indeed the Greek *eulogia*, might well be better put as praising, speaking well of folk, although the word can speak of conferring gain (Heb.7:7). [191] Nor, incidentally, was James against praise/blessing where appropriate, and rebuke/cursing where appropriate: Yahweh operates in this dual mode. What James condemned was retrograde randomness, moving from our new to old natures/mindsets.

James here was making an observation, not giving an instruction for us to follow. He was prefixing the larger lesson about the opposing ways in which we speak in asserting our opposing natures. There are various ways to make this contrast between natures. We may contrast the First Adam, to the Second—the Last—Adam; the sinful nature, to the Christian nature; the uncrucified, to the crucified.

James was not saying that what we speak has intrinsic power to spark life, or to spark death, into our circumstances. But he did say that if we give free rein to our two natures, we'll find that we'll wrongly offend as well as rightly praise, rightly help as well as wrongly harm, wrongly discourage and rightly encourage, output both truth and lies, both godly love and evil hate. Our words are a litmus test, showing us how far we've come, and how far we've still to go. I've used qualifying terms like 'rightly' and 'wrongly', for at times we can wrongly praise, and rightly offend.

∞

---

190   https://www.getbibleanswers.org/command.html

191   Accordingly most Bible versions nowadays translate as *praise* when God is the receiver, since he cannot receive gain—as if he lacked and we were greater! But he can receive praise.

Declare and Decree doctrine is textually selective (Gerizim not Ebal), ignores textual situations, and overplays human sovereignty. And being false faith it can damage true faith.

∞

I am quite happy to declare what I believe has been done, what I believe God can do, and what I believe will be done—and I have varying levels of faith. I am less happy to decree (Jas.4:16), without at least tacking on the rider, 'only if the lord is willing' (15)—and that's about decreeing *my* plans. On earth, there is no record of the lord saying that he declared and decreed (an abracadabra), and no mention of his praying for folk to be healed, or when healing of saying "in the name of the father".

Yet, as I taught at Huthwaite AoG in the late 70s or early 80s, then "on the block" at Mattersey Hall in '83/4, Jesus (God the son as a mortal human being and as our pattern) only worked miracles in his father's name and by the spirit's power. Likewise we—in delegated authority—are not commanded to say "in the name of Jesus" (as if an abracadabra), though sometimes it can be wise to flag up his name, just to inform other folk. I believe that if we are truly in tune with God's active will for a situation, then we have as much justification as the lord had, to simply command a healing, a walking on water, a multiplication of substance, an exorcism. That's a big *if*, but not an impossible one. For what use is a pattern which cannot be followed?

But not all of God's will, will be achieved on earth by us commanding left, right, centre, and up and down, merely making ourselves a little hoarse (or an ass). Our pattern, Jesus, was not to be exceeded in the miraculous, as if he was an Elijah and we are the Elishas.[192] Did Jesus go around declaring and decreeing that Satan's worldwide kingdom

---

[192] We do not know which performed more, or greater, miracles, since the records are selective, not exhaustive. However, the records attribute more miracles to Elisha, which some claim went with the 'double blessing'. The double blessing, incidentally, was merely a way of saying that someone was the prime inheritor/leader, not a numerical doubler. No one could bequeath *double* what they had. Some say that Paul had ups and downs because he didn't claim the prosperity gospel and word of faith. Tush!

was bound, and heaven's angels loosed? Not that we read about. Well maybe he did, but it simply wasn't deemed important enough to tell us? If so, is it important enough that we need to be told about it now?

If the church at Rome followed Paul's advice, he declared a good outcome to it: "...I want you to understand what is good and not have anything to do with evil. Then God, who gives peace, will soon crush Satan under your feet...." (CEV: Rm.16:19-20).[193] But Paul was not binding Satan. It strikes me that Jesus, our pattern, also saw a more or less immediate justification of his commands—he spoke, and it immediately happened. It's not Promise Box mentality.

When it comes to selecting what to declare, I really wish to see what God in Christ has or has not said about Christians at large. And such is worth a song: *I am a new creation, no more in condemnation, here in the grace of God I stand.* But we should fact-check texts.

Some encourage Christians to declare that if they confess their sin, according to 1 Jhn.1:9, God will forgive them. I think that the coat is good (postconversion forgiveness), but that it's hung on a wrong peg (conversion forgiveness). For IMO, the aorist tenses[194] of 1 Jhn.1:9 were only directed to non-Christian folk within that church.[195]

---

[193]   That Paul said 'your feet', not 'our feet', shows that he was neither declaring the return of messiah, nor binding Satan's kingdom. He foresaw for that troubled church a soon and swift shalom, as their ethnic factions reintegrated. The previous emperor had banished ethnic-Jews from Rome, and their return was creating new issues which Paul addressed.

[194]   An example of an aorist tense is water-baptism—biblically an emphatic one-off event per person. (Confusion leads to some being water-baptised more than once.) By way of contrast, an example of an indicative tense is the eucharist: we are commanded to repeatedly enact this drama. That said, aorists don't always mean one-off.

[195]   I am an amateur, not a master, of NT Greek. But here are a few points which I think are valid. Of the five aorists in theses verses, we find ειπωμεν/*eipōmen* (*we say*). It's not a bad expression in itself, but its three uses in *First John* are all aorist-emphatic *false* declarations (1 Jhn.1:6,8,10). I think that John used the 'we' of identification—we are all Churchians, fellow church members—though

So rightly or wrongly, for me to declare 1 Jhn.1:9 would to me be like declaring that I am not a Christian. No, I don't believe that those Churchians were Christians. I suspect that they were probably mixed up with some form of proto-Gnosticism which mixed in some Christian themes and was church-based. Gnosticism basically denied sin as we know it, though it wore many different faces. Gnostics could say that only their bodies, not they, sinned. Thus, I think, John hit them between the eyes with the idea that anyone making an all embracing and emphatic denial that they had ever really sinned, was emphatically deceiving themself and was emphatically mistaken big time. Yet, he added, if they asked God for forgiveness, he would emphatically forgive-clean them (conversion).

Similarly I don't like to sing, "Just as I am without one plea."[196] That's a conversion song, and just as I have no need to be water-baptised again, I have no need to be Christian-converted again. Such conversion is an emphatic one-off (aorist tense). There is an ongoing sense of cleansing, of course, but John had already covered that.

I'd also have problems with 2 Corinthians 5:20, in that IMO that was Paul talking about he and his colleagues being ambassadors *to the*

---

he toggled between Non-Christian, and Christian, Churchians. Some Churchians had already left the church (1 Jhn.2:19)—they hadn't been Christians, and had perhaps given up the fight to convert the church. Well, said John, if our everyday walk is in darkness (sin), any claim to Christian fellowship with God, is false (1 Jhn.1:6). But if our everyday walk as believers is in the moral light, then we'll have common fellowship with other believers, and for us a result of Jesus' death will, in the background, always be cleaning us up from sin's almost inevitable darkening of daily life (7). But if in fact we Churchians are claiming that we've always lived in sinlessness, we're actively fooling ourselves (8). Yet if we will in fact confess our sin, why, God the father will emphatically one-off forgive and emphatically one-off cleanse us: that's conversion forgiveness/cleansing. If we don't switch from our aorists to God's aorists, we continue to call him a liar, for he's declaring what we're denying.

196   If it's being sung, I can happily rejig to the past tense: eg "Just as I was, I came to you. O Lamb of God, I came, I came." The etiology of the song is quite moving, written by a Christian invalid and published in a hymnbook for invalids. Miss Charlotte Elliott had, I think, become a Christian as an invalid— "physically fit for nothing", as a family member said.

Christians within the church. For by *you*, didn't he mean the Christian recipients of his letter? It's all too easily to evangelicalise his pastoral words. That said, church leaders might need to declare that they are ambassadors to their errant sheep, as I guess Paul did.

Is God bound?

When we start talking about what *we* can achieve, it's good to get a good grip on the idea of sovereignty. If we say that we can decree anything, it's good to ask if God can do as much. There are far weightier tomes on this, such as D A Carson's *Divine Sovereignty and Human Responsibility*, a book I have deeply enjoyed. In *The Last Battle* (C S Lewis), we see Aslan saying that "they will not let us help them" (ch.13). Effectively that's about God's inabilities. When Jesus spoke of nothing being impossible to God, he spoke within the orbit of possibility, not about intrinsic impossibilities.[197]

Let's ask about ideas impossible in themselves. Can God create an uncreated being which has more power than himself? Can he create an absolute contradiction? Can he become Satan, become evil? Can God cease to be? Can God forget his creation? Surely not! Can God make a rock too heavy for him to lift? Indeed, moving beyond measurement into infinity, moves beyond rockiness into supernature, and 'rock' is defined by cosmic-time limitation! So no, he cannot make what cannot exist. Can the source and sustainer of reason, become irrational? Can the unchangeable change? Too often we ignore the jump between the temporal and the eternal. God, by definition, cannot become, cannot eternally change, as Plato pointed out long ago. If the Perfect becomes more perfect, it wasn't perfect. What do they teach in schools?

Within creation, is God self-limited? Let me kick off with a biblical story of limitation. The Syrians was gunning for the Israelis, but wished to avoid fighting the Jews—to use familiar terms in an unfamiliar way. All three got into a fight. In 1 Kg.22 we're told that

---

[197]   Mt.19:26 has its obvious context in the fact that salvation (25) is humanly impossible, that salvation is possible, but possible only by God: it is not a philosophic assertion that God can violate the Law of Non-Contradiction.

---

when the Syrians "saw Jehoshaphat in [Ahab's] robe, they thought he was Ahab and started to attack him." Later, we read that "a soldier shot an arrow without even aiming, and it hit Ahab where two pieces of his armour joined" (CEV): bye-bye Ahab. On the one hand, Yahweh did not direct the chariots that attacked the Jewish king, but on the other hand, Yahweh did direct that one arrow at the Israeli king. Seemingly his one act of intervention, in a big battle of randomness.

Every now and again, someone will decide that there cannot be a universal creator if even one bad thing happens within nature: it can be their church letting them down; it can be a world war; it can be a cat killing a mouse. Some say that either God is all-good but not all-powerful; or God is all-powerful but not all-good; or the idea, *God*, is false. After about 20 years of atheism, C S Lewis wrote a book called *The Problem of Pain*, a Christian perspective on the existence of pain. After about 50 years of atheism, Anthony Flew admitted in *There is a God*, that the negative evidence of pain in creation, did not trump the positive evidence of God as creator.

Still, a seeming conflict between God as sovereign, and evil in the universe, can be a theological timebomb for some. It can also be a background confusion within Christian circles and an obstacle to evangelism. Let's look at forms of God's will, his sovereignty. Let's be open to the idea that he sovereignly has shared sovereignty to mankind, allowing himself, as Lewis said, to be defeated by human rebellion. How else could we be meaningfully free to love or not to love? Little tin soldiers can be loved but cannot love. J R R Tolkien said that to be in God's image, meant to be a subcreator under the creator. I'd add that it's to be a sub-sovereign under the sovereign.

The sovereignty of deity is in non-watertight terms, in somewhat overlapping circles. For simplicity, I have used three terms for his will—three circles, so to speak. They are 1# Active, 2# Allowable, and 3# Advisory.[198] Let me give a few examples of each.

Firstly, let's look at his active will. This is when he directly intervenes in creation. Some, misunderstanding God, misjudge him or deny

---

[198]   We could marshal these under the terms, Decretive (decrees/pronouncements), Permissive (allows) the Preceptive (advises).

him, by assuming that if he is, then he determines each and every action within creation.[199] That is unbiblical. Deism was an idea that he never interferes in any way, shape, or form: don't blame the watchmaker for how time ticks. The biblical position is inbetween—he is semi-interventional, and the deists are semi-right. His active will can be either fixed, or fluid.

Think of the plan laid out in *Genesis*. There the incarnation and subsequent crucifixion of God the son as a man, was a fixed response to man's fall. Perhaps it could have varied as to generation and nation, but it was going to happen. Likewise, it is his fixed will that messiah shall return, whether we like it or not.

God's active will can be fluid, adjustable, negotiable, reactive to human choice (Dt.27:12-3; Jr.18:7-10; Am.7:1-3). Basically, the Bible teaches that if Yahweh decrees that he will punish, and we repent of our vice, he will repent (ie change his mind) and bless, and if he decrees that he will bless, and we repent of our virtue, he will repent and punish, instead. By the way, punishment/curse is often capable of leading to good repentance—it can be educative, a blessing.

Secondly, let's look at God's allowable will. This is God as passive, noninterventional, sitting in the chair of deism with his feet up, spectator not player. This is the universal setup of cause-and-effect. He does not cause me to jump from the aeroplane without a parachute, but if I jump without he causes me to land with a bump, because he has put in place the law of gravity and has walked away.

For as C S Lewis in his book, *Miracles*, and Perry Marshall in his book, *Evolution 2.0*, pointed out, humanity has an ability parallel with the laws of cause and effect, an ability which Lewis called ground & consequent, the ability to make free choices within certain givens. In philosophical terms, Determinism coheres with Non-determinism—compatibilism, semi-determinism. But though a sovereign, I *cannot* choose to here and now jump out of an aeroplane, if I am not actually in one. People who say that they can do anything they want, are not thinking sensibly, and talking sovereignty into absurdity.

---

[199]   Incidentally Charles Darwin developed his theory of random evolution, to shield God from such base attacks. See *Darwin's God* (Cornelius Hunter).

Thirdly, let's look at God's advisory will. An example of this is his gift of common sense, which would generally advise me not to jump without a chute, from a high flying aircraft. Imperfect common sense would have advised Jesus to avoid the cross. Jesus advises us to take up our crosses, and to follow him—that's counterintuitive. But we are taught that to die to gain the father, is to live unto him. So we can be faced with conflicting sources of advice. Adam was advised not to eat a certain fruit, but decided that he knew better. Do read Francis Schaeffer's book, *How Should We Then Live?*.

God's advisory will can link to his active will. Sometimes—because we have not taken his advice—he steps in with a rescue plan, even as *active safety* on a car can kick in if we go wrong, or a satnav recalculate a new route if we miss a turn. Sometimes he intervenes with a plan that will yield sorrow before it yields joy (Heb.12:2). Ethnic Israel entered Babylonia with weeping but came out singing. Still, some died without seeing the light at the end of that 70-year tunnel: it is sad to die in sadness. The race of Adam was captured by sin, and has never fully emerged—look at global politics. It seems to me that not all will ever know the joy at the end of misery.

So, God as sovereign has always had a range of involvement in creation, sometimes moving in, sometimes standing back, generally offering good advice. Seldom does he micromanage. If we come to understand this, we come to understand him better.

Binding and loosing

Let's get back to things we're presumed to be able to do, namely to bind and to loose. Firstly, when it comes to binding and loosing, it's good to keep in mind that if the king has made us *his* ambassadors, but then must approve of all *our* ideas, he would have become *our* ambassador. Do we seek to bind God to our loosing? That won't fly.

This is not the same as decree and declare, since the one is a method, and the other is a result. But they can go hand in hand, even when the phrase, *I declare and decree*, is not used. Both are sometimes spoken of as being our God-given authority of command.

Binding and loosing can be to us a no-man's-land, between on one side, a sacerdotal trench, and on the other side, an anti-sacerdotal trench, both sniping at each other. One side shouts that heaven will loose from sin whoever their priests first decree loosed. The other side shouts back that no, whoever heaven/God has already decreed loosed, their prophets then declare have been loosed, and that by bridging heaven and earth, their words of power and authority materialise God's loosing/binding on earth. Is it just possible that neither side is right, that both are fighting the wrong war?

After the older grammarians argued on both sides, biblical Greek was revisited in the late C20 and became understood a little bit better, as regards its aspectual nature.

Mt.16:19

Here, *loosed* (λελυμενον/*lelumenon*) in heaven, is in the perfect, remaining, tense, yet "the perfect tense does not by itself establish time relations" (Carson 2010:688). So in itself it neither says "shall be loosed", nor "has been loosed", but merely "stand/s loosed". Are we talking about things, or people, standing loosed/bound?

Arguing partly from the *personal* context of Mt.16:19—and partly from the related Mt.18:18 where in context the neuter ὁσα/*hosa* (*whatever*) implies people (*whoever*)—Carson flagged up that ὁ/*ho* in Mt.16:19—while also formally neuter (*whatever*), probably also means people (*whoever*). Let's look at the idea that Jesus was talking about evangelism loosing or binding *people*, that whoever we either loose or bind is either released from sin's prison or remains in its jail.

This can tie in with Lk.11:52, where by mixing their rules with Scripture, well-meaning Pharisees[200] had taken away the key of knowledge, thus binding by their error their audience from the heart of the covenant: alas, blind guides. In contrast, Peter's revelation of messiahship was the key of knowledge to loose his audience into the Christian kingdom.[201] Jesus had proclaimed the Sinai kingdom (Mt.4:23: ethnically based). In line with the Baptist, he had called his ethnic people back to it. And in line with the Baptist, he focused

---

[200] IMO they were students at the Sinai Level, but, failing to enter into a basic understanding of Yahweh and his messianic plans, were spreading misinformation rather than information.

[201] Obviously at that time he no more understood the prophecy about himself, than he understood that Jesus' death would begin that kingdom.

---

attention of its messianic content, the prophesied messianic level of *kingdom*, which would soon begin by the cross.

The keys[202] (the *preaching*: κηρυγμα/*kērugma*) were first formally handed to Peter to lead the way, and soon given more generally. They were the dual role of a message that, by being exclusive, would both loose/allow some to enter (2:14-39; 3:11-26), and bind/preclude all others from entering (Ac.4:11-2; 8:20-3), Christianity. Those precluded would either hear and reject, or simply not hear.

With limited keys, Peter bound both the Australian aborigines and the Inuits, simply by not evangelising them—but he could no more loose them than he could reach them! They remained bound in ignorance until being evangelised.[203] Until the cross, heaven had partially loosed Peter, in that like the Baptist, he realised who messiah was but didn't realise what messiah was. However, generally Jesus kept his ethnic people bound (Mt.16:20) until his resurrection, and God has bound (hardened that people generally) by the resurrection (Rm.11:32).[204]

An element of a future meaning was appropriate, since once Peter became a Christian—still future from Caesarea Philippi—he would bind and loose by preaching/not-preaching the exclusive message,

---

202 *Keys* not *key*, a plural in line with then rabbinic speech, and perhaps to indicate positive kingdom fullness. Some singular words were put at times in a plural form but without plural meaning. Eg Mt.16:19 speaks of *heaven* as *heavens*. We may still speak of looking into the heavens at night, or the sky at night, but seldom of the skies at night.

203 This need not imply their ultimate damnation—"but no one told us!" Naomi loved Ruth but didn't think she had to evangelise her into Sinai's level in order to gain Ruth ultimate salvation (Ruth 1:11); the primitive church delayed before reaching out to the Roman world (Ac.10:28): inexplicable if they believed that all the unevangelised would ultimately burn in the Lake of Fire; explicable if they believed that their salvation message was the exclusive Christian Level, allowing them to be choosy and to strategize. Going back to Ruth, she was loosed into the salvation people by Yahweh—those salvation people were not mandated to loose.

204 An admittedly difficult chapter to untangle, and where we should not think that hardening by God (at the Christian Level), necessarily means ultimate damnation (at the Everlasting Level).

---

which would by that soon future time of the resurrection, have been given. True preaching is in line with heaven. Evangelists work together in the gospel, building the eschatological church, until the Eschaton—the Age of everlasting life—comes with Christ's return.[205] That not just Peter would have these keys, fits the Matthean data that *together* they would fish for people (4:19), be salt and light (5:13-6), preach the kingdom (10:6-42), and disciple multiethnically (28:18-20).

Putting all this together, the key formally given first to Peter was key insight about the gospel message of conversion into the messianic community, not a jump into letting loose angels and binding demons, nor about ethical virtues and verbotens. Otherwise we might have expected that so important a theme would have also been presented in the Caesarea Philippi accounts of Mark and Luke,[206] who both well covered the themes of opening up Christianity, in their Gospels.

Nor had the Gates of Hades/Hell, anything to do with satanic opposition. Yeshua used common terminology for death itself: death itself could not kill off messiah's community, though would naturally kill off its members, generation by generation. That was the undying community which Peter would be privileged to open up/loose.[207] Jesus gave Peter the bigger picture, though Peter still—rejecting the cross—was confused about how that stage would begin. But he would

---

[205] The Christian Level is not essential for the Everlasting Level, but gives assurance of the latter, and the cross was essential for both levels.

[206] Mk.8 focuses on Peter's negative side; Lk.9 quickly moved from Peter.

[207] That he was to kick-off as leader is not to be doubted. After his key speech at Pentecost, he teamed up with John, who played second fiddle. Ecclesiastically, it was Phillip, not Peter, who first successfully reached out to ethnic-goyim, whereas Peter would need a kick-start to do so. Even so, Peter's last words in *Acts* were about how he had apostolically breached the Gentile barrier (15:7)— a first for him but not for the church. And after his last words in this account, decision making was chaired by James (19), affirming Paul's position but urging some basic cultural prohibitions for cultural harmony—cultural interface. Converts owe a certain deference to local cultural norms: when in Rome, eat as the Romans eat; when in Jerusalem... BTW, James did not say that Peter was the first Christian to evangelise the ethnic-goyim.

weather the crucifixion storm, refloating his crew until the master of the seas stepped in (Lk.22:32).

Mt.18:15-20

Jesus said, "...if two or three of you come together as a community and discern clearly about anything, my father in heaven will bless that discernment" (TVB: Mt.18:19). Were these words about conflict resolution? Here the loosing/binding theme—broadened out from Peter—was again pitched before the community began. It follows the same idea, but applied pastorally rather than evangelistically: "...the terms also naturally apply figuratively to judicial action, given the literal use for detaining and releasing prisoners" (Keener 1999:455).

Once begun, the church at large—having messiah at their hub—would be able to discern heaven/God's will in fallout situations, and follow biblical binding or loosing parameters. According to Carson, this setting was not "a promise regarding any prayer on which two or three believers agree" (Carson 2010:738). But if it includes prayer, he added, the context (περι πραγματος/peri pragmatos = about any judicial matter) would limit prayer to wisdom for in-house fallouts.

It might well begin with an offender and an offended, the basic 'two'—though there could be more. The type of offence[208] would be small scale, thus initially hidden within the private domain. Remedy could range from agreement by offender and offended, to local church excommunication.[209] At whatever stage, if after talking it through the disputants will agree a solution to whatever problem is being pursued (αιτεισθαι/aiteisthai: NIV's 'they ask for'), God will endorse their 'out of [church] court' agreement and consider the case closed. By submitting to the lord, their decision might have been *factually* correct, and would have been *attitudinally* correct (Rm.14:23).

---

[208]   We do not know whether "against you" is, or is not, what Jesus said.

[209]   It was not the sort of serious public example sin of which Paul immediately told off Peter publicly (Gal.2:14). As regards church networks (denominations), the possibility of denominational censure exists. The idea of church heresy might not have been what Jesus had in mind, but it is certainly what networks often have in mind.

What if the offender has not sinned, can't prove it, and simply submits for the sake of harmony? Civil double-jeopardy law arose to protect the innocent from the Sword of Damocles, but could protect the guilty from retrials as well. [210] Is Mt.18:19 meant to be final? Though the initial settlement could meet with God's approval in seeking peace over justice, arguably he permits retrials if substantial new evidence arises, in order that the church maximises harmony.

On the other hand, if a forceful disputant falls out even with the local church—even if for egoist justice they refuse discipline—excommunication will maximise the bigger picture of righteous harmony. Let the ill-disciplined believer be treated as if they are an unbeliever/traitor/disturber of the peace (17). The church at Corinth got into and out of a mess when a star convert sinned against God's grace, was reluctantly excommunicated, repented, and returned. It is likely enough that a local member had tried to get the man to repent earlier, before handing the case on to Paul—the local church hadn't wished to know. We should restrict pastoral judgements to fellow Christians (1 Cor.5:12).

Jhn.20:23

Going back to the trenches, one trench holds that whatever a priest forgives, heaven/God must then confirm: "If you forgive anyone's sins, they will be forgiven. But if you don't forgive their sins, they will not be forgiven" (CEV). The other side holds that all evangelists, seeing that heaven/God has forgiven, must declare that forgiveness: "If you forgive the sins of any, their sins have been forgiven them; if you retain the sins of any, they have been retained" (NASB).

Well, that might reflect previous thinking about reading time-settings into Greek tenses, instead of reading aspect-meaning out of Greek tenses. But "aspectually, they will be rendered, 'they are in a state of forgiveness', ie, 'they stand forgiven' and 'they do not stand forgiven'; but even so the passive voice implies it is God who is acting.... it is simply the result of the preaching of the gospel, which either brings people to repent...or leaves them unresponsive to the offer..." (Carson 1991:655).

---

[210]   It could also prevent a wrongly imprisoned innocent from release.

Again, the point is that by the time that Christian evangelism began, the general principle of forgiveness into that kingdom had been put in place by the cross, so that forgiveness flows through the invitation, as water from a reservoir flows through a tap that's turned on.[211] By saying "the door is open", I am not saying that I opened the door, though I might have played a part in folk going inside. Nor, if I know that the homeowner unlocked it for all who wish to enter, do I need to hear from the homeowner each time for each person, a "him, yes, her, no, her, yes, him, no" guest list. Priest-evangelists are not gatekeepers but guides.[212]

Under Sinai, only Aaronic priests dealt with forgiveness that kept sinners within Sinai. Jesus claimed higher authority than Aaron, and was falsely accused of playing God (Mk.2:7) when in fact he merely played messiah. In short, he did not forgive *because he was God* (*pace* C S Lewis), nor do we forgive *because we are God*. He forgave messianically, and we forgive messianically, anointed under the anointed one, if the water of life which we offer, is drunk. We are

---

[211] For the repentant to be forgiven into Christianity, an evangelist need not formally declare forgiveness. Indeed preaching might be as seed that germinates at another time, but an evangelist eventually forgave/loosed them at that later date. And that they 'forgive' is no worse than saying they 'heal', so long as it is understood to mean that they share the act of God forgiving/healing (Mk.2:9).
On the other hand, an evangelist might formally yet falsely declare to someone, "You are forgiven, ie you're now a Christian". A false pregnancy does not a child produce, whatever the woman or her husband declare in faith. The church believed that Simon the Sorcerer was forgiven, until Simon Peter realised that he was still bound (Ac.8:13,22-3).

[212] A separate issue would be church membership, where existing members decide whether or not they believe an applicant to be genuinely a Christian: even Paul scraped home (Ac.9:26). Should sheep welcome wolves into the sheep pen? Foregoing discernment, do not many wolves now wear sheepdog collars and ravage the sheep? I would suggest that for water-baptism, a low threshold of trust is biblical—a seemingly genuine confession of faith should suffice. On balance, I would not presume that anyone water-baptised was a Christian (see Ac.8:13,23).

authorised to evangelise, so like the pioneer Peter, we are able to loose by proclamation, or to bind by withholding proclamation.[213]

Prayer and power

Speaking of greater things, Yeshua referred to the greater privilege and effect of the conversion miracle, over the mere miracles he did (Jhn.14:12).[214] We neither exceed him in power, nor in authority. We have his authority as we walk in his will, and I believe that if we pray as he did, we will better know the power he knew. Let's look a little at how prayer featured in his life and death.

He prayed more than the Gospels recorded, even as his miracles far exceeded what were written down. The Gospels were not a straightforward A-Z chronology. They sometimes grouped different timeslots together for thematic unity, though a fairly clear chronological account of his travel narrative can be drawn up. Sayings in one context were perhaps sometimes—because of their theme—slotted in to different contexts, and sometimes he said the same things more than once, as we all do. Anyway, that's the way folk wrote in that culture, perhaps from a more organic mindset than a Western organisational one. I have not sought out a thoroughgoing chronology. The question is, *What can we see from what we have?*

---

[213]   Noting the connection between sickness and sin, Carson made the point that the spiritual side of Is.53:4 was taken up by the LXX and followed by 1 Pt.2:24—"That interpretation of the verse is legitimate because the flow of the Servant Song supports it", whereas the physical side was kept by Mt.8:17 (Carson 2010:407). So long as not proof-texting from *Matthew*, perhaps we may legitimately argue here that secondary pastoral binding/loosing exists distinct from evangelistic binding/loosing. Pastorally application would include good pastoral counselling, and personal devotions. By its proof-texting from Mt.18:18-20, I would dispute Elmer Darnall's prayer-command idea, though commend his overall pastoral aim to "excite an active faith" to help heal the patient (Darnall 80).

[214]   That was the mid-game; his cross was the end-game; his resurrection was the new game.

Mk.1:35: His privacy setting could be entirely private. He could rise before the crack of dawn, perhaps to be ready to pray according to Ps.113:3—*from the rising of the sun, Yahweh's name is to be praised.* Perhaps he also sought wisdom. For instance, should he bask in his popularity in Capernaum, or move to a different stage? Moreover, there is the likelihood that his power stemmed from his intimate fellowship with his father. We should not picture him as a divinity walking upon this earth, doing some kind of Jedi thing. He truly shared our humanity, and our need to walk with God.

Lk.5:16; 6:12: He could seek total privacy in reaction to popularity. In the face of growing threats, he might pray alone overnight, and presumably in prayer he received guidance as to which of his followers he should select to be the core group of twelve—the symbolic number of the Twelve Tribes of Jacob. And no, in choosing Judas of Kerioth, he did not get it wrong—horses for courses. We could call this Prayer Planning.

Mt.14:23//Mk.6:46: After a hectic day of excessive popularity, he might go solo to pray outdoors overnight—to avoid fans and fame?

Mt.26:39,42x2//Mk.14:36x3//Lk.22:42: The final setting was in Gethsemane, where Mark alone retained Jesus' rather unique use of the Aramaic term, *abba*.[215] While we're here, something should be said about the oft repeated phrase, "not my will but yours be done". But before we consider that, let us note that Jesus could plead for himself, and that even he could pray more than once for the same thing. Some Christians ask only for themselves—that is selfish. Some Christians ask only for others—that is fearful. Being too afraid to ask God to help your personally, is sinful since maligning him.[216]

Now let's spend a bit of time on Gethsemane, which is problematic in various ways, and can influence our christology—that is, the way we

---

[215]   One of the few Aramaisms in the NT, kept thrice, always with translation. That implies a theme that was outstanding to Yeshua and to his people.

[216]   If we may ask friends for personal help, how much more our heavenly father, who loves us more than friends?

think about Christ. Though their wording varies, [217] the Synoptics agree that 1# Jesus prayed about his θελω/*thelō*, but 2# effectively *willed* with all his heart and soul to follow his father's plan to the letter. *Thelō* can sometimes mean *I plan/will*, and sometimes mean *I wish/incline*. Did this word-range come into play? Admittedly the Gospels don't say *the father's thelō*, but they imply it, even as you might say, "Terry, would you like an ice-cream? Tom, what about you?" The offer clearly made to one, is clearly implied to the other. But for various reasons, I hold that the key word, *thelō*, should be read as the situational 'wish' of Jesus being subject to the 'will' of his father. But what about the big IF?

Some are puzzled that, so late in the game, Jesus apparently didn't know his father's plan about the cross. But might something else have been the negotiable? The Synoptics are clear that from Caesarea Philippi, Jesus had been teaching that he, the son of man, had to be crucified. Pitched shortly before his arrest we read this prayer: "Now my soul is deeply troubled. Should I pray, 'Father, save me from this hour'? But this is the very reason I came!" (NLT: Jhn.12:27). Talk about his 'hour' meant his appointment with death, when the seed would metaphorically 'die' to produce results (fruit) after death.

It might help to see that the Passover meal involved several cups. I'm not saying that each one was symbolic to Jesus, only that they could have symbolised that there are many cups in life's journey. Maybe for Jesus, Jhn.18:11's 'cup' meant Golgotha, and Mk.14:36's 'cup' meant Gethsemane. [218] After all, Jesus *knew* his father's will about the cup of

---

[217] πλην ουχ ως εγω θελω αλλ ως συ (Mt.);

αλλ ου τι εγω θελω αλλα τι συ (Mk.);

πλην μη το θελημα μου αλλα το σον γινεσθω (Lk.).

[218] An alternative thought is that the sense of Golgotha was so strong that the human Jesus was tempted to run and hide, speaking about his own spirit being willing but his flesh being weak and warning his disciples to pray for their own spirits to come through the temptation to run and hide. I can see this, but I cannot see why he would question whether Golgotha was his father's will—"if it be".

Golgotha. I'm sure that along his road, he walked into many unforeseen hardships and delights. "Who touched me?" was a genuine question seeking a genuine answer (Lk.8:45). Under intense hardship, was he simply saying that he didn't know whether his mission required the particular pain of that particular cup? May we not in prayer, question whether particular suffering is or is not in God's plan for us? John Alexander Dowie, confronted with the claim that an epidemic was God's will, denied it and moved into healing.

Another question is whether Jesus had one primary will overriding a secondary will, like a rider overriding the horse.[219] IMO, translations juxtaposing his *will* to his father's *will*, fail theologically, not grammatically (Jhn.10:30). It's better to translate that "he chose the

---

Jesus had long known that his father's will was the cross, so to ask him to take away the cross *if* it was undecided, was a non-starter. However, if by *cup* he meant the cup he was drinking then and there, Gethsemane, it would make sense. Gethsemane could have been an unknown factor to Jesus. We drink many a bitter cup not given by God's hand. If Jesus spoke of Gethsemane, we are not told if the cup was withdrawn.

[219]   This has long, rightly or wrongly, been mixed into a debate as to whether Jesus was truly deity and truly human—and if so how. Monothelitism (ie one will) tends to assert a completed fusion of deity and humanity. Assuming a distinction of wills, Chalcedon chose dithelitism (ie two wills) as the best way to affirm both in perfect partnership, yet without confusing either side.

It Jesus was a totally fused person, in this life we couldn't be like him, so Chalcedon has an advantage in being able to say that we are like him as to his humanity, but not as to his deity. But it raises the idea of an imperfect human will being subjugated by a deific will—had Jesus imperfection?

It is common today to assume an instance here of a human vote (if it is possible...) succeeded by a deific vote (nevertheless...). Eastern Orthodoxism remains dithelite, and Oriental Orthodoxism remains monothelite. Their debate is based on the idea that two natures had united—sides which disagreed on the how.

Another approach is that God the Son transposed (depotentiated) himself into humanity as a new Adam, an unfallen image of himself. "Fully human" meaning "as humanity unfallen would have been", not bespeaking a relationship after a merger. Thus one deific will reformatted/bowing into unfallen humanity—not one will, not a fusion of deific and human, but deific-become-human, incarnated will.

---

father's *plan* over his own *desire*" (Keener 1999:639: highlighting added). On balance, I think it was a case that Jesus didn't know his father's *plan* regarding Gethsemane, honestly stated his preference to avoid it, but was more than willing to face it, *IF* required. We do not *wish* to have a splinter pulled out, but we *will* it to be done, if the nurse *wills*.

Lk.9:18: Jesus also prayed with others. That could be alongside—as with disciples—or towards the needy. One big occasion was at Caesarea Philippi, where after a long stint in Galilee, it was time to turn around and head towards his death (22). First, his disciples had to be primed. Here, although Jesus prayed solo, his disciples were there (18), I guess listening in. Our prayers can be a teaching base for people to learn from how we pray. That is one reason why we should be the more careful how we pray when others listen in: God won't be misled, but others might.

Perhaps his wording was such as to raise questions in their minds about who he really was, for no one prayed the way he prayed. His was—and in a sense remains—a totally unique filial relationship with God the father. [220] That raised the game for them to more clearly define him. Simon 'Peter' heard from heaven—had Jesus prayed that he would? Although obviously not fleshing out what the messiah was meant to be and to do, at least Simon bravely committed to the idea that Yeshua *was* messiah, an idea that had frankly faded earlier— Jesus had neither fitted nor confirmed their messianic expectations. [221]

---

[220] The so-called Johannine Thunderbolt. Or Synoptic Seed, in the sense that the synoptics had the seed thought which John developed further.

[221] Some had been disciples of the Baptist and had heard him call Jesus, the messiah (Jhn.1:42). Messianic expectations were unbiblical and strongly nationalistic: the people wished messiah to fit their agenda; messiah wished the people to fit his agenda. Because of that disconnect, he kept his identity under wraps, what Wilhelm Wrede called, the messianic secret, although Wrede 'explained it' in a very different way. Significantly, once Jesus had defined himself by his death and ascension, the church happily dropped the enigmatic term, son-of-man, and spoke of messiah.

Lk.9:28: A little later, probably travelling via Mount Meron, he had a prayer time with his inner circle. We are not told whether they too were praying, but it is likely enough. Prayer once more was a backdrop to a defining time, also picking up on Jesus' death (31). Perhaps it was one of many times when his father was speaking to him, hammering home the nails of his fate. Group thanks could be sparked off by good news (Lk.10:17,21). [222] Seemingly there was spontaneity, a jumping for joy rather than any waiting for a Tuesday prayer meeting. Well, Tuesday prayer was a traditional evening slot in my circles, and weekly prayer meetings aren't such a bad idea.

Mt.11:25-6//Lk.10:21: I suspect that Mt.11:28–30 prophetically spoken to the Jewish nation, much as OT prophets had spoken oracles to the nations without them hearing (eg Is.14:29). Thus, I presume this prayer was within his discipleship group. Incidentally, hiding things and hardening hearts can be part of God's design for the greater good, and a judgement call as to whether others are good to hear/see. [223] A takeaway theme here is that to some at least, God had been opening up. Though some religious and social opposition remained blind, Jesus' disciples (*children*)[224] were beginning to see the light.

Lk.11:1: 'Friends' (φιλοι/*philoi*)—as they later became—asked him to teach them more about how they should pray (Lk.11:1). [225] Although

---

222   Mt.11:25-6 relates it to the other side of the coin, the majority rejection (20), rather than the minority uptake (Lk.10:17). Incidentally, some older versions spoke of the father's *pleasure*. That can mislead a little. The biblical meaning, is that what seemed good to the father, was what fitted his redemptive will/*plan*. What pleases him should please us.

223   I do not assume that hardened to Levels 2 or 3, means hardened to Level 4.

224   He could call them children in an educational, not a parental, sense. Jesus is not our father.

225   But be aware that there are various levels of friendship. Friendly fire, means one ally firing in error at another ally, not two buddies in a fight. Abraham was a friend of God; God was not a friend of Abraham. The death of Jesus upgraded their relationship from servant-disciples, to friend-disciples: they would *gain* understanding *if* they obeyed him. Had it meant that Jesus became a buddy to them, it would have meant that he would *gain* understanding *if* he obeyed them. We should not read our ideas of friendship into what he said, but we should read his idea of friendship into what he said.

Matthew did not draw attention to the setting, he did pick up on this general guidance for prayer (Mt.6:6–13). Luke, perhaps reduced the rhythmical construction for his ethno-Gentile audience, or simply drew from another teaching session of Jesus.[226] The latter is quite possible. Indeed, we have no more reason to expect Jesus to stick word to word to what he might have earlier said, than Paul to have copy-pasted between Eph.6:14-7 and 1 Ths.5:8.

As an aside on Paul, as it stands, is the *helmet* the hope of salvation (1 Ths.) or salvation without any hope attached (Eph.); is the breastplate of righteousness (Eph.), or of faith and love (1 Ths.)? Military gear simply provided some useful pegs on which to hang important thoughts, and Paul could doubtless have used a Roman helmet to illustrate many spiritual truths about protecting our heads. Likewise Jesus could have rephrased teachings along similar principles, giving prayer outlines when teaching his disciples.

This model for prayer wasn't for word-for-word prayer,[227] but rather a theme-for-theme foundation on which to pray. And it would have been as meaningful for the sinless one to ask that his sins be forgiven, as for me to thank God for my recent PanAm flight to Space Station 5 and back. He framed some core themes for their prayer life. And those themes had application for the kingdom of Sinai, and have application for the kingdom of Yeshua.

For instance, before he died, his kingdom had not come, so when his ethnic people prayed for God's kingdom to come, they were praying for the messianic kingdom to come. After it came, his people of the covenant pray for the next kingdom stage, for which messiah will return. Further, the relationship of God as father, valid under Sinai as the father of the nation, became individualised in a deeper sense of family, once the messianic community began. The 'our father' (Mt.) is now possible as 'my father' (Lk.), and although now individually praying *my father*, together we may pray *our father*. I guess that

---

[226]   That's how Luke started off. In the history of copying, his account came to look more like Matthew's.

[227]   But even if a parrot could recite it, that parrot would not pray it sincerely. Praying it word-for-word with sincerity is commendable.

Matthew kept the corporate sense—still relevant—and that Luke upgraded it in line with the new covenant. I doubt that the disciples opened up with, father/abba, *before* the resurrection.

Mt.26:26-7//Mk.14:22-3: At the Passover meal—which he transformed into what is now the eucharist—he thanked God for the symbolic elements of bread and wine, which bespoke both his harrowing death and his victory for humanity. Incidentally Lk.22:17-9//1 Cor.11:24-5 have a wine/bread sequence, perhaps reflecting how the eucharist had been adopted into Gentile communities.[228]

Jhn.17

Incidentally for this section I shall prefix verses with a v, when they belong to Jhn.17. Now, obviously a night of prayer is more than a chapter in *John*, though this is the longest account we have of Jesus praying. For John to cover such prayer in such detail warrants a little more cover of content here, for surely Jesus meant it to double as basic Christian teaching. Incidentally Norval Geldenhuys showed that John and the Synoptics writers show Jesus eating the Passover meal on Nisan 15. Only misreading *John*—based partly on not knowing Jewish customs of the time—has ever suggested that John sought to picture Jesus as dying when the lambs died on Nisan 14.

Misreading has spawned theories of a supposed setting of a Nisan 14 Meal, such as different religious calendars, an unofficial Passover meal, or simply John preferring symbolism to chronology. Church disputes arose between those who committed to this misinformed date—who were named Quartodecimans (ie fourteenthers), and Rome, which settled into a Sunday-based liturgical calendar. I suspect that primitive Christianity didn't give a fig about annual celebrations, but that if it had, then it would have been Quintodeciman (ie fifteenther). Early distancing from ethnic-Jews, such as *Romans* shows, IMO sadly reduced the flow into the church of ethnic-Jews, along with their

---

[228]   Thus, focus on the symbolic elements, not their sequence.

biblical and cultural perspective. For their part, their people generally followed their leadership which unilaterally persecuted the church.[229]

But back to the story, the lambs were killed in the daylight hours of Nisan 14 (our Thursday), hours which handed over to Nisan 15 with the going down of the sun (roughly 6pm). Then after nightfall—the beginning of *their* next day (still *our* Thursday)—Jesus ate the Passover meal, was soon arrested, and after dawn (our Friday morning) was tried and sentenced by Pilate, and died before the special sabbath which began the next day (Nisan 16)—which began roughly at 6pm Friday. Nightfalls were 'close of day' for community life, acting as our midnight handovers to the next day.

After eating the Passover meal, he had left the upper room (14:31), but not yet left the city (18:1). Thus he taught and prayed in the dark streets of Jerusalem. How and what did he pray? Strangely, we often shut our eyes and bow our heads, even though Yeshua looked up with open eyes. Mind you, I once read that an Australian pastor (Barry Chant), who deciding to follow Jesus on this, looked up in church, only to see uninspiring cobwebs way before the World Wide Web. So shutting our eyes might be better. But seriously, it's a matter of private choice, is based on a number of factors, and might take some getting used to.[230]

---

[229]   Another reason to suspect that salvation into the church is not essential for ultimate life with God (Level 4), is God's sovereign hardening of this race. Either 1# they must proportionately be ultimately damned (showing the Christian road is essential for all); 2# must have their own road to heaven (showing the Christian road is not essential for all); or 3# without their own road to heaven will not proportionately be ultimately damned (showing that neither Sinai nor Christian roads are essential).

[230]   I remember in the seventies that my pastor Gideon Gardiner (Hull), would prefix prayer meetings by saying, Lie down of the floor, kneel, sit down, stand up—whatever posture suits you best, do. The Bible records people praying prostrate (Nb.16:22; Jos.5:14; Dan.8:17; Mt.26:39; Rv.11:16), kneeling (2 Chr.6:13; Dan.6:10; Lk.22:41, Ac.7:60; 9:40; 20:36; 21:5), sitting (2 Sam.7:18), and standing (1 Sam.1:26; Mk.11:25; Lk.18:11,13). Sometimes people go for 'prayer-walks' as they pray for neighbourhoods; I used to pray as I bicycled— those were pleasant days.

Anyway, this prayer within a group setting, was to his father, "the only true god" (John used the outgoing polytheistic garb of his day), or as we might say, to the only one who was/is truly God (v1,3). Incidentally, this does not in itself rule out trinitarianism, though biblically the emphasis of the term is on God *the father*.

In its life setting, this prayer affirmed that those that other nations worshipped as divinities, were not deities, for Yahweh [231] alone is deity. Having written of the 'word' (λογος/*logos*) as *with* God, and *being* God,[232] presumably John wasn't printing a retraction here. Similarly Php.2:9-10 does not place Jesus' position as lord, *above* his father, nor does 1 Cor.8:6 *deny* lordship to the son's father, nor deny deity to the father's son. Biblically, exclusive language is not always literally exclusive (1 Cor.15:27), but its setting will be clear.[233]

Sadly the LEB/NKJV say that Jesus has authority over *all flesh* (v2).[234] It's better to say, authority over/within mankind.[235] This authority was proleptic, spoken slightly before activated, spoken in the mortal shadow of the cross about what lay on the immediate horizon, and was the authority that his victory gained, that of panethnic lordship (κυριος παντων/*kurios pantōn*: Ac.10:36; Rm.10:12) [236] over what we call the multicultural church (Eph.2:14-6). His *hour* (v1) was his crucifixion, which would physically and coronationally exalt him, lift him up (ὑψω/*hupsō*: 12:32). By his death he would open up the glory of God the

---

231 Again, this doubles as a monopersonal way for the person we call God the father, and a tripersonal way for the society we call God. John could have correctly substituted the term Yahweh, for God. See note on Jhn.1:1.

232 Jhn.1:1: this must be taken as being *with* God the father, and *being* deity in substance, to add systematic meat to the bones of data.

233 Our main focus on God should be the father, and on lordship as the messianic life (neither Sinaitic nor pagan).

234 Will he give fish and fowl, eternal life?

235 A technical Jewish term for humanity in general: πασα σαρξ/*pasa sarx* (Ac.2:17; Jhn.17:2).

236 The immediate context of Rm.10:9 shows that in v12, Jesus is this lord.

father, and his own messianic glory as lord of the church.[237] His father's *name* (v6) is also about authority—God's son had come in his father's name, authorised by him.

Eternal Life Now (v3) is Christian life, with God as our father, Jesus as our lord, and the spirit (Jhn.14-6) as our helper—he comes quietly with the Christian package. Jhn.14 has 1 mention of the term, *God*, and 23 mentions of the term, *father*. The Christian 1-2-3 chapter? Okay coincidental, but is not its emphasis the theme of inexclusivism? That is, if granting that Eternal Life Later (Everlasting Level) is inclusive of all who welcome God *as God*, we must grant that Christian Life is exclusive to those who in mortal life welcome God *as father*—through his son as lord.[238] Jhn.14:6 puts the exclusivism well: Jesus is the only (the exclusive) way to God *as father*, and to himself as brother.

I used to have the concern that Christianity was a glorious relationship which folk may enter and leave repeatedly, but that they only had everlasting life if they died within it.[239] Some—not without some proof-texting—get around this concern by dismissing any who seem to leave, as never having been in. That position is sometimes branded as Once-Saved-Always-Saved (OSAS). I now think that

---

[237] I dislike songs that sing of us 'lifting Jesus higher', if they imply that his uplifting is something we should do. His *lifting up* was his *crucifixion*—should we seek to hammer nails into him once more? Alternate words such as *glorify/exalt/publicise/proclaim* are fine for biblical songs, for clear blue water between what we should do, and nailing him to a cross which we cannot do, nor should if we could. Incidentally the legend of Longinus (a hero in my *Vampire Grail* story) promotes the good idea that even those who literally crucified him could find grace.

[238] Some think this simply means that only those who get eternal life now, have it beyond death. I think it has more the idea that something of what many will have beyond death, can be enjoyed by those who hear and welcome the good news of messiah in the here and now.

[239] Interestingly Calvin held that Cornelius would have had *Everlasting* Life had he died just before Peter arrived. I had had concern that Demas had lost *Everlasting* Life when Paul lost him. But if one can have it before, can one not have it after? Calvin would have said that Cornelius lacked *Christian* Life before Peter arrived; I'd say that Demas lost *Christian* Life once he left Paul—that is, if Demas had walked out on *Christ*.

---

anyone serious enough to enter the Christian Level, must already be in the Everlasting Level, and will remain in the latter *according to their underlying nature*, whether or not they remain in the Christian Level. I do not deny that leaving Christ is hellish—a death, a falling below, a burning waste—in mortal life.

Talk of the father's name (v6,11-2,26) carries ideas of authority and plan. There is a hierarchy in prayer, in that God's son came in his father's name, and has deputised us in his own name. To us, predominantly the son—not the father—is lord. That's a big NT theme. And that's another reason why it's generally better not to call the father *lord* in prayer, or by verbal equivalence. In Bible translation, calling Yahweh [the LORD], confuses lordship, covenant, and relationship.

It is worth noting that in prayer we may acknowledge our achievements under God, without unbiblical boasting (v4,6). In one sense glorifying his father was yet to be, but he spoke as if it had been done (proleptic language)—as in v12. And yet in another sense it was something he had done, in that his teachings and miracles had been in his father's name, glorifying his father.

So before the cross, as a seed he had glorified his father, but as seed which would soon die and glorify the father in being fruitful through the cross. Jesus saw both what he had done, and was about to do, as a package deal, to be sealed by the cross—"I have finished" (Jhn.19:4).[240] He asked that his mission would succeed, namely the setting up of the prophesied messianic community, in which the connection between God the son and God the father, would be clear, even as it was/is beyond creation.[241] That clarity would be the bedrock to define Christian Life (v3).

---

[240]   *Teleiōsas* (aorist of *teleioō*: package visualised as complete: 4). The final cry would be 19:30 (*tetelestai*, the perfect of *teloō*: package stands complete). Both forms of *telos* speak of completion, job done.

[241]   Time terms, like 'was', were given as handy pictures in popular language. Philosophically put, the eternal (supernature) is beyond cosmic-time (nature),

He implied a real incarnation (v5), using space-time terms to picture heavenly existence *before* and *to follow*. He would not detransition, deincarnationalise into [a] spirit-life, but he would be the *aparchē* (the new beginning: 1 Cor.15:20), the dawn of physical, human, immortality. Rising physically, he raised physicality, maintaining his solidarity with humanity, in which the fatherhood of God is now individualised, not simply a corporate identity (v6).

Historically, they still didn't fully understand his identity or plan, but they had the seed-thought that he had a one-of-a-kind relationship with God as father. But their knowledge was unstable, and needed to be shaken so that the unshakable alone would remain (Lk.22:32; Heb.12:27). For in order to grasp who Jesus was, and what was his plan, they still needed to grasp the resurrection. And in a sense they were the next seed, awaiting spiritual death for spiritual birth into his kingdom (Jhn.3:3,7).

Talk of *the world* (κοσμος/*kosmos*: v4) was talk about opposition (the serpent-bitten Adamic human nature), although in some contexts the Bible can use the term as morally neutral. He prayed for people who were in the *kosmos*, and for those not of it, but he did not pray *for* it. He prayed against the 'world' for its people's sake—that while their bodies are 'in' it, their minds should not be 'of' it (v9,14-6).

This is independent of the smaller picture of important environmentalist issues, but it is interesting that Paul linked the joys of the animal kingdom to the ultimate revealing of God's people (Rm.8:21).[242] While literally Jesus was still in the world, his focus had already moved on, as if the corner had already been turned (Jhn.17:11: CEB/CEV/NKJV/NRSV).[243] The name/title he spoke of, was probably that

---

and time exists only within deity—a servant, not a master. "The glory I had before the world" thus meant, "The glory I have beyond the world", beyond the universe in his noncarnate being.

[242] The havoc of 2 Pt.3:7,10 is probably metaphorical for the ending of human power hubs, a burning away (*per* Peter) to the blessing of the natural world (*per* Paul).

[243] *Eimi*: softened by most to a future tense, for easier reading.

---

of supreme lordship over the 'world' (Php.2:10-1),[244] a name which also connects to the name, Yahweh.

Again, literally speaking, Judas had not yet perished (v12): Jesus spoke with a proleptic eye. While on Judas—a confused wolf in sheep's clothing—I would but say that God had selected someone who sided at heart with the devil, to play the devil's part. Judas was not an innocent victim forced by God to play an unwilling part, and his fate is neither better nor worse than had he not played that part. Our ultimate destination is desire-based, not deed-based.

Moral overtones of *hagios/hagiazō* (holy/sanctified: v17) are secondary for those made holy (phase 1), who have been put into God's domain as Christians. Being holy, we should tune our moral life to God (phase 2). All Christians are phase 1 holy: Jesus prayed for his disciples to become Christians.[245] The father had sanctified his son (10:36): that is, mission-ally com-mission-ed him.

The disciples needed spiritual birth/insight to enable their witness of Christ, the word (*logos*) of truth (*alētheia*), the *Logos* (1:1) himself *alētheia* (14:6). He who prayed for their safety from attacks, pledged to send them to attack—part of spiritual warfare (v18). In short, mission is engaging in warfare (2 Cor.10:4). There is also a hierarchical paradigm here: Jesus came in his father's name; we are sent in Jesus' name. As we have seen, that name is a shared name, allowing both his subordination and his lordship (Mt.8:9).[246] Arguably we will be

---

[244] God the son eternally shares that lordship *vis-à-vis* creation, but as Jesus *vis-à-vis* the new humanity, would be given it. The name, Jesus, was given at conception/birth; the name above all other names, lord, was given at his exaltation. At Jesus' name, *lord*, all shall bow, glorifying his father.

[245] The name of our community is a secondary issue. Initially we were simply called The Way (Ac.9:2), then at Antioch were called Christians (11:26). Such names are not sacrosanct, but our oneness in messiah is.

[246] The term subordinationism, is not a no-no word, even if it can be used in a no-no way. Some, speaking of both an economic/temporal (job based) trinity and an ontological/eternal (or immanent vs transcendent, personhood) trinity beyond creation, affirm a willing subordination of the son to the father to get

---

everlastingly subordinated (harmonised) to the father and his son in liberating joy, as we freely range the universe. His connection to his father was one-of-a-kind. We are tapped into it through him, making us both like and unlike him.

"...in language that applies equally well to the consecration of a sacrifice and the consecration of a priest, Jesus was said to consecrate ('sanctify') himself" (Carson 1991:567). What did that mean? Not that Jesus become moral for us [247]—for he was born moral—but that God's son, by becoming Jesus, had *set himself aside* for us, had dedicated himself to us (v19). Jhn.10:36 shows him as having being voluntary sent. Entering into Christianity [248] is being voluntary *set aside* unto God the father, sanctified, holified, made new.

Some still say that Jesus, the church, or both, expected an imminent return, and that an age of the spirit was a church idea mooted to

---

the job done within creation, but disaffirm that the son is subordinated within the eternal society beyond creation. That is somewhat based on the idea that subordination is somehow oppressive, at best a load carried for a purpose. So we have this distinction between act (temporal) and attitude (transcendent). Some suggest that beyond creation, non-oppressively the son, as in an eternal dance, eternally bows to his father (eternal subordinationism), a joyful attitudinal subordination. It might be that our terms are simply inadequate to fathom the eternal—the guesses of children.

[247] I once heard a State Ed teacher assert that even Jesus needed to repent of sins, since even Jesus was water baptised. I've long given up expecting good theology from the State. John's baptism was to express covenantal coldness (sin) turned away from—with regards to (εις/*eis*) sin. Jesus identified with John's prophetic call back to his nation, not as a personal sinner—as his cousin well knew—but to fulfil righteousness, ie God's messianic agenda.

[248] Not church on the organisational, secondary, level, but church on the organic, primary, level (Jhn.14:6). Togetherness in fellowship, is not the same as togetherness in Christ in fellowship. The secondary door of Churchianity, does not in itself take us through the primary door of Christianity, but the primary door (in Christ-ness) will encourage us to enter the secondary door of togetherness in fellowship. Not all Churchians are Christians; all Christians should be Churchians at heart.

explain away that non-event.[249] I say that Jesus knew that he didn't know when he would return (Mk.13:32), and taught a realism of delay, an attitude of readiness, and an age of the spirit, in which many more would hear and heed his message (v20). His prayer extended beyond his earthly timeslot to believers (Christians) won by believers (Christians). His emphasis was on belief through the message—not of miracles (Rm.15:19), nor of godliness (Php.1:18): Rm.10:17.[250]

On an ontological level, the father and son are one society (Jhn.1:1), two persons. In biblical academics, that's called perichoresis (eternal interweaving/intermingling/indwelling). But the context here is rather the unity of missional will. Thus the son eternally wills his father's will (plan), and Mt.26:39 is no exception. [251] Us indwelling God's son (Jhn.15)—indwelling the unity of father and son (v3)—highlights the definition of eternal life now (v3).

True discipleship is dedication to God *based on* living with God, and highlights our mission to the needy 'world' (*kosmos*). It is a glory and an honour to be a Christian, even if we bring dishonour to that name. It is an honour that unites us, and this unity involves both a gateway event (conversion) and a maturing process—Heb.5:8. Saving others is in view, and our unity in the apostolic message—not in an emasculated Churchianity—needs to be seen by the unconverted.

Jesus focused several times on who it was he prayed to. We too should maintain our focus of addressee along trinitarian lines, not 'confusing the persons'. Jesus had/has a one-of-a-kind sonship, yet has given us a relative family status—we are his brothers/sisters, and not his children. I think that his *thelō/thelēma* (plan/will/desire/wish/preference)

---

249 The CEB prefers the then present, "do believe". All other MEVV take the present participle (*pisteuontōn*) as future-referring. The KJV's narrow band TR, had made the implicit explicit, by *pisteusontōn*. The general denying of an authentic delayed parousia, is anyway an immature position, though common in circles—even evangelical—where the Bible must give way to our will, and where allegations of biblical errors must be believed. Freud called such psychology *wish-fulfilment*.

250 Not *God's* word (NKJV), but the message about/from *Christ* (NIV).

251 I'd paraphrase as, "I willingly submit my wishes to your Gethsemane plan, whatever that plan is".

was an "agreeing with you" declaration (see 4:34; 5:30; 6:38; 10:30; Mt.26:39).[252]

Request can be for what we know God seeks, and this leads to the question, *Would the outcome not happen without our prayer agreement?* The outcome here is the church, where God the son's glory shines through. He is the *kurios pantōn*, that is, the panethnic lord over—and unifying—the redeemed across the world (Ac.10:36; Rm.10:12). The NABRE suggests that this is only for after Christ's return (the parousia). Well, it will be more so then, but it is so now.

Can an unjust *kosmos* understand the just father? The son could (v25). And in contrast to the *kosmos*, 'they', his disciples, would really know the sending: *apesteilas*, a verb form of the more familiar noun *apostolos* (Heb.3:1)—those he loves he sends. Heb.1:3 packs a christological wallop, or as Jesus put it, whoever had seen him had seen his father (Jhn.14:9). They had looked inside the tent, lifted the flap, and opened the book. Christ's ongoing work would be via the spirit (the paraclete): Ac.1:1. The idea is not of gateway love (Rm.5:5), but of maturation in love, growing in eternal life (v3), of ongoing christification. In our exodus, God's son has pitched his tent among us (1:14), even as Yahweh walked alongside ethnic Israel via the Tent of Meeting (Ex.33:8). It's good to know that knowing God's name is knowing God's love (v26). Educationally, this prayer doubled to teach his soon to be friends the bigger picture of the soon to be church.

Lk.24:30: In the last friendship setting, two disciples—possibly husband and wife—encountered Jesus, unaware that it was him. Having left him for dead, they were sceptical of reports to the contrary. I don't believe they shared an extra weekly Sabbath meal, or an extra annual Passover meal—both inappropriate in the Jewish setting. I don't believe that they shared a Christian eucharist—that only became a norm after he was known to have risen from the dead, and now has become linked to weekly Sunday meetings.

---

[252]   Young's Literal Translation: "not as I will, but as thou" (Mt.26:39). For various reasons, I think the idea is that Jesus didn't know God's plan for the Gethsemane 'cup', and subjected his 'wish' (*thelō*) to God's plan.

No, a common meal. Common meals expressed thanks to God, so unsurprising he gave God thanks. By the way, *breaking bread* could simply mean sharing a meal, their meals commonly involving tearing off chunks of bread to share. Some use this text as a basis for *saying grace*, the idea of giving God thanks at each meal. That's not a bad idea, even if it is not a mandatory idea.

But how did they recognise him? Possibly, if cloaked, they saw his face in the lighted room for the first time, once he lifted his head to pray—had he been wearing a hood? Or perhaps, by seeing crucifixion scarred hands uplifted: the Greek *cheir* covered what we call hands and wrists—nails had been hammered into his wrists, yet English translations say *hands*, leaving you to guess.[253] I find it interesting that, after his resurrection into a new kind of humanity, he humbly gave thanks, a reliance still on God the father.

Prayer: public

Lk.3:21-2: His first public prayer, so far as we can see, was at his water-baptism. What he was praying, we do not know, but likely enough it was a public commitment to God. After all, the setting of John's baptism was basically to do with committing to Sinai. What we then can see is God's verbalised response, perhaps harking back to Yahweh being pleased with Moses (GNB: Ex.33:12-3): "…You have said that you know me well and are pleased with me. Now if you are, tell me your plans, so that I may serve you and continue to please you…". Also Is.42:1,

---

[253] Incidentally there's a similar guessing game over some other words, such as σαρξ/*sarx*. Virtue signalling, the ESV generally says, "We're not going to tell you what we think it means here". The NIV has generally said, "We're going to tell you what we think it means here", but under pressure it has backtracked. Ironically, translating as *flesh* (Wycliffe) is as much interpretation as translating it as *carnal* (Tyndale): Rm.7:14. Rm.3:20 doesn't relate to the *flesh* of birds or fish, but globally specifies *humanity* irrespective of ethnicity, saying *no individual human being*. So why not do readers a favour, and translate sarx in its contextual meaning, as translators often do with other words which range in meaning? MEVV Grades: CEB/ERV/NCV/NLT (A+); CEV (A); NIV (B+); LEB (B); NABRE (C+); NRSV (D+); NKJV (D-).

modified from mere servanthood to the Davidic sonship of Ps.2:7.[254] Public prayer in non-Western countries is less likely to freak people out, but even if British we should not be too reserved to do it—even if we opt to be discreet.

Mt.14:19//Mk.6:41//Lk.9:16//Jhn.6:11: I have already covered the next public prayer recorded, namely, the feeding of the 5,000+ (see page 105). I think that he thanked God for what he had, for the promise God had made to supply his needs, and that he himself was appointed to be the true bread and 'fish' that would satisfy spiritual appetites. This latter point was brought out best by John.

Some call this story, John's eucharist—otherwise did John skip the account of the eucharist, even as he skipped the account of water-baptism? But why should he not skip what was not his own focus, and which the Synoptics well covered? Actually, one might say that John's whole Gospel was his eucharist account. Moreover, note that his use of *flesh* (*sarx*) is not the eucharist word translated *body* (*sōma*) by the eucharist accounts of the Synoptics and Paul, and that John used it as a one-off, aorist, tense, more akin to non-repeatable baptisms—one-off events—than to repeatable eucharists. And John seems to have paralleled *eating and drinking*, with *believing* (6:54,40).

Mt.15:36//Mk.8:6: The feeding of the 4,000+ is like to that above, so similar that some suggest that it was the same event, whether historical or nonhistorical (ahistorical). That's a little off topic, but we can note that like miracles of healing, miracles of multiplication could have happened more than the Gospels actually show—the Gospels were selective, not exhaustive (Mk.8:19-20; Jhn.21:25).

The dull disciples operated in the naturalist mode in which they often operated (Mk.8:4), perhaps more understandable in a Gentile setting where they might not have expected miracles to flow as freely as

---

[254] Mk.1:11 is also put Luke's way—as a public word; Mt.3:17 is put a personal way. The Evangelists took the gist of the voice (*ipsissima vox*), and directed the gist at their choosing. In short, the heavenly voice functioned both ways, although it is likely enough that most of the crowd did not understand the voice—see Jhn.12:29. It was identification of a pre-existing fact, not an adoption of a mere mortal into sonship.

among God's chosen people: the 4,000+ were seemingly a Gentile (ethnically non-Israelite/Jewish people) crowd. Disciples could easily link the 5,000+ as sketching out the messianic banquet then to come, but would not expect a similar miracle to speak of Gentiles sharing such a banquet. Prayerwise, Jesus publicly thanked God.

Jhn.11:41-2: Next we can read of the death and reanimation[255] of Lazarus. Jesus had moved about four days away (Andreas Köstenberger's *John* (BECNT), 2004:328), had heard the report of terminal illness, then had waited two days until the spirit bade him go because Lazarus had just died. Lazarus had been dead for four days when Jesus returned, and rabbis insisted that God could only return folk to mortal life *before* the fourth day.

Jesus had waited until death claimed Lazarus beyond doubt, in order that the glory of God would be shown clearer to those with eyes to see: "Did I not tell you that if you believed, you would see the glory of God?" (Jhn.11:40). Any sooner, and some rabbis would have dismissed the miracle as simply done by the devil.[256] Since his prayer began with thanks for having heard him, presumably he had already prayed for his father's help. Besides publicly showing before the miracle his confidence in God as his individual father, he also committed to the miracle. Failure would have discredited him, and his enemies would have ridiculed, not crucified, him (53). This prayer shows a pattern of request, thanks, and action. He shouted a word of command: *Lazarus, come out!*

As an aside, I am bemused by the idea that if Jesus hadn't specified who was to come forth, that all the departed—at least within hearing range—would have returned to earthly life, saying "You called?" The operation was done by the Holy Spirit, who would not have tapped each on the shoulder and said wakey-wakey, so to speak. But well, it makes good sermon fodder.

---

[255]   I forego the term *resurrection* here, to differentiate between any raised back to mortal life—to once more die—and any raised to immortal life.

[256]   As it was, this time opponents settled somewhere above that (Mt.12:24), and admitting it was by the spirit/finger of God (Ex.8:19): Jhn.11:47 (contrast 3:2).

As to why many times Jesus' "Be healed"—when he didn't specify who was to be healed—didn't heal all those at least within hearing range, I don't know, *if* the limiting name thesis holds true. No, Jesus personalised his command to Lazarus because he knew Lazarus personally as a friend, as elsewhere he said "little girl" to a little girl he hadn't known.[257] Problem is, this all-named idea assumes Jesus acted as deity, rather than as man—it is an Apollinarian-type error.

Jhn.12:28: Shortly before his arrest, he was asked to speak with some Greek-speaking Gentiles, probably either fully-fledged or borderline proselytes (20). We're not told whether he did so, but I suspect that discourtesy would have forbidden him not to. But that was not John's focus here. To Jesus, that request, that sense of being ready to go global, signalled his death, his *hour*, which would annul Sinai and open up a global panethnic kingdom not of this world.

He would become the world tree. He spoke of a seed having to metaphorically die and be buried, in order to fulfil its mission to be fruitful. He went on to speak about being lifted up to—as the NKJV best puts it—draw all peoples/races to himself (32), a text which some amusing sing to encourage us to follow the Sanhedrin and, like the Romans, to crucify Jesus afresh—*the crucifixion was lifting him up for the world to see!*

It was a daunting glorification, and he had on his mind such horror as many psalmists had lamented. He knew he had to face it, and told his disciples that though they didn't wish him to be killed, he must not pray for his deliverance (27). Some prayers don't make natural

---

[257]   Ex-Spiritualist medium, Raphael Gasson, held that idea (my *Revisiting The Challenging Counterfeit*, 2020:69). We could go on—would any other dead "little girls" have opened their eyes and asked, *Sir, is it I to arise?* C18 John Gill similarly asserted that the name was to limit reanimation, adding that it "showed [Jesus] to be truly and properly God." By erring on Christ's deity side, Gill underplayed Christ's humanity side. Elisha raised the dead; Jesus raised the dead; Paul raised the dead. Did they all show themselves "to be truly and properly God"? Those operations were done by the Holy Spirit, who can still raise the dead to mortal life. C S Lewis once depicted Lazarus as the proto-martyr, for, having escaped this world, he had to face it and die yet again.

sense but might make spiritual sense. Instead, he affirmed his readiness to die: *Father, glorify your name.*

Incidentally glorify (δοξασον/*doxason*) is an aorist tense, having ideas of one-off and focus. The cross glorified his father's name as *father* individualised, the new covenant focus. It was a prayer request based on submission, and others heard the reply. Sometimes we cannot hear our father because we are not open, and if we cannot hear him, how can others hear him through us? God's reply was for the benefit of the general public milling around, listening in (30).

Lk.23:34: There are some genuine doubts about this text. [258] Its request for forgiveness, goes back at least to Tatian, around AD 170,

---

[258]　There is a strong case against this text, in that from what we can see—and we see but in part—textual study suggests that early on it was added in. But some suggest that some scribes, presuming that it could not have come from Jesus because it had seemingly failed, dropped it out. The patristic comments, based on the textual evidence they then had (whether it was right or wrong), shows that in spite of the possible objection that Jerusalem's fall negated Jesus' prayer, his prayer perhaps spoke of eternal, not temporal, loss. Paul specifically sought the temporal loss of a sinner to urge him to repent (1 Cor.5:5).

Theologically it is difficult to square a Universalistic forgiveness, with the prerequisite of repentance (Lk.17:3-4). On this point, Ac.7:60 (also penned by Luke) might assist. Did Stephen simply mean, "Please don't punish them for this particular sin by hardening them to the gospel"? Paul came through. It wasn't about their ultimate salvation, as if rewarding them for his death. Since even Jesus' father had handed him over to death, asking his father not to punish 'them' (?) for their active part in his father's plan, could have been a public declaration that though sin had motivated them, mercy would withhold punishment, even as Yahweh withheld punishment from Joseph's brothers (Gen.50:20). Nor should Jerusalem's fall be put down as God's punishment. Yet if the text is authentic, why was forgiveness of that act based on their ignorance? Had Jesus meant that had they known who he was, they would not have crucified him, so should be forgiven? But was forgiveness needed? After all, capital punishment was objectively sinless and legally justified, and weren't they just executing their job? Now exceptionally his execution was objectively sinful since he was sinless, but since they didn't know that, they were

---

but must have predated him, and might have been spoken by Jesus, even if not recorded by Luke. We can see in the text the biblical idea that we should pray for our human enemies.

Mt.27:46//Mk.15:34: My own rendering of this would be something like, *"God, O God, you are mine, so why have you surrendered me up?"*[259] Jesus was not against using the language of his day, but that language is not the language of our day, though translators are loth to take certain steps against polytheistic language. [260] The inner message may be sealed in different envelopes, yet retains its own validity. It is the letter within, which is sacrosanct, not the envelope (cultural style) in which it was posted. This is one of my rants.

But as to the message to us, it is surely that we too can feel terribly abandoned by the one most basic to our lives—sometimes we are right to lament aloud. Perhaps the immediate context is also worth a mention: at midday it should have been bright, but dark depressing thunder clouds probably rolled in and lingered, hours before Jesus died (Mk.15:33). And like Jesus, who knew how Ps.22—with which he identified—panned out, we too can know that all will be well. But it can be tough getting there: public prayer-lament.

Lk.23:46: After unjust arrest, flogging, nailing to a cross, publicly facing the painful indifference or callous torment of many, he surrendered his life—his spirit—to his father, to God as his father. Many who have suffered far less, have turned away from God as father. Even in—perhaps especially in—days of darkness, we should pray-declare our yieldedness—and perhaps make it public.

---

subjectively sinless (Rm.14:23)—unlike Pilate.

Yet if it is inauthentic, why was it added? Again, we can but speculate. Did a church Q&A on their possible forgiveness, lead to a stirring sermon along the lines that if Jesus had been asked his thoughts, he would have said something like dot dot dot, with a church scribe (initially most were amateurs) jotting down this idea as a side note, a note thought by later scribes to have been displaced from the authentic text and needing to be added back?

[259] That's my take of the Greek text. Matthew used the Hebrew *eli*, and Mark the Aramaic *eloi*.

[260] The CEV is perhaps inconsistently best, on this issue.

Chapter 07   <u>Prayer and Blemishes</u>

Some expressions, some ideas, are better avoided in our prayers, partly because besides them misleading us as we pray, they can mislead others. Here I'll look at prayer-songs, sung-prayer.

<u>Blessing God</u>

Let's look at the abuse of the term *bless*, when it's related towards deity. Although nowadays we find the same Hebrew word for the root word, BRK, translation should be sensitive about its object. In short, generally it's *bless* when the object is simply human, and generally it's *praise*, when the object is deity. For as Heb.7:7 says, blessing is never from the lower subject to the higher object. Are we higher than deity? No? Then don't talk about *blessing* him. You can't do it; I can't do it. To those in the know, it can sound painfully arrogant to hear folk talk in prayer about *blessing* God.

Sadly, some Bible versions are on the problem side—for instance the NKJV/NRSV. But some are on the solution side—for instance the NIV/NLT. Songwriters are a mixed bag, too. Take for instance, the Redmans' *Blessed Be Your Name*, which, amended in various ways and sung from the gut, is a very wonderful song. *Praised be the name of the Lord*, improves one step. *Praised be the name of the <u>LORD</u>*, another step. *Praised be the name of <u>Yahweh</u>*, yet another. *Praised be [the Lord] Yahweh*, another step: I add back lordship as a title to balance the line. But if we change its direction towards unifying this misleading song, *Praised be <u>you</u>, [Lord] Yahweh*, is perhaps best. But can we ever ~~bless~~ this song too highly? "It is beyond dispute that the inferior is blessed by the superior" (NRSV: Heb.7:7).

Jesus: buddy, boyfriend, baby, or boss?

Now onto over-bubbliness in prayer-songs. That can take the form of Jesus being our best buddy at the pub, or Jesus being our bachelor boyfriend, or Jesus being our bouncing baby.

As to the buddy thing, it's good to see that even talk of Jesus—or God—as a friend of ours, can be misleading. Augustine made the point. C S Lewis made the point. D A Carson made the point. The Bible makes the point. *Philos*, translated as *friend* in Abraham to God, and us to Jesus, is about a one-way friendship, a blessing of alliance between unequal partners, a befriending. Abraham was a *friend* of God; God was not a friend of Abraham. The disciples became friends of Jesus—his befriended; Jesus didn't become a friend of theirs.

Consider Jhn.15. They would become—so hadn't been—Jesus' friends *if* they obeyed him, and then he'd let them into his plans, treating them more as *co-workers*—than as servants. What did that mean for us? On balance, I suspect that he spoke of the impending Christian relationship, which after the cross we're now born into by the spirit. That's spiritual befriendment, not buddy theology.

But if such friendship is two-way friendship, then it'd mean that Jesus will become our friend *if* he obeys us, and then we'll let him into our plans, treating him more as *co-worker* than as servant. By the way, Jesus was friendly towards publicans (KJV: Mt.11:19), not to prop up the bar with them, but to rescue them from the bar, so to speak. Hardly a reciprocal, symmetrical, friendship![261]

Talking about the related word *hetairos* (friend), "the absence of the word elsewhere in the NT shows that it is not thought to be appropriate to Christians, for in relation to Christ *doulos* [slave] is the proper term for believers, and in relation to one another *adelphoi* [siblings]" (Rengstorf: Kittel and Friedrich's *Theological Dictionary of the NT*, abridged by Geoffrey W Bromiley, 1985:265).[262]

---

[261] Yes, I know that the Latin *publicani* meant public servants, and that we're talking about tax collectors who were deemed to be collaborators with the enemy (Rome), but the KJV makes much more fun here.

[262] Admittedly this quote goes too far the other way.

Let's face it, Jesus spoke of unilateral, not bilateral, alliance—not about us being buddies, but about us benefitting asymmetrically. In fact in WW2, Uncle Joe was an ally-friend of Uncle Sam, not a buddy-friend. In Yeshua we are more than mere servants/slaves, but we are not on the pally level of best buddies. Respect, trust, obedience.

As to the girl-guy thing, one blogger picked up on a Vineyard song: "No mention of God, Jesus, or the cross—just 'I' and 'You.' How is this a worship song to God? It could be me singing it to a girl!"[263] Is Jesus our boyfriend? No. There must be clear blue water between God and girl/guy love. Still, if that's what floats your boat, *Bethel Music* (also rich in yuyu songs—see page 167) might be the go-to place for you.

And was *Let My Words Be Few*, co-attributed to Matt Redman's wife Beth because he needed her permission to turn a song he'd written to her, into one written to Jesus? No, I'm not the first to ask, and yes, it is cheeky, yet it's asked to make a point. Matt acknowledged that it wasn't ideal for church singing.[264] Too much syrupy sweet candy, and not enough meat and potatoes, is bad for our health. What of Scott Haslem's (1999) *I Keep Falling In Love*?[265]

Chris Idle lamented how so-called *Liberal Christianity* (a.k.a. Quasi Christianity), likes to encourage feminine terms such as *mother*, and enjoys the "delightfully ambiguous 'Partner' and 'Lover.' Charles Wesley

---

263   http://lestyouforget.wordpress.com/2008/04/11/bad-worship-songs

264   https://www.youtube.com/watch?v=qFljv_wit4k

265   *I am found in your embrace, covered by your love / Beyond my deepest dreams I know your love so strong, spirit come / You lift me up to heaven's door, you restore my soul / I can't live without your touch, I need you so much, need you more / You're my rock and my redeemer / The rock on which I stand / I keep falling in love with you, lord / Every beat of my heart, breath that I take / Through the seasons that change, your love remains / My hiding place, my home.*

Or Oneness Pentecostal Lanny Wolfe's (c.1975), *I keep falling in love with him over and over and over and over again / He gets sweeter and sweeter as the days go by / Oh what a love between my lord and I?*

To some extent, one person's meat can be another person's poison, since some process differently. Loving God is to be enjoyed, but not perhaps the idea of frequently falling in then out of love for him.

of course wrote *Jesu Lover*...but even then brother John was not so keen, omitting it from his 1771 book" (Reform 2013).

Idle also warned about songs which treated the spirit as some Pagan Age *thing* or *she* in the sky, of fatherless songs, and of wishy-washy songs in general. He warned of a "new stream of 'divorce' hymns" in which the "'spirit' apparently releases us from old obligations and ties, in the name of freedom and fulfilment" (Reform 2013). He warned of *free love*—meaning our costly worship of human emotions, rather than obedience to Love himself. This warning is not idle.

Some missionary women are told that Jesus will be their husband in place of any mortal man; nuns are often called brides of Christ. On the flip side, will he—or perhaps *she*?—be the *wife* of single missionary men and monks? And to subsequently marry, must a mortal—whether monk or missionary woman—*divorce* Jesus?[266]

As to the infancy thing, I also object to Baby-Jesus prayers, often the bane of Christmas. Besides googahism, ideas of him in Pampers yet prayed to, undermines true faith and evangelism. Jesus as a baby, does not exist. I as a baby, do not exist. Such carols also miss the point of not asking Jesus for things. When the docetic *Away in the Manger* plays, if I can I scurry away to self-isolate, covering my ears.

<u>My god Poly?</u>

Let's look at polytheism talk, the implication of more than one god.[267] Sure I nitpick, but that can usefully prevent lice infestations, since nits become lice, and that's not nice—unless you're a louse, then I'm a grouse. IMO the Old Testament should often use a small g in god, to underline what was going on. As an outgoing tide, such language lingered a bit into the New Testament, although a strong

---

[266] Paul spoke of Christ being like a husband, with the whole church pictured as one blemished bride, not as a husband to each, or some, Christians.

[267] *Poly* comes from the Greek word, πολυς/*polys*, which carries the ideas of many/much.

monotheistic tide swept in with the C1 church.[268] We have often failed to upgrade our theology and our talk.

Under Sinai, the aim was not to teach philosophy. Though dropping some hints about monotheism, the idea was to generally assume alternative deities, then to challenge Israelites to forsake all others and to cleave only unto Yahweh as *their* god—monolatry (Jos.24:14). Similarly a husband believes that his wife is one woman among many women, yet ought to cleave only to her—he has made his covenant.

You may have noticed that Bible translations tend to capitalise the term *god*, when it relates to Israel, but not when it relates to other nations: "the god of Ekron" (NIV: 2 Kg.1:2); "the God of Israel" (NIV: 2 Kg.9:6). That's like the petty capitalising of pronouns, when they are so-called *deific* pronouns. That's something the NKJV did but which the KJV did not do. But whenever the Old Testament talked like polytheism, I'd translate as, for instance, "the god of Israel".

From there, I'd translate away such talk from the NT, at least from when Israel went global by the resurrection. As the church integrated more with biblical philosophy, so such poetical talk became more and more out of place and time. Today, many songs have an *our god is...* structure. My god is wonderful, your god is precious, our god is healer, etcetera. But talking about *types* of god, is not talking about God, since God is not a type of god—there aren't types of gods. However, ingrained talk isn't easily outgrown.

I can say that of all the Bible versions I've compared, the CEV most often goes the right way when following the Greek, though willy-nilly it drops in egregious clangers when not. Compare, say, Php.4:9: "And the God of peace..." (NIV); "And God, who gives peace..." (CEV). If the NIV insists on polytheistic translation, at least it should use a small g— "And the god of peace"—as it should in the OT. Fixing Bible

---

268   I'd propose that at least we generally translate θεος/*theos* as God when it's about the father, and *deity* when it's about the son: saying "Jesus is God", is misleadingly simplistic. The Logos, the son, was with God—as with God the father—and was, as is the father, deity *in essence* (ουσια/*ousia*): Jhn.1:1. We may translate these two *meanings* of the Greek NT, by two words from languages, namely English—*God*—and Latin—*deity*.

translations could help slowly fix our polytheistic hangover, which painfully comes out in our talk, our songs, and our prayers.

I refuse to sing that *my god* is such and such a *type*. I don't want any god. I have God, and he has me. As one Roman Catholic said, "we do not even believe in a god, for this would imply a possible or conceivable multiplication of gods: but only in God" (Tyrrell 76). Okay give the man some slack. There *is* a god, a transcendent being, but he is God, not a *comparative* god (adjectives compare).

Amusingly, some Muslims speak of *the Christian god*, and some Christians speak of *the Muslim god*—your god vs my god. Yet both sides agree that there is no god but God! They both converge (there is only one god) and diverge (is he is monopersonal or multipersonal/monosocietal?). We don't have *gods* which diverge, but we do have divergent *ideas*.

Polytheism factors into prayer. If in prayer we tell God that he is a wonderful [type of] god, would it not be better to stop and unsay that—to renounce all such language? Knock it on the head, until it is dead? Yes, with good mental discipline we can wean ourselves off the language of polytheism, which helps no one nowadays.

Unitarianism

Let's look at unitarian songs. I've already beaten this drum a fair bit. Suffice to say that some songs are what I call soft/quiet unitarianism, some are what I call hard/loud, and some are what I call hyper/deafening. You can quietly exclude the trinity, simply by softly saying that Jesus *alone* saves, *only* is lord, is *all* we need, and other silly stuff like that. Even the Five Solas of evangelical circles, undo the Athanasian Creed.[269]

---

[269] I reject the five *Solas/Solae* (Onlys)—which the Reformers didn't come up with—partly because they can sound as if they each stand alone, rather than only *together* as a package deal (as all being needed), and partly because some do disservice to trinitarianism. Eg, saying *Christ alone*, formally discounts the father and the spirit as saviour. I replace them with the five *necessaria*: Scripture is necessary: *Scriptura necessaria est*; grace is necessary: *gratia necessaria est*; faith is necessary: *fides necessaria est*; the cross is necessary:

I can also exclude the trinity, simply by saying that Jesus is deity, and leaving out any trinity references. Or I can make trinity denial absolute, explicitly ruling out the trinity. If singing that Jesus *alone* is deity, I implicitly am singing that the father is *not* deity, that the spirit is *not* deity, and ironically that the noncarnate son is *not* deity—as persons. Such songs I call Sabellian, as if such deity names are subsumed as modes under the personal name, Jesus. Again, it's a choice: *Hillsong* might want you to sing Sabellian songs; I want you not to sing for Sabellius, but to sing for Yahweh. But it's your choice.

But if you sing such songs, be aware that you will degrade whatever trinitarianism might be within you, and probably degrade it among other singers. We should act responsibly in what we sing to others. And this carries into prayer, whether spoken-prayer or sung-prayer, if it is public. Now if Sabellius was right, then sing his songs. Conversely, if our spoken-prayers or sung-prayers are rightly trinitarian, we enrich congregational trinitarianism as we pray. Thus *Elim Sound*'s theodirectional *One*, upgrades us. While unhappily it sings of *blessing* God, and uses *the lord* instead of *Yahweh*, happily it's explicitly trinitarian without gaffe: *We have come to bless the lord.... To praise the father, spirit and the son.*[270]

Proseuchological blemishes

Misdirection and misvisualisation

Let's look at both misdirectionalism and misvisualisation. Misdirectionalism misunderstands and misdirects prayer, particularly petition. It's like you phone the police about your bubbling stomach, the doctor for your burning house, and the fire brigade about your boisterous neighbours. Misvisualisation misunderstands and misdirects vision, particularly towards the trinity—it is fuzzy vision. It's like you picture the police chief as also

---

crux necessaria est; giving glory to the trinity is necessary: *trinitatem glorificare necessarium est*. Necessary for what? That's a biggy, which I cover in my *Israel's Gone Global*, 2018, and *Salvation Now and Life Beyond*, 2024.

[270]   *Elim Sound* is capable of more problematic songs, such as *New*. IMO the Christian songwriter stables produce a mix of songs to sing, and songs to shun. Don't idolise the stables; examine the horses one by one.

being the chief medic and fire officer, and in fact being one person with three different names (Sabellianism).

In fact, sometimes misvisualisation even becomes nonvisualisation, in that we're not visualising deity at all in our mind's eye, but blinking between what in theory are prayer lines, and congregational—*allēlous*—lines to others in church. In short, pretence prayer, sham prayer. Undermining prayer is the bane of polydirectionalism.

Put the latter this way. Imagine I visit your local church as guest speaker—perhaps less likely if you read this book! I invite you to close your eyes (and of course to bow your heads) in prayer. A hush descends. Reverently standing at the front, I close my eyes and bow my head. "God, please bless us this day. Pastor, I noticed that your building project is getting along well. God, please meet our needs. It is good to see that your flower bed is blooming. Who looks after it? You are Jehovah Jirah. We'll sing a song I've written, after we've taken up the collection. Lord, thank you for your blood. I've some books for sale, which I've put at the back of the church. And please anoint my words. Amen."

Then we sing...in fact, let's do this right now, shutting our eyes when we sing to deity, and opening them when we sing to each other. Are you ready?

First song...

Eyes open: "*The Lord's* my shepherd, I'll not want..."

Eyes shut: "And I will trust *in you* alone..."

Eyes back open: "*He* guides my ways in righteousness..."

Eyes shut again: "And I will trust *in you* alone..."[271]

Second song...

Eyes shut: "Up from the ashes *your* love..."

Eyes open: "To *our god* we..."

---

[271]   To focus on how we degrade prayer, I've ignored other issues with these songs. Lest you justify Townsend, consider that Ps.23 was antiphonal, set for one party to sing/chant to another party, who would sing/chant their response. The CEV modernises the structure to be unidirectional. Modern lyricists should follow suit to fit congregational praying.

Eyes shut again: "Chains have been broken... *You* are alive..."

Eyes back open: "*Hallelujah*... Make *his* praise glorious."

Now I hope you closed your eyes for the prayer-bits, and opened them for the us-bits. If so, you might get the point, which is, *Do these songs really get into prayer?* Honestly, it seems to me that the prayer bits scattered within are hollow, even as pretend-prayer-bit songs make a hollow mockery of prayer. They nominally encourage song to deity, without really getting up close and personal, and are about as genuinely prayer as my pretend-prayer above is.

As has been said, the order of petition is basically to God, through the lord, and by the spirit: Eph.2:18. Knowing this, if we maintain good visualisation, we should not err in the direction of petition. How we develop our individual ways to do this, can vary. I'll offer some suggestions, not recommendations.

One way, might be to face forward whenever you are addressing God, turn your head to his right, your left, when addressing the lord, and turn your head to his left, your right, when addressing the spirit. And perhaps lift your head upwards, if your focus is on the togetherness, the oneness, of the eternal society.

Or, if you pray with your eyes open, you could sometimes select three objects or icons, each to represent one member of the trinity, and perhaps a forth object if your focus is on the togetherness, the oneness, of the eternal society.[272]

A danger is that you might become too dependent on, say, an external image. Thomas used to travel a lot on crowded trains. Whenever he travelled with his back to the engine—as he had been taught to do when a child—he'd end up feeling sick. His wife suggested that he simply ask someone in an engine-facing seat, to swap places. Fine, he was never ill again on trains, until one day, when he had travelled with his back to the engine. His wife asked him if it was because no one had been willing to swap places. No, he replied, apart from him

---

[272]   If you generally shut your eyes in prayer, you could visualise sky for the father, land for the son, and sea for the spirit, and the starry heavens for their togetherness.

the carriage had been empty, so he simply hadn't been able to ask anyone to swap places. If you select icons to focus prayer, will you be able to pray without them? For they should be treated as learning aids, not as crutches.

Another danger is that we treat such externals as being what they represent, treating the means as the end. Orthodoxism issues safety warnings with every icon issued: use only as a venerable window into the sacred; do not venerate as sacred. Similarly, Catholicism employs idols, three-dimensional icons. For if they are treated as sacred, they become demonic. At best they are a healthy means to an end, never the unhealthy end.

The terms we use are also important. That's semantic visualisation—visualisation in words. Word association games look to see how we link words. If I say red, you might say blue, or you might say sunset, or you might say blood, or you might say setter. If I say lord, do you say father, do you say Jesus? If I write LORD, do you say father, do you say Jesus? With the latter, seeing the word in capitals might get a different association. As said, many songs downgrade LORD to lord, thus changing association. Tyndale, like the HCSB, tried to get us back to God's name, whereas Wycliffe used *lord*.

The spoken word *lord*, can also begin as a word-visual for the father, then slip into a word-visual for the incarnate son, while we are still vaguely addressing the father. So under cover of the sound, *lord*, we attribute deeds of the son to the father. Thus we thank the father for being born of Mary, while asking the son to grant our prayers. But to not upend biblical theology, we should thank the son for being born of Mary, and ask the father to grant our prayers.

And as I've said, for good trinitarianism we need to get back to a Yahweh/Yeshua difference. Incidentally, in a corporate sense, Yahweh is not simply God the father. Nor in a corporate sense, was Adam simply Adam the man. For in some contexts, *Adam* could double as Adam the man and the woman together—a corporate name: Gen.5:2. Likewise in some contexts, *Yahweh* doubles undercover for the trinity, even as does the term *God*, although when used of one person, it is best kept for the father. Maybe translators could make the text much easier for us to see this, as they do with most words which have a range of meanings.

Personally I prefer Paul's way of joining the terms *God/father*, and *lord/Jesus* (1 Cor.8:5-6), and mentally keeping these two persons distinct, yet united in one tripersonal being/society.

I suggest that we drop the Dominus Factor, introduced by Wycliffe into English, and instead drop calling God, *lord*. Tyndale began the process, but like the HCSB, was inconsistent, whether from fears of readership turn-off, or hopes of readership drip-feed education.[273]

I suggest that we follow the rule of thumb that the father is God, Jesus is lord, and ask only God (not the lord) in Jesus' *name*, that is, being a part of Jesus' family and mission. And though talking with the spirit is part and parcel of Christian life, see that the spirit is the person of deity alongside us who inspires, not receives, our requests (Rm.8:15,26-7). In short, ask only the father, and don't call him *lord*.

<u>Halleluyah, Yuyu & Noyu</u>

As to the word *halleluyah*, when lobbed at deity that's merely a low-level folly, though it can annoy those in the know. Yep, that's literally asking Yahweh to praise himself! The Hebrew word calls upon fellow believers (*u*) to praise (*hallel*) Yahweh (*yah*). "Extol him who rides on the clouds, by his name Yah" (NKJV: Ps.68:4).[274]

As to yuyu-prayers, if I pray, "You (pronoun), you (pronoun) love me", I am misvisualising, blindly telling I say not whom, that they love me. Such prayers undermine trinitarianism, simply by inattention as to who we are supposed to be praying to—who is the you? They can wear down the meaningfulness to us of the persons of the trinity. Be specific, be consistent, lest he who is the destination, he who is the way, and he who is the navigator, seem to us mere fuzziness.

I love the piece in *The Taming of the Shrew*, when at last softening into marriage, and as a good wife prepared to play Petruchio's little

---

[273]   Very sadly the HCSB upgrade, the CSB, dropped the attempt begun with Tyndale, seeing that it was inconsistent—as was Tyndale—without seeing any virtue in that. Tyndale had more sense.

[274]   Incidentally, even as words can change meanings, so letters can change over time. The original KJV spelling (like the Geneva's) was Iah. Later KJVs had Jah. Today we have Yah, to represent the Hebrew ' (jod/yod).

---

game, Katherine says: "Then God be praised, it is the blessed sun! But sun it is not when you say it is not, and the moon changes even as your mind. What you will have it named, even that it is. And so it shall be so for Katherine" (45). They made a game out of fuzziness. But let's be clear about who *we* mean, whether in sung or in spoken prayer.

As to noyu prayers, if I say "Lord *Jesus* (noun), *Jesus* (noun) loves me", I'm sounding as if I'm taking to one Jesus about another Jesus, or otherwise that I'm being artificial, not really normalising my speech. I heard only the other Sunday, a pastor pray something like: "God, may *God's* kingdom come." If you go onto Facebook you can tune in to many churches, and hear such prayers—is that what you wish?

But yet again, it's talk to, presumably, one god about another god's kingdom. The pastor had a fixation on a certain biblical phrase, and instead of translating it into normal speech when speaking *to* God about it, made the whole thing sound like he was throwing in something without real visualisation, without really praying.

Here's a quick test for you. Assuming that besides myself there is only John and Jack in the room, which shouldn't I say...

1. "*John*, please pass me *Jack's* book"

2. "*Jack*, please pass me *Jack's* book"

3. "*Jack*, please pass me *your* book"

Of course, if I'm not looking at anybody and not really visualising them, I might absentmindedly say "*Jack*, please pass me *Jack's* book", but that wouldn't be real life; that would be fuzziness. Prayer should get a little deeper than it sometimes does, by lifting the artificial fog, and by visualising biblically. Reality check, please.

Sadly, some corporate prayer-songs reflect this absentmindedness, this unreality. I still hark back to my Bible College days, when as a group going around some churches, we were taught to sing, "Spirit of praise...let me know, Holy Ghost liberty." Archaism aside, there was not a ghost of a chance of getting me to sing that! At most it's, "Spirit of praise...let me know, your glorious liberty". But nowadays I'd rather not ask the spirit for anything, period. Even then, I think my pneumatology had developed enough to ditch pitching requests to him. But whatever, my plea here is for us to ditch unnatural prayer-talk. Let our prayer-talk be natural, as if we really are face to face with deity: "God, may *your* kingdom come."

If you have heard even half the prayers I have heard in my circles, you will have been able to meet Jesus in his human body. That's right. It turns out that he has many different faces, both guys and girls, and many different voices which each claim to be God's son speaking. The Bible says: "God did not keep back his own son, but he gave him for us" (CEV: Rm.8:32a). Yes, but we know better, don't we?

Some songwriters seem to think so. For instance, having spoken of being a son among his sons, in *Now Are We* (1990), Kayla Parker crossed both gender and deity boundaries, and sung that she was chosen to be God's son. Adding confusion, she called the father both *lord* and *prince of peace*, perhaps thinking him to be his own son, too, although that meant actually...herself. So a lot of misvisualising there, Kayla, with Bible terms thrown willy-nilly into the pot.

The biblical writers differed in approach, as whether or not to call Christians *children of God* (John), or *sons/daughters of God* (Paul). John kept the term *son* (υἱος/*huios*) exclusively for Jesus. Paul used it also for us, but for us it was only as a plural, generally linked to adoption, and in Greek best meaning sons/daughters.[275] If I speak like John, I'd say that I was a child of God, and that Jesus is the son of God. If I speak like Paul, I'd say that I am *a* son of God [by adoption],[276] my wife would say that she is *a* daughter of God [by adoption], and we'd both say that Jesus is *the* son of God. Either way, Jesus and I are both in God's family, though he through incarnation, and I through spiritual adoption/birth.

---

[275]   *Hebrews* drops Paul's link to adoption.

[276]   D A Carson noted that insisting that Paul called Christian girls and women 'sons', because assuming that only sons could inherit, is mistaken: see Carson 1998:131-3 on the ESV fallacy.

Chapter 08   <u>**Prayer and Anselm**</u>

In *Prayers and Meditations*, Anselm of Aosta, Italy, sought to extend Christian meditations beyond the closed doors of the C11 monasteries, and to share prayer with a larger catchment than clerics. We may commend his aims, even if the methods are no longer ideal. Similarly, improvements to archery might have been helpful in the age of arrows, but no longer ideal in an age of bullets. However, what about certain principles, such as prayer and meditations being for all Christians? Such is surely an ongoing good, being part of a biblical framework somewhat uncovered by Anselm.

He has been called the father of Scholasticism, an academic-devotional framework within which theology and philosophy once more got back together. It was rife in the Middle Ages, and sought to understand what was good from the past pagan world, and to rebuild its wisdom, enriched and corrected by Christianity. It was a process needing several centuries, but once it had done what it could to incorporate past wisdom, it needed to decline—as it did in the C14—to allow for new reflections. It was, so to speak, the plant stem connecting the prior bulb to the future flower—an organic bridge.

Anselm worked with the then given position—which is still held by many—that one prayed via the good offices of canonised saints. That was a term given to rare individuals within the church at rest, deemed to have been outstanding in holiness and openness to deity. That prayer-through method is not for me. I commend his conscientious approach to such, which has benefits within it. In my circles, there are many prayer-songs—either set prayers or sham prayer. And quite candidly, many prayer-songs in my circles are either meaningless to pray, are downright dangerous to prayer, or are both.

"...we do not have a high priest who is unable to empathize with our weaknesses, but we have one who has been tempted in every way, just as we are—yet he did not sin" (NIV: Heb.4:15).

Anselm believed that if you were going to ask a saint to help, you should really get to understand them, so as to match your request to a sympathetic saint. A lady of the night might well wish to pray to Mary Magdalene, for instance.[277] Anselm offered a set/pattern prayer to Mary Magdalene, partly based on the idea of her being the woman disdained by Simon the Pharisee. In this prayer, switching as he sometimes did to the lord, he wove this little gem: "You made yourself a mortal in order to give us immortality" (Ward 205).

Likewise in approaching *Saint* Peter—or so he doubtless believed—Anselm had done his homework about fisherman Peter having being made a pastor/shepherd by Christ. And with the added church idea of Peter being heaven's door-keeper—has heaven a door-keeper?—Anslem then sought to approach Peter as "as a scabby sheep addressing the shepherd of the flock, as a wounded desperate soul addressing the door-keeper of heaven" (Ward 10). It's as if a saint responds to your address with a, *Why ask me?* You've just got to be ready to give your reasons.

By the way, we could extrapolate this idea to actually getting to know about deity. This might sound too radical an idea to some Christians, but not I think to any who have got to this point in this book.[278] But how many adult Christians have never left Sunday School, paddling on the shores rather than swimming in the waters?

It's also good to note Anselm's humility. It's a virtue based on fact, and not a bad idea for us, although some may question whether he went too far into self-abasement. I wonder what Christian realism says about this. R W Southern noted how in later years, Anselm's tone

---

[277]　It's been mere speculation as to whether Mary had been such a lady: https://aleteia.org/2018/04/02/was-mary-magdalene-a-prostitute/. My point is that if we so believe, we might as well speak—a *best guess* policy—and she won't mind.

[278]　I think of a tragicomedy song by Amy Grant, *Fat Baby* (1982).

had moved "from the personal and effusive self-examination of the earlier prayers" (Ward 14).

As to Christian meditations, it's what today we might call, doing theology. It's about spending time thinking about biblical things, Christian things, Christian books, Christian songs, meditating on them, mulling things over. It can marry in with personal devotions, prayers. It's a blessing, not a curse, though like most things the good can go bad if unbalanced.

Among the 19 Prayers we have of his, Anslem wrote some for Countess Mathilda of Tuscany. He added that he hoped that they would stir up both love and reverence for God. In a prayer *To God*, unsurprising he spoke unmindful of his polytheistic tone—if Ward's translation does him justice here. He dubiously linked the father with the lord, and deemed himself to be a sinner needing forgiveness.[279] Negatively he asked deity for protection against temptation towards the un-Christian. Positively he asked for help towards the Christian. Per Eph.4:22-4, God helping we ought to put off evil (anti-Christian nature) and put on goodness (Christian nature).

Anslem highlighted God helping us to play our part, and prayed, "Help me to love you". He prayed for the knowledge of God's will, too. God's general will is within the Bible, but his situational will might require him to speak to us, though sometimes biblical principles (indirect speech) may be enough to choose well. Anselm prayed to have right attitude (humility), and to avoid wrong attitude (arrogance). Now and again he fell into the still common glitch of not differentiating the father from the son, by using the term lord, for both: "Always, lord, let me go on...through the lord" (Ward 91-2).

In a prayer *To Christ*, he looked at Christ's turning points, such as his death and resurrection, and the blessèd hope of his return. He praised and thanked him, aware that verbal offerings were but poor offerings, but were better than none. By contrast, I am disturbed at how often we seem to deem Christ fortunate to have our thanks and praise.

---

[279]   We should distinguish between evangelical and pastoral, forgiveness.

On the minus side, Anselm unsurprising but unfortunately here overlooked the order of prayer, and asked Jesus directly: "By your powerful kindness complete what in my powerless weakness I attempt." And he referred to God as having died, as if Christ was God, an unnuanced statement that as a standalone is unbiblical.[280]

On the plus side, he desired to love Christ more. He spoke of having lost the grace of his baptism. I presume he meant by that that he had been brought up in Christian ways, backslid, then returned to them. Was his *return* his *conversion*?

Interestingly, he switched from Christ to himself—"Why, O my soul?" And after that he switched to Mary, who had been Christ's mother.[281] By and large he visualised well, I think, spending dedicated time on one person, before moving to another, and not confusing the persons. At one point, having returned his vision to Christ, he switched as a short aside: "Alas, lord, alas, my soul". That's like talking to someone about you-and-I, a natural style.

There seems to be an understanding that the emotions are not always up to the highest prayer. And an understanding that one can tell God that they are feeling low—or caught up in distressing fear—and yet pray through into a sense of serene love. In three prayers *To Mary*, Anselm prayed: "Good Lady, a huge dullness is between you and me",

---

[280] The very term, christ, means anointed one. If we say that Jesus is simply God, are we saying that God is anointed, and if so, by whom? That Christ was deity incarnated, God the son (not simply God) as a human being, I wholehearted believe. It's how we put that that can mislead. And like the *Servant King* song by Graham Kendrick, Anselm also mistakenly spoke of the creator's [nonmaterial/nontemporal] 'hands' being pierced.

[281] In my aioniology, motherhood is a function/relationship which ends by death, as does marriage (Rm.7:2). Thus I say that I *had*, not that I *have*, a mother, and that she who was my mother is, but is not my mother. Our language is imperfect for biblical categories.

However, Roman Catholicism holds that Mary remained Christ's mother, and as at Cana, plays a part in intercession, and has a mothering role to Christians. I have little wish to critique Anselm's then Mariology, which I presume has improved since his death. I will only note that he noted Mary's subservience to Christ as to her lord, although doubly wrong in calling him her god.

and spoke of being "held back by despair" (Ward 107). One may recall how many psalms are lament based.

In his second of these three prayers, Jesus and Mary are treated as always son to mother: "Dear lord, spare the servant of your mother; dear lady, spare the servant of your son. Good son, make your servant's peace with your mother; good mother, reconcile your son to your servant" (Ward 112-3). Anselm reasoned that to offend a mother offended her son, and offending a son would offend his mother. He feared that his sins offended, well, both really. Given that, did it not make sense to ask both to pardon his offence given to both? He feared judgment of sin unpardoned. He asked on the one hand to "escape the sorrows of damnation" which he deserved, and on the other hand to "enter into the joy of the blessed" (Ward 114).[282]

In the third of the three prayers *To Mary*, Anselm did flag up his sense of spiritual separation from grace, but told himself off for being too melancholy, and affirmed to 'Mary' his reliance on her to see him through to safe waters. After all, he reasoned, without her bearing Jesus in the first instance, no sense of grace could ever have come. But she did bear him, and grace did come with him. Therefore, is she not the one to affect any second coming of grace? Is she not the "gateway of life, door of salvation, way of reconciliation, approach to recovery" (Ward 177)?

Anselm questioned whether he was too hung up about himself, and too small minded to forget his pettiness and instead to praise Mary's sublimity.[283] Personally I look to the sublimity of the stream, not of any human sluice gate, but I strongly agree with Anslem that the incarnation was the grand miracle of miracles, of supernature being born into nature, married to nature, and far more remarkable than any Big Bang. Thus Miriam's part was far greater than what she

---

[282] "If there lurks in most modern minds the notion that to desire our own good and earnestly to hope for the enjoyment of it, is a bad thing, I submit that this notion has crept in from Kant and the Stoics and is no part of the Christian faith" (Lewis 1949:1).

[283] Anslem seldom erred in misvisualisation—picturing as you pray—but in line 140 he spoke *to* Mary about "the blessed fruit *of* Mary's womb" (Ward 119).

realised, and she was more than justified in being called the most blessèd of women (Lk.1:28?,42),[284] indeed of human beings.

In this prayer, Anselm rejoiced that "all just people who died before [Christ's] birth exult" (Ward 119). Elsewhere he painted the picture of a falsely dishonoured king who, following a great act of nobleness (in short, the cross), issued a general pardon to apply to any rebel who came and claimed it on a set day. (Any penalty-free offence is a meaningless offence; payment implies meaningful offence: serious offence; serious penalty: death was needed to satisfy the inbuilt need for penalty.) Later the king extended it to any who confessed that they would have come if they could have come but couldn't have come. They would also be pardoned from former guilt. Name it; claim it.

This can picture those who died before Christ's birth, if they would have and had been, good people. How many, before human aviation, would have flown if they could have flown? Not all who never flew were ever anti-aviation. Indeed, the king's pardon could extend to those who, subsequent to Christ's birth/death, did not turn up and bow down, since not having heard the king's offer.[285]

---

284   The phrase "Blessed are you among women", belongs only in Lk.1:42. The term 'full', as in 'full of grace' (πληρης χαριτος is only in Jhn.1:14/Ac.6:8), was not written here by Luke, but was an interpretive change to his text, carried in the Latin, and preferred by some Catholics. Hence lacking in the RSV, it bobbed back in the RSVCE (Catholic Edition). The NET footnote says: "'favoured one' (a perfect participle, Gk. 'Oh one who is favoured') points to Mary as the recipient of God's grace, not a bestower of it." Granting the NET on the Greek, it could still be argued that unstated by Luke the recipient of favour became a granter of favour. The Catholic *New Jerusalem Bible*, and *New American Bible (Revised Edition)*, both get it right. The *New Catholic Bible* gets it wrong, and its cheeky little footnote sidelines the correct translation as a lesser alternative translation. Incidentally, in a wider comparison of these three versions, I gave the NJB an A, the NABRE a B+, and the NCB a D+.

285   Anselm argued that for meaningful justice, penalty ought to be paid for sinful offence, yet that by the cross penalty was paid on our behalf, so pardon by grace could be issued. His Satisfaction picture—that unoffending deity alone could satisfy offended deity—was held strongly by John Calvin. Some would say that it is one imperfect picture among several, all capable of hinting in differing ways, of the reality of salvation.

Anselm spoke his Marian devotions to 'Mary'. I do not say that he actually spoke to Mary, or that he spoke true about her. Some would affirm him on both counts. But imagine that I blindfold my eyes, take a bow and arrow, about face and shoot, and that I believe both that there is an unseen target, and that I have shot the arrow into the target. I have shot my arrow, but if there is a target, have I hit it, whatever my blinded belief? Anselm's arrow was shot towards an idea, *Mary*, but was his idea in line with reality, objectively real?

Nevertheless, I commend meditating on the woman whom God picked to fulfil the plan of incarnation, what Anselm called the recreation, the reestablishment, and what we might call the Christ dimension. The arrow is not illusion, even if fired at illusion. May we not have a rich love for Winston Churchill? And though unable to speak to him, we are able to speak to our idea of him. In Christian Spiritualist circles, sitters are seemingly able to see apparitions of him, and would believe that they could express their love for him, to him—though of course they would be mistaken in the target.[286]

But the love Anselm had, even if misdirected, was well fixed on the great intervention, and the particularity of God's plan (Mary as the mother of messiah). Personally I would rather direct my love for Mary— and for Joseph—to he who selected her and her husband for such a wondrous task. But boy, how easily we overlook those in the past who have done so much towards our benefit. Looking back at their tasks, as Anselm reminded us, is good.

As to Mary's virtues, real or fancied, our mediations can be rich in love and appreciation. Indeed we can well meditate on idealised womanhood (perhaps as Mary or through Mary?),[287] and idealised manhood

---

[286]   For the misdirection of Spiritualism, see my *Revisiting The Challenging Counterfeit*. At a more casual level, many mourners address sentiments to a likewise illusory target, as if Poor Jane or Rodger was within the grave, listening to every word.

[287]   We lack sufficient evidence that she was an ideal woman, though we see various virtues which God saw in selecting her. Some would add that she was also in the right family line of King David. I am unconvinced that she was, but I am convinced that her husband was, and was probably King David's heir.

(Jesus). After all, did not the psalmists marvel in prayer at the exaltation, the crowning, of humanity (eg Ps.8)?

Some say that only deity is worthy of praise—bother the you-alone songs, all too common in Christian circles![288] More sensibly, Paul told us that whatever was worthy of praise this side of heaven, should be praised (Php.4:8). Paul praised the Corinthian Christians for certain things, and not for certain other things (1 Cor.11:2,17).

In a prayer *To John the Baptist*—do Roman Catholics pray to Baptists?—he told John that he, John, baptised God (Ward 127). It would be better to say that John had baptised God the son, since there is more to God than God the son: neither father nor spirit were baptised. And if I have baptised a human, have I baptised humanity? And it would be best to say that John had baptised God the son in the son's incarnate mode, that is, baptised the man Christ Jesus. John had baptised his cousin; was God his cousin? Anselm proceeded to tell John a lot more things which, arguably, John had never known before.

This really boils down to the question as to whether we really know what we are talking about. It raises the challenge of us being self-critical with our theology. In extenuation, it may be that the bulk of Anselm's theology lay within his restricted circles, so that he assumed that what he and his circle believed, must be true belief. To be fair, his supporters might fairly accuse me of being in too restricted an evangelical/ecumenical circle. We judge from where we sit, but should be aware that our seat may not be the ideal perch.

He also interposed a section which I presume was about Satan. Anselm revelled, as elsewhere, in contrasts: "He hardened his heart when he was punished; I hardened mine when I was kindly treated. So we are both set against God: he against him who does not want him; I against him who died for me" (Ward 129).[289]

---

[288] Anslem also had his you-alone talk, about the lord (Ward 216).

[289] Again I note with disagreement the *Death of God* idea, though unlike Nietzsche (who really meant the death of the idea, *God*, and illogically believed that the idea, *morality*, could live on), Anslem believed that *God* had been resurrected from death.

In his *Prayer to Saint Peter* (Ward 135), he as usual contrasted himself to the great saint: Paul was chief of the apostles; Anselm was the poorest and weakest of men. And as usual he reflected on how 'merciful Peter' had once been in need of God's mercy.

In his *Prayer to Saint Paul* (Ward 141), he picked up on the feminine side of the Bible. Here he "explored every aspect of Paul's career to find an avenue of approach along which sinners can travel with confidence. But all in vain. Everywhere he came up against an impenetrable wall of sin. Then he stumbled on some words of St Paul in...*Thessalonians* and *Galatians* which suggest the contrasting images of a nurse and a woman in labour. With this flimsy aid Anselm found a new approach to St Paul, now depicted as a tender nurse and mother" (Ward 11). [290] This nicely puts the idea that prayer can be an exploration, a seek and find.

In his *Prayer for Enemies* (Ward 216), Anselm addressing Jesus as God, proceeded to ask 'God' to bless his, Anselm's, enemies. Here he recalled the dominical injunctions to pray for those who persecute us, to bless and to curse not. Moreover he also had the spirit of messiah, putting this command into his heart and soul. Christianity extends the grace to personal persecutors, to state persecutors, though limiting God-backed aims (Rm.13:4) and saying that where they and God depart, go with God (Ac.4:19).

Anslem prayed aloud his awareness that his heart could hold evil towards his enemies, and he sought God's love (God's seed/attitude) to flow from his heart towards his enemies, not the devil's seed to flow. In praying for our enemies, we should first face our inner sins of hostility, and be transformed by the renewing of our hearts. Otherwise, will our prayers not be sham?

He prayed that whatever he sought for his enemies—if in God's love—he should seek for himself. Do you love your enemies as you love yourself; loath your enemies as you loath yourself? He begged God not to give him, nor his enemies, what he might otherwise wish upon his enemies. He prayed that he wouldn't always get even what he asked for, for he might blunder. He prayed that his enemies might

---

[290]   Paul and his team sometimes acted like a mother (1 Ths.2:7) and sometimes like a father (1 Ths.2:11). Statistically, fatherless children lose out in life.

repent of their misunderstandings, and instead live in God's light. In this, I think he was aware that any personal bitterness towards them could work to their spiritual detriment: he fought shy of such sin towards them. "This is the punishment that I ask for those who serve with me and those who hate me—let us love you and each other" (Ward 218).

Moreover he reflected on how he himself had been, and was, at enmity with the lord. If the lord sought Anselm's good, paradigmatically should not Anselm seek his enemies' good? He ended on a trinitarian note: "O Saviour of the world, who with the Father and the Holy Spirit lives and reigns, God throughout all ages. Amen" (Ward 219).

<u>Prayer meditation</u>

Anslem also wrote some mediations which could lead into prayer. One abbot, Durandus, fed back how one such meditation had blessed him, and begged Anselm to pray for him. Asking mortal saints to pray for us, was well known, however much they in turn might seemingly pray to immortal saints.

As to the mediations, Anselm used a soliloquy, the idea of internal conversation, talking to yourself, perhaps aloud. Indeed the idea of even reading without talking, was unfashionable until much later. And every now and again he spoke a few words aside to deity: from looking within, to looking above, so to speak. As you read, keep looking up now and again. But he kept such redirection clear.

So, there is a lot in Anselm which I would recommend, and plenty of premises which I would not recommend. And of the latter, there is perhaps much which would nevertheless be useful in the personal devotions of many, whose ways are not my ways, yet who are fellow brothers/sisters of my lord. *Romans* 14 tells us to treat gently the devotions of others. They are secondary issues. I would argue that as we teach the primary issues, those of us misguided in the secondary issues, might be guided out of them—given time and openness.

In this context consider physical-circumcision. The primary issue, the new creation, rendered it superfluous, even misleading. However, Paul himself held that in a social setting in which it was customary and where needless offence needed avoiding, his own mixed race colleague should be physically-circumcised (Ac.16:3).[291] That was for evangelical purpose, but I think that his principle of avoiding needless offence applies in the pastoral also, to avoid spiritually stumbling others, not merely displeasing them.

Let me take something of Anselm's approach to personal communion with deity, and put it into a trinitarian prayer setting. The particulars of these prayers below may be taken, dismissed, corrected. They are quickly drafted and are secondary. The primary idea to consider is private relational prayer. As with Anselm, here we may meet personal prayer-letters, letters written to deity in a casual yet reflective style.[292] I suggest that the style of each person should reflect their personal style.

God/father/destination

"Dear father, I call you dear, for you are precious to me, and I call you father, for you are father to me. Once I was not in your family, but now I am. Some say that like the Prodigal Son, in that story that your son told us, we have been brought back into your family. I demur. For would that not mean that we were simply reintroduced to a prior state, rather than introduced into a new one? Is the new creation merely a restoration of the old creation, a going back to old Adam, rather than a going unto the new Adam?

---

[291]   Contrast Gal.2:3: he who needed for evangelism to be physically-circumcised in a non-Christian setting, would not have needed to be physically-circumcised for salvation in a Christian setting. Whether, now after the teething times, any Timothy should be physically-circumcised within enculturation, to evangelise among ethnic-Jews, is another matter. But the primary theology was that physical-circumcision had had a fundamental place under the now defunct ethnic covenant (Sinai), partly as a token of God's plan of making spiritual-circumcision the entrance into his spiritual covenant (Golgotha). But not to contest against Sinai now, is to not contest for the fundamental change in salvation history. In in-house Christian circles, Sinai membership rites were nonnegotiables, not given credence.

Presumably other than being with Paul in Jerusalem, Timothy would have got away with not being physically-circumcised.

[292]   Many overseas missionaries will write prayer-request-letters, asking fellow believers to pray for their witness and wellbeing.

"Perhaps it says something about humanity since its beginning. For after all, humanity, but not I, once knew you, was part of your family, walked away from Eden. Humanity, not I, became prodigal, but can it repent as humanity? I of course was born with a prodigal nature, since part of prodigal humanity, but I personally did not depart from Eden, and humanity has no personhood to repent and return to Eden. Could any individual humans even *return* to Eden as the prodigal returned to his home, other than Adam and Eve? And even if we could—though we can't—should any human wish to return, since your son became the Second Adam, offering redemption into the New Eden? Should we put new wine into an old wineskin, or into the new?

"No, since my beginning I did not walk away from your family, not having been born into it. Yet now I am within. Once you were not dear to me, nor had ever been, but now you are. Indeed, I am overjoyed that I am within your family, and to know that you know me personally, and that you love me personally as a child of yours, one among a teeming multitude.

"Some say that all human beings are children of yours. They are right, of course, at the old creation level—children by creation, children born to the prodigals and away from the old Eden. Yes, as you have said, all human beings are in your image—*imago dei*—and thus murder is inherently evil. Yet with your son came a new creation, and only since his death and resurrection have we been able to be born spiritually into your family, your new creation family.

"And with him came a new creation image, his image, the *imago christi*, even as he is the true image of you, and Adam was but a dim prophetic type of your true image. Moreover, your word speaks about some humans being children of darkness, and some being children of light—you are the light. None are in Old Eden; not all are in New Eden.

"So not all are in your new creation family. Even Moses was not spoken of as a child within your family, but as a servant preparing your house for your son, Yeshua my lord. For him whom I first met when I was but a young child.

"And to him I was taught to pray in my early years, even before I welcomed him. And then largely wasted years, before I was taught, and saw in your word, that much of my prayers were misdirected, though I doubt not that you heard and heeded me. Only then, upon my knees did I look up, and half in fear dare to address you, rather than the lord.

"Is it not true that theology leads, and prayer follows, and that false theology leads falsely? But you now, as you did then, transcend Jesus. And the clues are everywhere before us. Your son came not in his own name. No, he came in your name, in your authority, in your mission. We can see chains of command in human circles. How would a private, though they casually address their sergeant, casually address their general? And yet your son's mission was to offer greater address. Indeed it made you, the general of all generals, our father.

"So when I dared not to bypass him and to speak with you face to face, had his mission not failed, at least in my case? For he came to become the way to you. So when I deemed him the destination, I had not understood his mission. But by seeing him as the way to you, I can now understand his mission, and for me it has neither fully failed, nor remained overly long below par. Thank you for showing me this.

"But then, who am I to say what is overly long? Yet oh that I had known you from the outset, not simply known about you. For knowing you is deeper, and richer, than simply knowing about you. The Creeds tell us a fair bit about you, and the demons know about you more than I do. Yes they know and fear you, but from a different perspective and in a different way, than do I.

"My knowing you is loving you; their knowing you is hating you. My fear is deep reverence; their fear is the fear of suffering. For they are unable to know joy, damned by their own freely chosen and unentrenchable bitterness, and a deeper gulf of dread lies now before their feet, set fast in damnation.

"As for me, I seek heaven, not to gain it for itself, but to gain more of you within your wider and deeper creation, and through your universal playground. And my knowing you increases within my mortal years. Yet in my folly it increases but slowly, far more slowly than needs be. For how often could I set time aside to focus on you, time in prayer with you—and yet do not? How often do I settle down with a good book, rather than with the Good Book? And how insular I am, when your son was so outgoing, so sociable.

"Still, my personality and my quirks, though they limit me so—yet I blame them but in part—yet it will not always be so. I yearn for the eschaton, when we shall know as we are known—when I shall know as I am known by you, and when others will know me, not for what I now am (please spare them full sight), but for what I shall be then. And only then will I be worth knowing.

"Worth knowing, say I? Is an unborn child worth knowing? To you, perhaps as worth knowing as any born child is known. But to us? I think not, but I think not as a mother. Marvellous as the human development is before birth, we deem it not worth knowing the real them, perhaps because we can't really begin to know the real them. Even within the first years from birth, we can only at most sketch a little of the inner infant.

"In the spiritual world, am I not even as an infant within your family, not worth much knowing, else incapable of being known? Am I capable of knowing the human heart? And if so, am I capable of knowing your heart, though unlike human hearts, you hide it not, nor is it sullied?

"I have some hope. As Paul has said, you are beyond full comprehension, but not fully beyond comprehension. You are knowable in part. Similarly we can prophesy but in part. And so I can know you in part, and can know and be known by others in part.

"How then do I come across to those who see me in part? In mixed ways, I doubt not. And likewise, they to me. Mixed ways, and misunderstandings. We share a common dimness of sight, but we are not blind. Even unto you, we are not—if in your family—totally blind. Even those of us without your son, are not totally blind, I think.

"But am I fit to be seen by my fellow mortals? In different pictures we picture ourselves, excuse ourselves, hide ourselves as did Adam and Eve, even from you. We are Christians under construction, we say, so please excuse the mess. Yes, our inner life is a jumble of mess, with a foundation perhaps not fully laid, or else with scaffolding around a partly constructed frame. What is humanity, that you care for it?

"And yet, we are worth being known by each other, even at this stage, for the knowers and the known are one, people under construction, similar messes making allowances for other messy sites. Yes, we abhor our messiness, and hide what we see as our shame, our weaknesses. Yet you encourage us—within wisdom—to be open about our weaknesses, for we are commanded to carry the weaknesses of others.

"Yet how can we carry what we do not know? How can a doctor heal, if the ill conceal their illness? Yet we fear lest our real self be made public. And we hide in darkness. Yet you are the light, you, with your son and the spirit, are the light. And you see us through and through, and have unrepentantly thrown your loving arms around us. You fully excuse the fully excusable, and do fully forgive, as we allow, the fully inexcusable mess which you see.

"And you see, infinitely better than I can see, the goodness within me, both the *imago dei*, and the *imago christi*, the goodness you have given me, the spirit of your son encoded into my spiritual DNA. A glory even I can but hope for, but which you see, a seed of your planting. Oh thank you father, that you stepped in to rebellious humanity, lovingly giving your son to live among us as one of us, howbeit he never rebelled towards you, never fell from you.

"Oh the son of your love! Not a biological son, I know, nor a son within time, but an always son, one coterminous with you, indeed one with you beyond time and space, beyond creation, eternal in eternity. Such is your love indescribable, which we can only describe in part, in figures of speech, in dim analogies. Such a beloved son, who entered time and space and took up residency as a human being. A biological mode, a creation mode, which he has taken into cosmic glory.

"And as such, as a human being, he became a sin offering, and carried our curse, carried my curse. Ah pictures, dim illustrations, fit for our dim sight. Him you gave up, for me, for us. To us, I, who had no worth, you have given worth through him. Beyond incarnation you called him your son. Within creation you have called me a son. Not, I know, the level of the son, for my sonship is rooted in time, whereas his sonship is rooted in eternity.

"I cannot understand your love in such a gift, and cannot give back love in the measure given, but only in part, even as I can but know you in part. Father, your graciousness towards me and mankind, is truly wonderful beyond compare, superlative beyond superlatives, even as measurement itself is immeasurable. But, glorious father, please excuse me now, as I turn towards your son, my lord."

Lord/brother/way

"Glorious lord, I call you that, even as I call my eternal father, God, and not lord. You are near and dear to me. As lord, you have the highest right to my obedience, under God. Yet I know that, within the patterns of understanding which we mortals have been given, he is the ultimate lord, for he is to you—my lord—as lord. You, even in your noncarnate self, bow before your father—or so I picture it. And that not perforce, but in love. Is it not what some call the Divine Dance, where you play your part in the timeless dance, willingly following, so to speak, the lead of your father?

"Yet what are these terms, *father* and *son*, to you? Was Bunyan not right, to write in similitudes? Are they not handles, human pictures, given to us to begin to know you? Approximations, yet approximations given by you, as the best pictures for us within our mental framework? And since it is a gift of a picture from you to us, I rejoice in the likeness of you as the son to the father.

"And within that picture, we are told that you sing your father's praise to us, brothers and sisters of yours, that you proclaim his name to us. For by your work, by your commitment to humanity, we have come to be covenant brothers and sisters of yours.

"C S Lewis spoke of 'us lions', for he knew that you identify with us intimately, not standing aloof, but happily mixing with us in our frailty. Indeed, we had all been as motionless as stone lions, but because you died on stone, we who have welcomed you have stirred into life, as your breath has touched us. And indeed, you welcomed us first.

"And your oneness with us is not to your gain, but to ours. You became one with us, not to get, but to give. How I love you, lord, yet how truly I confess with a hymn writer, that weak is the effort of my heart, and cold my warmest thought towards you. And yet I am more amazed at you loving me in spite of my black ingratitude, than I am at my own coldness, my own ingratitude and casualness about awe.

"Much of mortal life is humdrum—perhaps it is my age. But at sea, how often all seems calm, until every now and again a storm stirs the waters, and we are then filled with awe and dread. Is our Christian life not as an ocean voyage, and at least in Western waters calm for the most part? And is my love for you, not humdrum?

"But how many, in some parts of this world, face the storms, not of your might, but of the kosmic rage towards them for holding true to you? How much brighter their love! And has that not been true since you rose from the dead, and began the new humanity? Even so, as with the mighty oceans, storms in the heavenlies affect one part of your people, and not another, then move from the one part to another.

"Has it not been that both storm followed by calm, and calm followed by storm, has been the lot of each country and people? The West itself, once a spiritual calm, has become choppy. Persecution need not be physical to be effective. The Pilgrim Fathers left one choppy shore, seeking to find a peaceful harbour. You, the light of the world, left the peaceful harbour for the choppy shore, faced the fury, and were slain. In your name, we now are the light of the world, and might too be slain. Oh whatever our fates, may our witness towards you never be slain, silenced in spiritual death.

"When you return, will you find faithfulness generally among your people? For you are lord, and as such have a right to be obeyed. Your loyalty to us is without doubt, but our loyalty to you is in doubt. But perhaps, what we need is the wakeup call of persecution. The church in Jerusalem was finally scattered, once persecution squeezed tight, and the blood of martyrs has birthed many churches in many places. While we are to pray for peace in society, in which to seed the church, you know that sometimes within peace, we become complacent, sleep and sow not.

"Lord, I marvel that you, knowing our weaknesses both within the old creation and the new creation—for you know the weakness of man's heart—did become mortal for us sinners. For sinners we were outside of your family, and sinners as we are within your family. Yet you did.

"I praise your love—and for your commitment to us, thank you. Your grace was both unmerited, and unrewarded in the eternal. And yet within the temporal, you saw the salvific results of your death, and were satisfied. For your heart is ever to give, and you have seen your gift accepted. You have seen our newfound joy. You have seen us grasp meaning to life. And you are well pleased.

"And at this I marvel, too, that you are the eternal uncreated son, and also Jesus, the temporal created son. Yet how can one person be as two? Is it that you have written yourself into the universal book, a character which is you the writer, and yet who, without variance of will, writes their own lines? As author, you are lord. As character, you have become lord over your redeemed church.

"Is it that the painted seed has grown upon the canvass according to its perfect nature, bloomed into flower? Within nature you are the first fruit from the dead. Beyond nature you are the lord of life. But lord, please excuse me, as I turn my attention to the Holy Spirit, he whom you have, under the father, sent in your name, and has also come in the mission of our father. And was the co-sending not right, if you are one in perfect will with your father? And was the telling us this, not to say that your mission would continue in your will? Thank you for abiding with us."

Spirit/helper/navigator

"Wonderful spirit, I gladly turn to you. And what a privilege! It's funny, but in the West, privilege, a Marxist no-no, is almost being repented of, as if none should inherit a class, or a rich family tree, whether rich in goods or in wisdom. Yet cannot the haves help the have-nots? Is not generosity a virtue? Nowadays is it not that some, wallowing in the narrative of victimhood, are being taught to bite the heel of those who stand, even as Satan bit the heel of the messiah?

"And yet through that poison we have been healed. And that healing has come through you, wonderful saviour. How privileged we are to be healed, and to walk with you, the healer. Did Luke not say that after Jesus had risen from death, he has continued to work and to teach through you? Had he not foretold that he would do so? For you who were always with us, had not been given in the new covenant way until messiah began that covenant.

"And of all the marvels which come by you, is not the greatest the only one which Jesus could not give before he died, the healing of conversion, of entrance into your family? Thus, with your help, we are able to do the great works which he did, and the greater work which he did not, but which by death he made possible. But oh, how many of us affirm the greater work, but disaffirm his lesser works, not going about healing everyone who is oppressed by the devil, though God is with us. Why do we not all revel in all you can do through us, and metaphorically clip your wings instead?

"Alas, how easy it is to blame others. The works do not get done because others do not pull their weight, because others do not believe. How often does the work not get done because I do not pull my weight, though I do believe? And perhaps mine is the greater guilt. For if others do not believe, why expect them to do the work? But if I believe, why expect me not to do the work?

"I take some comfort in the idea that not everyone is to do everything; that we have different jobs. Still, to whom much is given, much is expected. But what of they to whom little is given? Even if I have been given little, is not little expected of me? Yet whatever I have been given, whether meagre, much, or middling, do I not wish to be as those to whom preferably none has been given? Much cake, no payment?

"Yet rather than wallow in my lack, I would revel in your abundance. Indeed I revel in the contrast. For such is your grace that you love me nonetheless, and continue with me as my guide. I knew a man whose driving instructor walked out on him.

"Is it not that you walk with me through mortal life, showing me wonderful scenes on route to the Celestial City, walking through green pastures and besides peaceful waters? Is it not that I, being wayward, time and time again insist on going, what I call my own way? Is it not that you lovingly walk with me even in my needless wilderness, wherein I suffer, though you too suffer? For do you not feel the pain my sin inflicts on me?

"Is it not that when from folly I come to my senses, and forgo the pigs' food, that you graciously guide me once more, never giving up on one who gives up on you so often? Yet is it not that because of my detours, the journey no longer allows you to show me glories I might otherwise have seen, which now we must pass by? And so I have bypassed times of profit, for times of loss. You are the wise; I am the fool. Is it not well said that fallen human wisdom at its best, is far below your wisdom at its worst? Well did the apostle Paul revel in contrasts.

"Truly by your love you guide a pack of fools, a pack of ungrateful fools, of whom I am one. I would not contend with Paul to be the chief of sinners. Perhaps he meant simply his stubbornness in resisting so long messiah, not his sinfulness as a Christian. For as a Christian he strove from the holy fire within him, to excel as chief of saints.

"Some might think that he meant that he led sinners, as their chief. And yet he revelled in sanctity, in sainthood, in the new creation. He saw Christians as seated in the heavenly places, seated with Jesus, with earth as his footstool, therefore as our footstool. As saints rather than as sinners, Olympians, winners not losers.

"Yes, he knew that Christians were removed from the sinful kosmos, though the sinful kosmos was not fully removed from Christians. Time and time again he urged Christians to put off what didn't belong to them, and to put on what did. Both these things are only possible with your help—you recreate our minds.

"But compared to him, I have been neither so bad before, nor so good since. A humdrum Christian am I. I think of Jean Darnall's book on life in the overlap. Truly, I live in the intersection between the old life and the new life, between the spiritual mind and the carnal mind. Do we not all, we who have you as our guide, we who are walking from the carnal? All the more does your patience towards us exceed our expectations and imaginations. What other guide would not give up on us, give up on me? Oh Holy Spirit, you are so wonderful, with God and the lord, you are beyond compare.

"Spirit of holiness, you abide with us who have been made holy, have been made saints, are set aside unto God. And yet we are still far from holiness of heart and mind. But as we walk with you—not simply as you walk with us—we are being made holy in attitude, not merely the holiness of relationship. What joy must be yours, as you see the fruit of your labours, the fruit of your patience. Is it not even as an artist who joyful in spite of their art, can still rejoice in their art? And yet you are not self-seeking. It is not some joy which you need, but is a superfluity of joy you can revel in. And it is a joy in seeing us enjoy your joy, in seeing us become more Christ-like.

"To that end we might have to suffer. Is that not as gold is refined, howbeit gold feels not the fire? Yes, fire can burn away our dross, helping us in mortal life to better know messiah, and to better know is to better become, and to better become is to better enjoy.

"For us that fire can come from without, but can also come from within. From those who hate us, and from you who love us. And did the christ himself not have to suffer, being lower than the angels, one with man for man?

"His sufferings were ordained, even to the tasting of death, that we should be able to taste life, immortal life, not merely immortality. As a mortal, he suffered sufferings without deviation, perfecting himself as the Second Adam, the new paradigm for the new humanity.

"Is it not a privilege to share in his sufferings, perfecting us as members of the Second Humanity? Thank you Holy Spirit, that you allow us to share such sufferings, to endure, to be transformed increasing into the new image, as being yielded we are guided by you."

∞

Joseph, saint

"And Joseph, what of you, do you heed me if I pray to you? If you don't you will not say No. Have I a direct line? Is there voice mail you will one day listen to? But if the latter, why bother, when any who have prayed to you will be with you, and will speak face to face? And if the former, why, when there is no need? Or maybe there is no need but there is grace. That if we feel a wish to speak to you, you feel the wish to listen to us, for our sakes?

"Yes one day we shall meet, perhaps on many a day. Although the term *day* will not mean then what it means now. But if we cannot speak in terms unfamiliar, we must speak in terms familiar, for now. For will we not as individuals, immortal and sinless, be free to roam the universe as our playground? Will we perhaps bless the biosphere of other planets, having different days, even as Adam and Eve once blessed a garden in Eden? By what planet would we then agree the term, day? Will the term be irrelevant to us within endlessness? And if we all roam through such now unfathomable distance, uninhibited perhaps by the speed limitations of light, perhaps once in a billion years—in Earth reckoning—we might meet and make merry.

"But are you not now awaiting that release into a universal body? Little are we told of what we may call the intermediate life mode. A seed is one mode. A stem is another. A flower is another. The mortal life is one mode, somatic and spiritual. The intermediate life is another mode, nonsomatic and spiritual. The universal mode is another, doxasomatic and spiritual. Is it, I wonder, like those who have been performers on stage, who having played their part, join the audience until the play is ended? And then shall we all put on our new coats at the exit door, our glorified bodies awaiting us, and leave the theatre to rove the universe, the greater play? If so are you not now off the stage, seated in the balconies, part of the great cloud of witnesses?

"And what was your part in the show? You were born the heir of David's kingdom, yet were neither anointed nor permitted to be king. What must have been your sadness in your youthful years, to recall a free kingdom under your great ancestor, but live as a subject among a people subjugated under the iron heel of Rome?

"Yet you were permitted to see the anointed one born unto your then wife. And you were promised that he would be given the kingdom of David, and the greater kingdom of which David's Throne was but a prophetic hint. Thus you were permitted to see and to adore he who was born the anointed, the set aside one, the messiah given by Yahweh, the king over all high kings. And you bowed to the firstborn of Miriam, as to your lord, even as it was prophesied that David would call his special descendent, his lord, to whom Yahweh the lord would subjugate his enemies.

"Great was your joy, your hope, your belief. Yet we are not told much about you. Does such silence speak of all who died before the cross, even if they lived when messiah walked upon the earth? For like the Baptist, you too died before messiah died. I wonder why it was so.

"Had you been an aged widower before being betrothed to Mary? Some say so. And if they deny that you had children with Mary—as if a normal wife—they hold that his brothers and sisters were either step-siblings or cousins somehow living with her. But had you been a young man, looking forward with hopes and fears for the future with your betrothed-wife, to the time when she would be your wedded-wife?

"Oh what shame and grief must have pierced your heart, to discover that she was with child, as if your wife was an adulteress. For you knew well enough the facts of life, and being righteous knew rightly that her child was not your child. Did you seek to discover the baby's paternity? You did seek to divorce her, quietly to walk away.

"Had divorce gone to plan, you could have kept her dowry, the *kethubah*, besides retrieving any bride indemnity lodged with her parents warranting your good behaviour. You could have left her and been a richer and a wiser man, and with your reputation intact.

"Yet you who had seemingly been shamed, while rejecting Miriam as unfit to wed, in kindness did seek to shield her from the full force of public censure, and perhaps from being slain for her seemingly infectious disloyalty against your nation. Thus you preferred to avoid a public court, and were content for a simple divorce to return her dowry, though you were entitled to it.

"But you who were open to the voice of kindness, were also open to the voice of God. Thus you heard the angelic voice, and you rejoiced that the right of kingship would not pass to a full son of yours, though through the full wife of yours. Yet your joys were unheard by those around. For they would have rated you as unclean, as having fathered a child outside of wedlock, though at least with your betrothed wife.

"In public you would be shamed, sharing the unjust names thrown at your wife. And you even became a shame to your parents, who had had such high hopes for you, the godly heir to Israel's hope. And did they not refuse you both the guestroom of their house in Bethlehem, leaving her to give birth in their ground floor utility room, where animals were lodged? How you must have awaited your wedding, when you might take Mary to be your lawfully wedded wife, when your parents would have had God's assurance that Mary's son was by his design.

"And what joy you must have felt, watching Yeshua grow up as a righteous child, and claiming the holy temple to be his father's house. Yes, your house was not his house, even as mere human kingship was no longer God's plan for your people. For would he not, by fathering no heir yet rising to undying life, preclude any others from your race from rightly taking the throne of King David? Would not the prophecy of kingship have been a rich historical symbol of what Yahweh's global plan had really been? Did you not rejoice at the moreness? Joseph, one day, I doubt not, we shall meet with our lord the king, once his enemies are but his footstool in salvation history. And you will hear me, and I will hear you. But for now, goodbye."

Chapter 09   Prayer and Malcolm

C S Lewis and prayer

Writing on C S Lewis' *Letters to Malcolm—Chiefly on Prayer* (1966) J B Phillips said that it "nowhere tells us 'how to pray' but...stimulates [a] hunger and thirst for God without which we should never pray at all." Over hopefully Hugh Montefiore suggested that it might "become Lewis' most enduring memorial." Let's quickly run through this book. Or skip it if you wish. For his part, Lewis rejoiced that for some people prayer is so simple that they just talk to/with God. Yet he wrote for those, such as "adult converts from the intelligentsia[, for whom] that simplicity and spontaneity can't always be the starting point" (Lewis 1966:79). Looking at philosophical issues to prayer, can help us see biblical issues to prayer.

Malcolm (and later his 'wife' Betty) was a pretended correspondent in Lewis' reflections on prayer. Lewis aimed to talk about private, rather than public, prayer, which within Anglicanism[293] he identified as liturgy.[294] As to prayer-liturgy, laypeople should "take what [they] are given and make the best of it", and the less chopping and changing, the easier to endure (Lewis 1966:5). Rejecting *liturgy fidget*, Lewis valued familiar ways for allowing easy access to and from God: a good

---

[293]   Lewis spoke of this network as if a Church. I bypass and replace this terminology, rejecting it as unbiblical. Globally there is one church (not Anglican, not Baptist, not Catholic, not Orthodox), which is represented by *local* (not *doctrinal*) churches around the globe. No denomination should refer to itself as The Church, or as a type of Church (Elim *Church*, *Church* of the Nazarene, etc).

[294]   Lewis 1966:5. In his days, pressure within Anglicanism to escape the 1662 *Book of Common Prayer*, led to the *Alternative Service Book* 1980, then superseded by *Common Worship* (2000). The soonest up-to-date, the soonest dated (Lewis 1966:14).

shoe is one you don't notice. Yes Jack, but what if the shoe has lost its sole?[295]

For spontaneous praying aloud in church meetings, some parts of the church switch off quality control, encouraging more personal interaction for men, women, and children. I think that whether we pray church-prayers (liturgy), or whether paraphrasing Paul, "all may pray" (1 Cor.14:31) individual prayers, there will be some content we should reject, and some we should respect, while favouring all serious prayers with serious consideration. For, as Paul said of prophecy ("all may prophesy"), we are surely under the obligation to "let the pray-ers judge" (1 Cor.14:29).

Lewis affirmed Rose MacAulay's approach of building a library of set-prayers to aid her own spiritual life. She had presumably repented of having had a sexual 'partner', had gotten serious with God, and Lewis had had the good "luck to meet her" (Lewis 1966:11). If nature is diverse, and God perfects nature, then he will perfect diversity, and it was bigotry to dismiss MacAulay's prayer life, though it wasn't a pattern for Lewis.[296] Might it be that either some rely too much on others, or too much on themselves, and that a combination is best? Personalised prayer fits our individual situations (1 Kg.8:38), but set prayers can help us fit into the body of Christ, and Lewis argued for God's intimacy and God's transcendence, our proximity and our reverence. But had Peter and Paul needed liturgy for transcendence and reverence, I wonder?

Underlining the danger of trying to perform eye surgery if you yourself are blind (Mt.7:3)—and perhaps he had once ridiculed MacAulay's method—Lewis admitted that he had once foolishly prayed too much through wordless imagination, poles apart from set prayers. But with the exception of "the Lord's Prayer", he didn't go for set prayers. He realised that while "praying without words" (Lewis

---

295   Lewis was well aware that living language changes, and that incremental updates and major updates are sometimes needed to read the original.

296   Lewis spoke of personal style such as he had witnessed within Greek Orthodoxism, not of the Hippy/Postmodernist idea that everyone's 'bag' is equally valid: if your bag's murder, murder, if it's healing, heal!

1966:13) was great when it worked, it had seldom worked well even for him, since he could not always do, what he sometimes did.

He said he wasn't bothered if some Christians asked deceased believers to intervene for them, but he warned both against the ideas of marshalling big names to twist God's arm, and of assuming that they'll share our pettiness. I think that whatever Abp. Thomas Cranmer meant by "With the company of heaven" (*Book of Common Prayer*), those who have died probably won't accept our prayer requests, but with us will pray for the return of Christ (the eschaton).

Lewis enjoyed the sense of church solidarity over time—the bigger picture. Talking of time, he said that praying was generally best done when physically alert, not tired. Better to pray in a crowded train on the journey, than resting alone after it. Our bodies, as well as our inner life, ought to be yielded to God: Lewis commended humble kneeling, as useful but unessential. Especially if unyielded to God, physicality can be dangerous, but it is a sensory gift from God to us: angels "understand colours and tastes better than our greatest scientists; but have they retinas or palates?" (Lewis 1966:19).

When it comes to prayer, why inform he who knows all? And why remind him who never forgets? Well, perhaps for our benefit, not for his. "The change is in us.... We offer ourselves to be known" (Lewis 1966:22). Effectively, prayer requests are inviting God into situations, thinking through in our own minds what it is that we seek in situations, and not assuming that he automatically intervenes. For Christians, asking God is a privileged way of 'meeting' God our heavenly father, and being real with him. Our requests should be serious to us. Not supercilious, but significant issues which we or others face, not generally what makeup to put on one's face. But on the other hand, let's not be too starchy about 'bothering God'.

We should yearn and pray for God's sinless harmony to have its way in our hearts and lives, and in human society at large. We should beg for it, even if disagreeable (Heb.12:11), indeed bowing in submission to it if asked. In fact, he might aim to give us a blessing that our hands— already full of old blessing, or seeking a different blessing—cannot hold. We should therefore pray with open empty hands, and for the basics for our daily overall well-being.

To play our part in forgiveness, it can help to see a time when we have offended in a similar way to how we've been offended. Lewis did not go into why we should repeatedly ask God to forgive us. The answer perhaps lies in ruling out the idea that ultimate damnation, like Damocles' Sword, hovers over *Christian* heads, and ruling in the idea that daily forgiveness is all about daily father-child harmony. In short, our bitter attitude against others—whom our father also loves—might block us from his grace, close our hands from receiving: can a clenched fist take hold of his blessings?

Nor should we ask God not to lead us into temptation, as if God were a fiend who might otherwise tempt us with what he forbids us.[297] What the Greek word πειρασμος/*peirasmos* means in different contexts is important, and in Mt.6:13 it means something like test, not temptation: we verbalise our wish not to be tried, even though we know that testing can have a positive value.[298] Lewis tended to drop the textual addition about kingdom, power, and glory, though they and other church comments can be useful.[299]

---

[297]　Jesus was tested to the breaking point, and did not break, but the ultimate leader/driver was not the ultimate tempter. "The spirit did not tempt Jesus, but he did lead him to be tempted": https://danielbwallace.com/2017/12/12/pope-francis-the-lords-prayer-and-bible-translation. Presuming that the disciples knew about Jesus in the wilderness, his pattern prayer for them could carry the idea that such ultimate tempting was something to seek to avoid, God willing—please do not lead us in the way you led your son, into [such?] temptation, but on the contrary [when tempted?] deliver us from the evil one—a confession of our weakness and God's ultimate strength. As Lewis noted, in isolation it presents problems: if God seeks to lead us into temptation's zone, should we doubt his wisdom as Peter did Jesus' commitment to the cross (Mt.16:22)?

[298]　A few English versions break away from the traditional wording, though end-age (eschatological) talk of *the* trial is too limiting: NABRE/NRSV. The CJB/GNB probably pitch it about right—please don't test us too hard. God can *test* (*peirasmos/peirazō*) us through trying times (*dokimos*)—for which we should be grateful (Jas.1:12)—but he does not *tempt* us (*peirasmos/peirazō*: 13). So knowing that trials can make or break us, in prayer we remind ourselves that in weakness we fear to face where he might lead.

[299]　Since to say that Jesus said what he did not say, is to misrepresent him, I agree with Lewis that these words should be dropped.

Commenting that "one wouldn't condemn a dog on newspaper extracts" (Lewis 1966:32)—which might once have been true—Lewis briefly contrasted a brighter side of Alec Vidler to a darker side of Cardinal Newman.[300] Newman confused heaven (the destination), with earth (the journey); God, with religion. Religion can sound like an add-on, a menu selection not to everyone's taste, an organisational motif, an idol. Atheists would demolish it as an unwanted department; Christians should raise it into an organic element of life.[301] A Sunday-only *Churchian* (my term), might be religious but sub-Christian, or simply a weak Christian. [302] Psychologists [303] are right that guilt feelings can mislead, but fundamentally wrong if they dismiss all guilt feelings—guilt can exist. Confession therefore can be good for the soul. Both healthy and unhealthy can think themselves unhealthy, and both healthy and unhealthy can think themselves healthy. Praying for forgiveness should be based on specifying the *guilt*, not on the fog of *feeling*.

Intellectually, though asking God might seem to lower the tone, Lewis cited both Ps.131:1 (Great)—"I am not high minded"[304]—and the Yeshuic Covenant[305] examples of invitations to ask God. Objections

---

[300]   When de-religionising rather than de-supernaturalising, Vidler was "rather good" (Lewis 1966:33). But confusing those ideas, Vidler sacrificed the tree to save some branches.

[301]   Jas.1:27 is clear: godly religion flows from godly hearts towards the needy (outward), seeks godliness within (inward), and looks to God as father (upward).

[302]   John Bunyan's *The Holy War* highlighted that Christian conversion doesn't (if ever) open us up fully to God, but does open us to God as father. Sunday Christians oppose further liberation, and some repel God. God seeks to be 24/7 in our lives, not 1/168.

[303]   Freudians went too far. But "they did expose the cowardly evasions of really useful self-knowledge, which we had all been practicing from the beginning of the world" (Lewis 1966:37).

[304]   Like the Great Bible, Lewis low-mindedly ignored God's name by a mere [Lord].

[305]   A.K.A. the Christian Covenant, or New Covenant. It is our covenant with God the father, through Jesus the mediator.

to asking God can be a bit like determinism:[306] it "does not deny the existence of human behaviour [but] rejects as an illusion our spontaneous conviction that our behaviour has its ultimate origin in ourselves" (Lewis 1966:39).[307] Yet if even determinists ask others for help, why should we not equally ask God for help? Nor, if God responds by changing circumstances, is the cosmos any less stable than by us changing circumstances, at least if he works—as do we— within the cosmic laws of his creation. In short, to ask and to receive, is not intellectually offensive in itself.

Lewis alluded to his widowerhood, and how his prayers for Joy's mortality (Lewis 1966:44: "a form of anguish..the torment of hope") were not (the second time) answered by a yes.[308] Such prayers can be Gethsemane Prayers, and afflictions are part of our humanity. Knowing that the cup was his destiny, Jesus "could not, with whatever reservation about the father's will, have prayed that the cup might pass, and simultaneously have known that it would not"—a logical and psychological impossibility (Lewis 1966:44). Lewis concluded that the hope against hope of imperfect humanity surfaced in, and was put down by, Jesus.[309]

We can agree that Gethsemane showed Jesus' humanity and his submission (even if we don't agree as to how such were shown), and that both should play a part in prayer. Lewis also implied that sometimes it is

---

[306] Why ask for what will be, any more than for the next sunrise? Yet unlike sunrises, James said that we don't have some things because we didn't ask God for them. Determinism is the materialistic idea that every action is an effect that is theoretically totally traceable to the original cause—Big Bang?

[307] A philosophy Lewis countered well in his book, *Miracles*.

[308] C S Lewis' *A Grief Observed*, tells the story.

[309] My reading is of two cups: Gethsemane's unknown; Golgotha's known. The former bitter cup he wished (*thelō*) to be withdrawn, yet if it was in the father's plan (*thelō*) then he willed (*thelō*) to drink it. In short, Jesus' will was always one, and always one with his father's. Yet humanly it's fine to prefer to avoid a bad unless it is a needful bad, but whether—unlike Golgotha— Gethsemane was needless, Jesus simply didn't know. "He chose the father's *plan* over his own *desire*" (Keener 1999:639: emphasis added). Lewis also invoked Lk.22:43-4, though this *floating* text might be inauthentic.

strengthening, not comfort, that we need in our sorrows, sometimes to face what can seem to be God's desertion.[310] Lewis made the point of "shared darkness", people who share deep sorrows in life (Lewis 1966:47)—in prayer we can share the dark valley.

Lewis made the point he had made in *Mere Christianity* (4.3),[311] that our requests in our time-dimension, interact with the eternal, and that the eternal heeds us and interacts with our time-dimension: 'God hears'—rather than 'has heard' or 'will hear'—is better from a philosophical standpoint, even if not from a pastoral. Requests—unlike the idea of spells enforcing their will—are "taken into account", and since the eternal considers them, the reply could begin before the request (Is.65:24?).

If we hadn't asked, it might have happened anyway; if we hadn't asked, it might not have happened. There is deific-human interaction: God did not make us to sin, but in *consequence* of our sin he offers forgiveness—our sin evokes response. And if forgiveness is God's response to our requests, may he not respond to our other requests, not by compulsion, nor by choice, but by consonance with his nature?

Based on the idea of deific impassability, some deny that God is interactive, even that he intervenes. Biblical images of God's reactions to us are just that, *images*, but intended to convey meaning that is richer than our theologies and informs them. Blaise Pascal's idea that prayer (by God's grace) commissioned God to do as we asked—we the agent, he the patient—underplays God's sovereignty: "we can bear to be refused but not to be ignored" (Lewis 1966:55).

Nor was Alexander Pope's *plan/by-product* idea right, about deific sovereignty having a set plan that willy-nilly displeases or at times pleases us, but which allows little or no scope for meaningful variations. Far from a general universal plan set in stone, God's

---

[310]   I deem *Jewish church* (Lewis 1966:46) to be both anachronistic and dubious.

[311]   To simplify, picture a human author spending years deciding what will happen in a split second to their characters. Yet God, beyond all timelines (time is within him), can spend—to speak in human terms—an eternity deciding what will happen in a split second to his characters.

---

awareness of 'every sparrow' is less unreal that Pope's anthropomorphism of God as absent clockmaker (*deism*).[312] We have the boon of meaningfully asking God.

Now, is the lord's promise of Mk.11:24 literally true?[313] Yet don't we, who ask but are denied, have as lord the one who asked in vain in Gethsemane? Did he not add an opt-out, "if it be your will"?[314] Let's not hide the problem behind the easier and more spiritual prayer forms of worship and reflection. If Jesus had made an open-ended promise, it might seem irresponsible of him. For it is surely obvious that if we always got what we asked for, we'd suffer, and how, in a shared situation,[315] could God grant believer A the exact contradiction of what believer B asked? While more mature Christians should ask, *Why then the promise?*—and get a good answer—it can be unwise to overload immature Christians with it. Huckleberry Finn, told he'd get what he asked, didn't get what he asked, and "never gave Christianity a second thought" (Lewis 1966:62).[316]

Whipping up our feelings into *faith*, might be psychological gymnastics, but whipped feeling isn't faith. Lewis suggested that the

---

[312] Within the Yeshuic Covenant, the raw data of Scripture can speak in terms of god-types (see my *The Word's Gone Global*, 2017:199-21), but translation theory should smooth them out for us. For my money, "..the god of peace" is better as "God, the source of shalom" (CJB: Rm.16:20); "God is not a god of confusion", is better as "God is not the author of confusion" (KJV: 1 Cor.14:33); "the Lord, the god of the spirits of the prophets", is better as "the Lord God, who inspires the prophets" (NLT: Rv.22:6). I cringe at Lewis' "The god of..." (Lewis 1966:58)—capitalising 'god' doesn't redeem such polytheistic claptrap, infecting our monotheism.

[313] Ten years earlier, Lewis had done a paper on this.

[314] This exact wording is missing from the KJV (see Lk.22:42: Weymouth), though its meaning is in the text.

[315] Eg, if for the same fleece and time, Gideon asks for the fleece be as drenched as a drowned rat, and Joash asks for the fleece to be as dry as a desert.

[316] Might the widow's assurance to Huckleberry have lacked Christ's assurance? If God does not give what he has not promised to give, why dismiss him as a liar or deny his being? The lord's assurance contains truth, but, Lewis suggested, a truth more for tertiary than for primary level Christians: a warning for charismaniacs.

situation of the promise to Jesus' there and then disciples, might have contained the obvious proviso that such asking would be based on what they knew they needed for God's mission.[317] To be a supplicant is fine (Jesus asked for himself in Gethsemane). But Lewis suggested that perhaps a supplicant is less likely to be heeded, than a servant's request to play their part. And the deeper in the servant, perhaps the more in tune with God's missional will, and so perhaps the more their variation-requests will be granted.

Thomas à Kempis' *Imitation* sends kitchen chatterers to devotional studies, but doesn't send students into the kitchen of life. In fact no book on prayer will suit everyone. Nor is it necessary that all should aim for the highest prayer levels. After all, some good hill walkers make lousy hill climbers, and some people cannot even walk hills. It's more important for our spiritual life, to do well within our prayer level, than to aim at higher levels.

That said, to fall below our spiritual potential, is to underdevelop our spiritual life (Heb.5:12). [318] At the highest level, what some call *mysticism*—or *spirituality* to ignore the snubbed term *religion*—needs grounding in godly religion. The Gnostics thought themselves too *spiritual* to be merely *soulish* Christians. Mysticism can be good, and can like Christianity sail the same sea, but it cannot guarantee the same destination, nor the same sense of direction: "out of this [world], but into what?" (Lewis 1966:67). LSD can also send one to sea,

---

[317]   Using the term "God's fellow-workers" (ASV: 1 Cor.3:9), he suggested a friend/servant (clergy/lay type?) distinction from Jhn.15:15. Yet the NT elsewhere shows no such distinction: Simon Peter remained a servant (*doulos*: 2 Pt.1:1); John remained a servant (Rv.1:1); Paul was a servant (Rm.1:1). He was right that some are more deeply into mission than others, whatever Jesus meant by *friends*. IMO he probably tried getting the blood of his thoughts from the stone of 1 Cor.3:9, on which https://danielbwallace.com/2014/03/17/what-does-we-are-gods-fellow-workers-in-1-corinthians-3-9-really-mean/ argues that Paul really meant that he and Apollos were fellow workers within God's mission.

[318]   It is sad if elderly Christians have given sixpence to church ever since their childhood days, and only prayed the set prayers of childhood: real prayer is real.

but to what end? The best spiritual map, Christianity, remains vital for top end mysticism, Christian mysticism.

Sainthood might prove one's mysticism, but mysticism doesn't prove one's sainthood. In fact not all saints are, or should be, hill climbers. Architects and builders are both needed for God's temple. Mystic prayers can be insightful, but the best can be the enemy of the good, even as devotion can work against practical deeds for others. In fact, even intercessory prayers can short-change others (Jas.2:16). Moreover, seeing what others need, can blind us to what we need. I see the sawdust in your eyes—may God sort your problems out. I do not see the plank in my eye—may God not sort my problem out (Mt.7:3). Sometimes we know so many needs, that we need God to help us to be selective. Jean Darnall once said that if the devil cannot stop you from doing God's will, he will overload you to depress you.

We might think that we pray to ourselves, soliloquy, yet the boot is on the other foot. Prayer should see God as both separate to us, and within us. And "moment by moment, [God] projects into us" his thoughts (Lewis 1966:71). The deeper our prayer, the more of God and the more of us it is. God is the pure actuality from which all humanity draws life, even if humanity abuses life (substance abuse). But praying with God is—though probably still with some distortion—praying in line with him, even in a sense him praying to himself (Rm.8:27). That, in a sense, is like anything he chooses to do through man. God is not all, but he is all in all, distinct from yet indwelling creation, raising humanity higher into his life.

Linking creation to creator, the traditional term *ex nihilo* was only meant to rule out creation from other than God: "it can't mean that God makes what God has not thought of, or that he gives his creatures any powers or beauties which he himself does not possess" (Lewis 1966:74).[319] Man, by God and of God, is somehow profoundly like God,

---

[319] Probably *ex deo* (from himself) is better than *ex nihilo* (not from anything). The Big Bang fits in well: God created matter/energy from his own eternal being, and gave it laws to evolve. Likewise, the kick-started code-based biosphere reflects something of himself who is life.

and profoundly other.[320] In looking at man's specialness, perhaps Lewis needlessly held that everyone must be in this *imago dei* sense, a sibling of Jesus (Mt.25:40).[321] Omnipresence is not some ethereal cloud, but, to cite a song, "something lives in every hue, Christless eyes have never seen": omnipresence is more weighty, solid, than ethereal gas, and indwells each created thing (neighbour, dog, cabbage-patch, stone) in different ways. We should perceive his presence. His presence might be distasteful, but we must not avoid the unpleasantness of reality, or we will live in the unreality of the always-pleasant: "dream-furniture is the only kind on which you never stub your toes or bang your knee" (Lewis 1966:77).[322]

---

[320] He believed (not covered here), that on Earth man alone is separated unto God by God's bestowal of a rational spiritual likeness, and he assumed (not covered here) that other planets might have such life. Theologians speak of the *Imago Dei*.

[321] Although everyone is conceived in God's likeness, to say that "it cannot refer only to the regenerate" (Lewis 1966:75) needs qualification. Based largely on Jesus' other references to his brothers and sisters (*adelphoi*) as being his pre-Christian co-workers (Mt.12:50), Keener 1999:605 dismisses the popular idea that this parable means that all humans are in Jesus' family, in which some sometimes need particular care. Likewise Keener dismissed the dispensationalist idea of whole nations being sheep or goats according to how they have treated ethnic Israel, and added that dispensationalism fails to account for "the shift from the neuter 'nations' to the masculine pronoun, suggesting individual judgement of [each nation's citizens]" (604). He argued that Matthew's context meant that the people of *all* nations (secularising ethnic Israel) would be judged by whether or not they sided with Yeshua's suffering workers/worshippers (605).

The NT underlines that each convert should have a helping heart for fellow converts as family members, siblings in covenant. Theologically every human is a child of God by creation (Adam 1), but only Christians are children of God by conversion (Adam 2), and I think that, *pace* Lewis, Jesus' spiritual *family* is limited to the latter.

[322] Sometimes people can dismiss the idea, *God*, because they dislike the idea, *unpleasant*. "If God existed, mother would not have died"—kneejerk atheism. Lewis wrote *The Problem of Pain* as a theodicy, and *A Grief Observed* of his personal pain. He had lost his own mother in childhood.

Finding the simplicity of prayer might be complicated. To place *myself* in the presence of *God*, sounds simple, but who is the *myself* that *I* am to place, and what is the *concept of God* that *myself* is to meet? If for instance, we have the idea of God being an angry old man in the sky, it would be that *idea*, rather than *God*, that *myself* would meet. And what am *I* beneath the surface? Dazzling lightness and dark clouds?[323]

Against the pantheism of Hinduism (which Lewis found attractive), he suggested that we are to our surround, not as *I am that*,[324] but that *that and I share origin*: creatures distinct from God and from others, within God's creation.[325] A real play—delusional unless recognised as a real play—can show us the natural world and beyond. The hand of God in nature, can show us the heart and mind of God beyond nature. Pray, being aware of the bigger spiritual background that's beyond our everyday 'world' of shifting shadows, this shadowland in which we must live and know God. Be real with God; know God for real. But "emotional intensity is in itself no proof of spiritual depth" (Lewis 1966:83-4).

If we pray with eyes closed, some kind of mental image of God is fine, so long as the image is not taken to be God: a bright blur, for instance, is not God. If we pray with eyes open, keeping our eyes fixed on an object—a neutral (a table) or for some a positive (an altar)—can help concentration. Western Catholics can use idols (statues) of saints to seek saintly intercession; Eastern Orthodox can use icons (pictures) of saints to seek beyond saints. Yet such visuals can distract, and work less well with the father and the spirit than with the lord, tending to sidetrack trinitarianism: "exclusively addressing our prayers to [the lord] surely tends to what has been called 'Jesus-worship'": Jesusism is charming but is not Christianity (Lewis 1966:86).

---

[323]   Jean Darnell's *Life in the Overlap* pictured Christians as living where the circles of the old and the new creation intersect. Do we affirm our virtue/vice in genuine prayer?

[324]   Philosophical Hinduism would say, I am that tree, I am that rock, etc, in the sense that I speak as a voice of the whole.

[325]   Using the term *creature*, with Aquinas, for any object in creation.

Mental imaging (*compositio loci*) can become so engrossing that it impedes devotion. Even imaging of the cross in its grim reality—needful at times—can, by the roar of horror, deafen us to quieter voices, such as compassion and gratitude. Nor are songs of the cross always helpful.[326] Lewis couldn't imagine not imagining, but found the spontaneous flittering images around his peripheral vision—like wheeling rooks in a windy sky—more helpful than sustained exploration of any given image, and more common in worship-prayer than in petitionary-prayer. Deity is personal, and very much more.[327] It is right to ask God, but sometimes we do not ask because we do not believe, or do not wish to be *shoppers*.[328]

For adoration and worship prayer-types, "begin where you are" can be a lot better than trying to fit our mentalities into images of glory. That can include even the natural pleasures of life, such as splashing in a cool stream on a hot day. Ultimately pleasures come happily from God through creation, and even "bad pleasures" are really just pleasures outside of a godly setting: the sweetness of a stolen apple is still "a beam from the glory", the abused is still holy (Lewis 1966:90).

For a freely given apple we can give thanks (gift: he has given to us), and through its sweetness praise (construction: he has done well), even adoration to the creator (message: he wishes us to enjoy). "To experience the tiny theophany is to adore...[through] the sunbeam to the sun" (Lewis 1966:91-2). Many mindsets—such as inattention, secularising, greed, and pride—oppose this perception of deity. Like love-making,

---

[326] Lewis affirmed the death of Jesus as the atonement, but songs about fountains filled with blood, were probably not for him. He knew that *blood* was a metonymy for *death*. I think too many songs crassly use *blood*, where *death* would make the point far better to the unconverted. Why tell non-vampires that we drink Christ's blood each week, then invite them around to have a drink? Such as 1 Cor.11:24-5's *estin* (is) is metaphor: wine merely represented Christ's blood, even as the tree represented, though the text says it *was*, Nebuchadnezzar (Dan.4:22).

[327] Not "a personal god" (*pace* Lewis 1966:88)—*are* there types of god?

[328] On this, if we are to love others as we love ourselves, we should seek our good as we would seek the good of others, and let ourselves be helped as we would wish other to be helped medically, psychologically, spiritually, whatever.

sunsets can be religious moments, and though not sacred in themselves, awakenings of joy and of adoration of infinitesimals, to which good books can safeguard, direct, and enhance. And "mere obedience is worship of a far more important sort" (Lewis 1966:93). The experiences of joy in even the little things, are festal rays of light into a sad dark world, promises that "joy is the serious business of heaven" (Lewis 1966:95).

That we seek pleasure wrongly—even an automatic relishing of anger—opens up penitential prayer. A sticky-plaster *Sorry, let's forget it*, overlooks longterm remedies. And asking God to 'calm down' takes human analogy too far: his wrath is rather the just, generous, scolding and indignant turning of his 'face' away from us, of the doctor seeking to kill the disease so as to cure the patient. The rebuked can turn into the repentant; the care can heal: both are based on seeking our best.

Human wrath isn't holy, because man isn't holy, not because wrath is unholy (Jas.1:20). The wrath/forgiveness picture is dim but helpful, so far as it goes. There is also a question of focus. The puritans sought to attend to inner corruption. Lewis agreed with that vision—even Christians, since morally contaminated, should surely seek freedom from their inner corruption. Yet, he asked, rather than an occasional glimpse, should it be "a daily, lifelong scrutiny" (Lewis 1966:100)? [329] Wasn't that unlike the Christian idea of rejoicing in our newness? "A spiritual emetic, at the right moment, may be needed. But not a regular

---

[329] Some churches have a regular confession of sins; fewer perhaps have a regular confession of our newness in Christ. How's this? "God almighty, we confess that in Christ we are heirs of your kingdom, seated in the heavens with him, and that Earth is our footstool, for we are seated with Christ. We confess that we have your spirit of peace, purity, and power, and can live victorious lives. We confess that we have authority over the evil one, and represent you in our communities and in our world, etc.."? Compare that to this copy-paste: "Merciful god, we confess that we have sinned against you in thought, word, and deed. We have not loved you with our whole heart and mind and strength; we have not loved our neighbours as ourselves. In your mercy, forgive what we have been, help us amend what we are, and direct what we shall be, so that we may delight in your will and walk in your ways, to the glory of your holy name. Amen." If our confessions are *mainly* negative, how do they feed us, or are we perhaps to vomit up wrong food we have eaten?

diet of emetics!" (Lewis 1966:101). Moreover we can become immune to emetics, even proud to have them. Besides, if emotions rule our confessions, they can mislead.

Adoration as a prayer-type, might be best with fellow believers, and can come through the eucharist. Fussiness about church services, fussiness about other people, can block our adoration of God. But through our fellow creatures and human operations, we can look to the creator, and so become more like Christ.[330] As to the eucharist, though the specified physical elements enable fellowship (κοινωνια/ koinōnia) with Christ, Lewis confessed himself "not good enough at theology" to guide. And truly, he failed to note that the very idea of Jesus' body being *broken*, was debatable (Lewis 1966:103).[331]

He humbly sought guidance: aren't bread and wine odd elements to identify with Jesus, and, if merely symbolic, aren't they a particularly strange combination—rather than perhaps the cross—if we are seeking to maximise the psychological benefit from reflection on Christ's death?[332] Yet when the mind is at a loss, we can rejoice in our smallness, that there is more to heaven and earth than our philosophy—let us hold our tongues![333]

The magical element in Christianity is its "permanent witness that the heavenly realm, [perhaps more than] the natural universe, is a realm of

---

[330]   Lewis' *Screwtape Letters* has more on how blocking others blocks God.

[331]   Lewis 1966:103. In short, beginning as a church idea, it became written into Scripture, though it faces biblical objections. We should not say, "Jesus said it".

[332]   IMO they identify us with the exodus and with Canaan in the newness of Global Israel: blood and wine; manna and harvest—fulfilment. Jesus' death created the journeying-arrived paradox. Perhaps tracing back to the ethnic exodus is the psychological ground for blessing. They are not to remind us of Christ's death *per se*, but of the *meaning* of his death. There are many ways to use such themes, such as God's son being the Release from Egypt, the spirit being the guide/paraclete through the Wilderness, and the father being the arrival into the abundance of Canaan.

[333]   Truly, we are always journeying and never arriving, although as 'pennies drop' we can arrive at definite stops along the way, growing in spiritual knowledge. The magic and the wonder of the fairy tale will always walk with us until Christ returns, and then the true magic will begin, world without end.

---

objective facts—hard, determinate facts, not to be constructed *a priori*, and not to be dissolved into maxims, ideals, values, and the like. One cannot conceive a more completely given, or if you like, a more magical, fact, than the existence of God as *causa sui*" (Lewis 1966:106). Adoration walks hand in hand with a mix of sheer wonder and understanding. Theological sawdust is what we get when we try shaving theology to model contemporary moods to please society, when we treat theological givens as elastic not inelastic truth. The eucharist is a remedy to sawdust, a window into the deific.

Repetitive prayers can seem to be riding the rapids, hoping to hit calm water and heart's delight. Trying to forgive can seem like that. And for fellowship with God, and for inner peace, forgiving others can be a bargain, fellowship restored with God's help. The nag to resolve can be like the widow begging for justice until the unjust judge repented, we being the unjust judge. And do we need to forgive those who have died unforgiven by us? A bigger question, the older we get, is how do we connect to the departed?

If for fellow mortals God is doing all he can, why—as he commands—ask him to bless them? Because God commands us to, that's why. Likewise even if the fate of the deceased is set (as saved or damned), why not ask God to bless them?[334] Just because Rome turned the idea, purgatory, into a commercial scandal—compare Dante's *Purgatorio*—should we dismiss the whole idea? Should we not desire a purifying Purgatory, even if it has much pain, if it is like having a bad tooth extracted, or pleasanter, like taking a bath and donning fresh clothes before approaching the majestic throne?

On this, Lewis sided with John Henry Newman against Thomas More and John Fisher. He wondered whether the idea flowed naturally from Scripture, and whether requests to bless departed saints in the richer life might be granted, even as they can be for saints before

---

[334]   Obviously if set in damnation, the request might not be possible to grant, or might lessen the fate, without suggesting a change of fate. His *The Great Divorce* was a aioniological dream, toying with the idea that after death some/all unredeemed spirits were still for a while fluid, capable of repentance and return to God, capable of a final vote to divorce from him or not.

death. With deference to Lewis, do "our [grubby] souls demand purgatory" (Lewis 1966:103), or—if resurrection makes us clean—do our souls merely demand the change of resurrection (1 Cor.15:51)? As an aside, one may add a caution against throwing 1 Cor.15:29 into the fray: it is too unsafe a peg to safely hang any substance.[335]

Because "prayer is irksome", we can prefer to talk about it rather than to actually pray (Lewis 1966:113). If we are Christians, shouldn't prayer flow from us as naturally as roses from a rose-tree? If we welcome interruptions to prayer, or even force ourselves to pray as a duty or penance, are we even Christians? Well, at best we are Christians giving way to the sin of darkness, still fearing the light of God, yet under construction, not yet what we will be.[336]

We have a problem. God is within his creation, but is intangible. And the mental hoop of speaking as if to an intangible being, is somewhat counter-intuitive—though mind itself is intangible. For objective and subjective reasons, we accept both God and the idea of a prayer link, and should try to connect. But for now, prayer might remain an irksome duty and practice. Similarly we have moral duties to our biblical neighbour, and our imperfections can prevent those from developing beyond duty. But moving from mere duty into delight is possible: the rose-tree has no *duty* to produce roses, it simply does

---

[335] Mormons cite this text to affirm mortal intervention into the postmortal, and grow their genealogical records. Paul's off the cuff reference, clear enough to his initial audience who were in the know, isn't clear to us: we cannot fully follow his thinking. But among hundreds of weird and wonderful ideas, some main contestants stand out. One, basically in line with Early Church Fathers, is that some Corinthian Christians ('they') considered themselves as *intrinsically* mortal—physically and spiritually—yet for spiritual resurrection in the body (spiritual hope only in mortal life: 1 Cor.15:19) were water-baptised anticipating their physical burial, howbeit blind to water-baptism's prophecy (even for unbaptised Christians) of physical resurrection to come: they lacked *aparchē* teaching. See David E Garland's *1 Corinthians* (BECNT), 2015:16420-46/28028.

[336] Conversion relocates us into light (Jhn.3:19), yet converts can either live with their eyes shut, or like a bud slowly opening.

what it is. "Aristotle has taught us that delight is the 'bloom' on an unimpeded activity" (Lewis 1966:115).

The activity of prayer—as that of loving our neighbour—might continue as a mere duty for now, as we by choice behave as if we love God and our neighbours. The imperative to be born anew[337] extends beyond conversion, seeking to birth imperative into normal nature. Unlike Milton's silly idea of military discipline in heaven, Dante got it right: angels don't need telling to be good (the *ought*), even if they do need telling what good to do (the *should*). Law still informs us.[338] Yet prayer, often in irksome obedience, blooms delightful at times, and the best of the psalmists had moved from mere duty, to delight in Yahweh's torah (Ps.119).

If we rightly question whether we *are* Christians who find prayer irksome at times, we should also rightly question whether some who claim the faith, are Christians. Having questioned previously a then bishop of Woolwich (J A T Robinson), Lewis called attention to the likes of Rudolf Bultmann who first *demythologised* what he deemed myth, then *remythologised* with a substandard myth: from riches to rags. In short, some change the Bible to say what they think folk wish to

---

337   Lewis used the term 'born again', which is more Nicodemean than dominical. Jhn.3:3 spoke of a *different*, not a *repeat*, birth, blurred by many Bible versions. In fact, by his own admission William Tyndale was not *born again*. The play on words went: "unless..born anew, it's not possible to see God's kingdom"; "How can a grown man ever be born a second time?"; "You must be born from above" (CEB/CEV/NRSV respectively).

338   Lewis held that Gal.3:24 was of a basic teacher preparing students for adult life, and that it holds true for Christians preparing for heavenly life. By adding "to bring us", the Geneva/KJV misled us: Tyndale's *unto* (or even *until*) or *with reference to*, was Paul's meaning. The Law/Nomos/Torah in its guise as *paidagōgos* was the Sinaitic overseer (not junior school teacher) to Ethnic Israel, until messiah came and that class closed. See Douglas Moo's *Galatians* (BECNT), 2013:6600-43/16965. "..the law was the guardian in charge of us until Christ came. After he came, we could be made right with God through faith" (ERV) with better guidance in life.

     Moral law (not '*the* law/Torah' of Sinai) teaches us in Christ, taught man before Christ, and will retire when Christ returns.

hear.[339] It's as if the Bible, rather than the people, must be chopped and squashed to fit the Procrustean Bed. Whoever reshapes Christianity as a way to sell it, is "a pretty mixture of fool and knave" (Lewis 1966:119). Not all bishops are Christians.

Lewis affirmed that supernaturalism is the only basis for true prayer, commenting that though he was converted to supernaturalism before he was converted to the idea, *heaven*, he had come to see that heaven should loom large in prayer.[340] Lewis looked a little at what memory both is and foretells—will we wallow in future in reality, we who wallow now in remembrance? Though corpses will not rise from tombs, souls will be reclothed in sensory bodies after resurrection—"as the flower to the root, or the diamond to the coal" (Lewis 1966:123)—and sensory perception enriched. And so Lewis ended his book on prayer, with thoughts on heaven. And so do I.

Gloria in excelsis Deo

---

[339] In today' world, one could equate the likes of Steve Chalke, who after coming across difficulties to the idea of biblical integrity, "genuinely believe that writers of my sort are doing a great deal of harm" (Lewis 1966:118). Perhaps we need not invoke Søren Kierkegaard's line—that they pretend to themselves to be unable to understand the Bible, because they know very well that the minute they understand, they are obliged to act accordingly. Perhaps it is simply a case that they, being genuinely uncomfortable with the Bible's position against the Western spirit of the age, pastorally prefer their own position that a new more liberated church should emerge from new cultural soil. A touch of 2 Tm.4:4? If spiritual birth is a picture of waking up to Christian insight, then spiritual death (or withering) can be a picture of sinking back to into sleep.

[340] Antony Flew made a similar point when converting from atheism to deism, and presumably his belief in heaven postdates his death.

Selective Subjects and Sources Index

A

Abraham · 10, 11, 15, 29, 30, 66, 97, 118, 119, 139, 158
Athanasian Creed · 78, 79, 80, 83, 87, 162
Augustine of Hippo · 58, 86, 158

B

baptism (spirit) · 54
baptism (water) · 53, 54, 55, 56, 57, 58, 59, 62, 75, 87, 98, 122, 133, 151, 152, 173, 209

C

Cho, Yonggi · 88, 89, 97

D

Dominus Factor · 167

E

eschatology · 33, 89, 94, 130, 182, 195, 196
evangelism/evangelical · 52, 53, 55, 59, 85, 99, 110, 115, 125, 128, 133, 149, 160, 162, 172, 177, 180

G

Garland, David E · 209

I

Islam/Muslims · 57, 162

L

Luther, Martin · 30, 65, 74

N

Nicea · 86

P

patripassianism · 51, 64, 68, 87, 96
polydirectionalism · 69, 164
polytheism · 10, 12, 13, 15, 23, 24, 25, 35, 80, 143, 156, 160, 161, 162, 172, 200

S

Sabellianism/unitarianism · 65, 66, 68, 69, 70, 71, 72, 73, 77, 78, 82, 84, 87, 99, 159, 162, 163, 164
sovereignty · 49, 109, 124, 125, 126, 127, 142, 199
Spiritual level
   1 Common · 11, 12, 13, 75
   2 Sinai · 11, 12, 39, 61, 75, 115, 128, 133, 140, 151, 154, 161
   3 Christian · 11, 12, 36, 48, 53, 54, 58, 59, 60, 61, 73, 75, 115, 128, 129, 130, 140, 144, 145, 154, 158, 202
   4 Everlasting · 12, 54, 55, 58, 60, 115, 129, 130, 144, 145
Spiritualism · 14, 17, 154, 176

T

Tertullian of Carthage · 87
The Five Necessaria · 162
The Five Solas · 162
trinity/trinitarianism · 43, 51, 52, 53, 62, 63, 64, 65, 66, 67, 68, 69, 70, 71, 72, 73, 75, 77, 78, 79, 80, 83, 84, 85, 86, 87, 88, 89, 93, 96, 102, 143, 147, 149, 162, 163, 165, 166, 167, 179, 180, 204

W

Wesley, John & Charles · 88, 159
Wycliffe, John · 167

Y

Yahweh/God's name · 66, 67, 68, 69, 70, 71, 75, 80, 101, 112, 143, 145, 147, 157, 163, 166

Works cited:

Pat Alexander's *Lion Handbook: The World's Religions*: 1994
Ronald B Allen's *Numbers* (EBC): 2012
Jane Austen's *Pride and Prejudice*: 1980
Edward P Blair's *Word Illustrated Bible Handbook*: 1988
F F Bruce's *International Bible Commentary*: 1986
Ken Chant's *Sitting on Top of the World*: 1972
D A Carson's *Jesus and His Friends*: 1986
D A Carson's *The Gospel According to John*: 1991
D A Carson's *A Call to Spiritual Reformation*: 1992
D A Carson's *New Bible Commentary*: 1997
D A Carson's *Inclusive Language Debate*: 1998
D A Carson's *Matthew* (EBC): 2010
Jean Darnall's *Life in the Overlap*: 1977
John Drane's *Introducing the OT*: 1989
Gordon Fee's *Listening to the Spirit in the Text*: 2000
Fee & Stuart's *How to Read the Bible for All Its Worth*: 2003
Getty & Getty's *Sing!*: 2017
Steve H Hakes' *Israel's Gone Global*: 2018
Steve H Hakes' *Revisiting The Challenging Counterfeit*: 2020
Craig Keener's *Commentary on the Gospel of Matthew*: 1999
Craig Keener's *Miracles*: 2011
K A Kitchen's *Reliability of the OT*: 2003
Alan Lenzi's *Reading Akkadian Prayers and Hymns: An Introduction*: 2011
C S Lewis' *The Pilgrim's Regress*: 1944
C S Lewis' *The Weight of Glory*: 1949
C S Lewis' *Reflections on the Psalms*: 1958
C S Lewis' *Letters to Malcolm—Chiefly on Prayer*: 1966
C S Lewis' *That Hideous Strength*: 1983
C S Lewis' *Mere Christianity*: 2002
I Howard Marshall's *Acts* (TNTC): 1992
Perry Marshall's *Evolution 2.0*: 2015
Elmer A Martens' *God's Design*: 1994
Nick Page's *And Now Let's Move into a Time of Nonsense*: 2004
Alan Richardson's *An Introduction to the Theology of the NT*: 1958
George Tyrrell's *Lex Orandi*: 1903
Willem A VanGemeren's *Psalms* (EBC): 2008
Benedicta Ward's *The Prayers and Meditations of St. Anselm*: 1973
James White's *The Forgotten Trinity*: 1998
Frances Young's *The Making of the Creeds*: 1991

Books by this Author

Theology

Israel's Gone Global

Israel's Gone Global traces salvation through the term, Israel. Was the covenant with the people-nation of Yakob-Yisrael, crossed out? How eternal is covenant? To examine that, we examine marriage. Can a covenant partner be truly divorced? Has Yeshua-Yisrael mediated a spiritual covenant with a spiritual Israel? Is evangelism of ethnic Jews needless, a priority, or neither?

No one could have everlasting life but for the cross, but has it always been globally accessible? Might any who die as Atheists, Hindus, or Islamists, make heaven? And is eternal life joyful? Is everlasting life fun?

Tackling the question of people who die in infancy (or as adults who never heard the gospel), we consider whether it is fair if only those who don't die in infancy get a chance of eternal damnation (if infant universalism), or alone get a chance of eternal heaven (if infant damnation). Does predilectionism make best sense of biblical revelation?

Opportunities to enjoy eternal life spring from the new covenant—reasons to rejoice. But what about salvation history before that covenant?

∞

Singing's Gone Global

Singing's Gone Global, briefly explores the background of singing, before and into ancient Israel. It examines the impact songs have on those who sing, and on those who listen, touching on spiritual warfare. It looks at how nonsense songs neither make sense to evangelism, nor to the evangelised, and asks, "Is there a mûmak in the room?"

Oddly some songwriters simply misunderstand prayer. Part two covers the basics of the trinity, focusing on the spirit in order to understand types of prayer (eg request, gratitude, adoration, chat), leading in turn to a better understanding of our heavenly father, our brother, our helper, and ourselves in Christ's likeness.

Next we look at some common problems. Part three focuses on problems such as buddyism, decontextualising, misvisualisation, and unitarianism. Diagnosis can help Christ's 'bride' to recover from suboptimal and unbiblical songs (Eph.5:18-30).

Giving a Problem Avoidance Grade (PAG)—an A+ to Unsatisfactory scale—in part four we examine specific songs. Weapons forged (Part three), the mûmakil can be attacked, seeking to save and be saved.

Subsequently the book concludes by showing how Christmas carols may be tweaked to better serve our weary world, rejoicing that joy to the world has come.

∞

The Word's Gone Global

The Word's Gone Global, examines Bible text (trusted by early Islam) and introduces textual critique. It looks at the Eastern Orthodox Bible and the Latin Vulgate. Did the Reformation improve text and translation? Were Wycliffe, Tyndale, and Martin, helpful?

Why did the New International Version begin, and why does it enrage? Why did complementarians Don Carson and Wayne Grudem, clash? Is marketing hype between formal and functional equivalence, meaningless? Which version or versions should you regularly read?

In English-speaking circles, Broughton wished to burn Bancroft's King James Version, yet many KJV proponents—think Gail Riplinger and Peter Ruckman—wish to burn all alternatives. More heat than light?

Grade Charts cover 30+ English versions on issues such as God's name, God's son's deity, marriage, gender terms, anti-polytheism, and various issues in John's Gospel. No, Tyndale was not 'born again'. No, John was not antisemitic. No, he did not disagree with the other Gospels.

∞

Prayer's Gone Global

Prayer's Gone Global, begins with ancient civilisations and prayer (the Common Level). Then it narrows into Ancient Israel and prayer (the Sinai Level). Then it deepens and widens into Global Israel and prayer (the Christian Level). Deity is revealed as trinity: Sabellians mislead.

Relating to the trinity includes the Holy Spirit. We should of course work with him, but should we worship him, complain to him, chat with him? Above the spirit stands the often forgotten father—oh let Jesusism retire.

Authority is another issue. Are we authorised to decree and declare? Is binding and loosing actually prayer, or is it evangelism? Is it biblical never to command miracles? Do we miss out on the supernatural which Jesus modelled for us, too fearful of strange fire to offer holy fire?

You can freshen up your prayer life—ride the blessed camel, not the gnats. Listen to Saint Anselm pray, and C S Lewis and 'Malcolm' discuss prayer, and be blessed.

∞

Revelation's Gone Global

Revelation's Gone Global, is a telling of John's future, as if by a then contemporary named Sonafets speaking to his church about how John's apocalyptic scroll related to their days, and about what was still future to John.

Encouragement is a big theme. Roman persecution was an unpredictable beast which ferociously lashed out here and there—what church or Christian was safe? But God stood behind the scenes, allowing but limiting their enemy, and messiah walked among the churches, lights to the world.

Victory lay neither with Rome nor demons, but with God, and with the warrior lamb who had been slain. Victory was guaranteed, and would finally be enjoyed.

Exhortation was given to believers, to play their part while on the mortal stage. They were to walk in the light, and not to let the show down by straying.

Angels of power, actively working out God's will, far exceed the puny forces against God and his church. His wrath was not pleasant, but could be redemptive until the new age begins.

C S Lewis' essay, The World's Last Night, is briefly examined to enjoin a calm awareness of the ongoing battle we are in, and the brightness to come when the king returns.

∞

The Father's Gone Global

Focusing from God as father, to the specific person of God the father, The Father's Gone Global looks at the biblical parent/child pattern from Genesis, through Sinai, and into the Church.

Abba as a new covenant word expresses deep filial affection even under deep anguish in our Gethsemane battles. Coming through God's belovèd son, it speaks into the church and into our lives.

Though to many the 'forgotten father', human parents/fathers should 'put on' God the father, and his children should 'put on' his son. We forget him to our cost.

Human applications aside, what is the Eternal Society? Is filial relationship modelled by God the son incarnate? Are we to be always obedient to our father and guided by the spirit?

Eschatologically the father will be supreme, but even now he is the one to whom the son points. Christian life should relate to God our father, God our brother, and God our helper, prioritising the father.

Renewal of the church is vital for our confused world, but renewal which downplays the father falls short of the good news which Christ created and the spirit circulates. May this book play its part.

∞

Salvation Now and Life Beyond

Salvation Now, divides the doctrine of salvation into the four main levels of common humanity, the old covenant, the new covenant, and life beyond.

A big weight is put on the term, Israel, as God's master plan. This too has four levels, meaning a man, a people, a new man, and a new people, respectively.

Various ideas of what Christianity—the new covenant for the new people—is good for, and how we get into it and best enjoy it, are examined, and a faith-based inexclusivism is suggested.

Everlasting life is seen as the ultimate goal of salvation, universal meaningfulness and love beyond all fears and pains.

∞

Revisiting

Revisiting The Challenging Counterfeit

Revisiting The Challenging Counterfeit, is an extended review of Raphael Gasson's 'The Challenging Counterfeit' (1966). Raphael was an ethnic Jew whose spiritual journey included many years as a Christian Spiritualist minister.

Today, when psychic phenomena captures the imagination and the bank accounts of popular media, it is useful to unearth the witness of one who had well worn the T-shirt of a medium with pride, only to bury it in unholy ground as a thing of shame and of sorrow and of wasted time.

Challengingly, his book exposes what true Spiritualism is. He had nothing but high praise for Spiritualists, and deep condemnation for Spiritualism. For he had discovered true Spiritualism to be itself a fake of true Spirituality, a mere Counterfeit that, in deposing death in the mind, enthroned it in the soul.

Counterfeit phenomena covered include apparitions, Rescue Work and haunted houses, materialisation of pets, psychic healing, Lyceums, clairvoyance, and OOBEs—to name but a few. This book surveys his exposé of Spiritualism's offer of fascinating fish bait, false food falling short of real food for the soul. Though it takes issue with

Raphael on a number of points, his core insights are powerful and timely, helping us to avoid—or escape from—a Challenging Counterfeit, and to discover true spiritual currency.

∞

Revisiting The Pilgrim's Progress

Revisiting The Pilgrim's Progress, is a re-dreaming of John Bunyan's most famous dream. An ex-serviceman and ex-jailbird, he found fortune, freedom, and fans worldwide.

This dream journey is substantially Bunyan's from this world, and into that which is to come. It is not a fun story, but it has lots of danger, and joy, and reflection on some big life themes.

Profoundly, sinners who become pilgrims become saints. But that can make life more difficult. One big question is, Is it worth it? One big temptation is, Turn back or turn aside. And if you see others do so, that makes it harder not to. Bunyan was tempted. And he discovered that not deserting, can lead to despair. But he also discovered a key to liberty.

Pre-eminently, it is a story of grace which many follow. Grace begins the journey, helps along the way, and brings the story to a happily ever after. Are all fairy stories based on heaven?

∞

Fantasy

The Simbolinian Files

From Simboliniad, a crystal planet long gone, came the vampire race, the wapierze, thelodynamic shapeshifters seeking blood. Most oppose Usen, King of the Light, so side with the Necros. Seldom do the Guardians intervene. These files, secretly secured from various insider sources, reveal something of what they have done, and will do.

∞

Vampire Redemption

Artificial intelligence, created by superpowers to save man, questions man's worth, and becomes The Beast. Escaping into the wild, many discover a wilderness infested by zombies and diabolical spirits. Who will help? Father Doyle? He's tied up with the mysterious Lilith.

Tariq? He's tied up with Wilma. Can the bigoted old exorcist deliver him from evil?

Radical problems can require radical solutions. But does man really need hobs, elves, and the more ancient of days? In the surrounding shadows, vampires and demons form an alliance, raising the stakes against Whitby and Tyneside. Powerful vampires live shrouded within Whitby, speaking of life beyond this galaxy. Is salvation in the stars? Is Sunniva, the despised woman of Alban, worth dying for? Big questions, needing big answers. Not even Guardian Odin can foretell man's fate and, as silent stars go by, one little town must awake from its dreams.

Though The Beast slumbers purposeless and undisturbed, in the far west a global giant slowly opens its yellow eyes and threatens to smother the earth in fire and ice. There is one chance only.

∞

Vampire Extraction

Bitterly long their imprisoned spirits lay, fast bound to Earth's drowsy decay. To the Simbolinian race, there was no hell on Earth, for Earth was hell, and Usen the cosmic jailer. Was it so surprising that as vampires they stalked Usen's children for blood? Most chose the Kingdom of Night, wary of both the Kingdom of Necros and the Kingdom of Dawn.

As queen of the Night, Lilith's story streams through the summer sands of Sumer, and through the green woods of Sherwood. It flags up both dishonour and joy, and cuts across the paths of Ulrica the Saxon and Robin the Hood, as tyrannies rise and fall in merry England. Bigotry seldom has a good word to say about Usen, nor about mercy. Reluctantly, Lilith examines what it means to show mercy, to show weakness. Wulfgar had enslaved Ulrica: is it mercy to let her burn; should mercy have spared Lona? Could Hamashiach turn daughter into sister? Could Count Dracula be turned from his madness? Has Draven really betrayed his mother? Life has many questions.

Tales picture ideas, letting us walk through the eyes of others to better see ourselves. This story exposes subplots behind common history. How these chronicles came to be written up is, in the spirit confidentiality, not for the public eye. What truth is within you must judge. Discrimination is a gift from Beyond, from which the words still echo: mercy is better than sacrifice. Indeed mercy can be sacrifice. Judge well.

∞

Vampire Count

Vampires were not always earthbound, nor are all evil, but being victims of Usen's Eighth Law, his Children became their fair game. Yet the Night Kingdom was divided: some veered to the Necros; some to the Dawn. Who was wrong; who was right?

Long ago one incited his people to racial violence against elven and human kinds. Ever he strove to be king of the Night, and unto Necuratu the Dark Lord he gave the dragon shape. He made war upon the ancient Middle East, even the Nephilim War. Against him the Light raised flood and division.

At last his own people, paying the price of his rampage, bound him in deep sleep. Yet the millennia seemed meaningless to him: even the rising of Hamashiach hardly disturbed his dreams. At last awoken, he and his brides stalked the hills of Transylvania. Only the fear of Lilith—and after her unforgivable sin, Queen Rangda—chained their bloodlust.

Dracula sought escape and autonomy. By cunning and devious means, he immigrated to London via Whitby. Pursuit followed swiftly, with a shadowminder helping a circle of human headhunters, though they sought the death of all vampires.

∞

Vampire Grail

Wulfgar is a vampire, a thelodynamic creature from another galaxy, now locked into our world by one called the Cosmic Jailer. He hides a tormenting secret from his queen, Lilith, which the Necros use as blackmail. She will only go so far with the Necros against Hamashiach—Wulfgar must go further.

Unknown to the Darkness, to bury Hamashiach is to plant the Light. From the buried seed springs life, and humanity must reimagine itself. Longinus turns to The Way, the nexus of the Seventh Age. His spear goes on a special mission to the island of Briton, where Wulfgar lives again.

Logres is centred on Avalon, but raises up Arthur, a man of mixed race, to carry its flag and to protect against the Saxons. But its main enemy is the Darkness, which ever seeks to extinguish the Light it hates and fears.

Finally, it seems as if the Darkness has won, and the dark ages descend. But does the Light not shine in the Darkness? Must Wulfgar remain in the Night?

∞

Vampire Shadows

Dark vampires, hidden within the ancient empire of Khem, fall out with the king who, stirred up by the Necros, enslaves the Sheep People. But Iahveh, the shepherd-divinity, is stirred up, and stirs up a hidden hero to force a way out.

Apprehensively the two vampire-magicians join the Sheep of Iahveh, on their long and deadly trek in search of a promised land. Can any survive?

Warily they ask deep questions. Is Usen evil, as prejudice says? Is he possibly a good jailer? Are his unusual regulations, meaningful? They risk ending up in death.

Neverendingly the Sheep's sorry story drags out in interminable peregrination. Weary of wandering, most would settle for some green pastures and untroubled waters. But as they well know, that would take a miracle.

www.ingramcontent.com/pod-product-compliance
Lightning Source LLC
Chambersburg PA
CBHW032117040426
42449CB00005B/171